New GLORY

OTHER BOOKS BY RALPH PETERS

NONFICTION

Beyond Baghdad: Postmodern War and Peace
Beyond Terror: Strategy in a Changing World
Fighting for the Future: Will America Triumph?

FICTION

Traitor
The Devil's Garden
Twilight of Heroes
The Perfect Soldier
Flames of Heaven
The War in 2020
Red Army
Bravo Romeo

WRITING AS OWEN PARRY

FICTION

Rebels of Babylon
Bold Sons of Erin
Honor's Kingdom
Call Each River Jordan
Shadows of Glory
Faded Coat of Blue
Strike the Harp!
Our Simple Gifts

…in Eastern countries hate and veneration are very commonly felt for the same object.

—A.W. Kinglake

SENTINEL
Published by the Penguin Group
Penguin Group (USA) Inc., 375 Hudson Street, New York, New York 10014, USA
Penguin Group (Canada), 90 Eglinton Avenue East, Suite 700, Toronto, Ontario
Canada, M4P 2Y3 (a division of Pearson Penguin Canada Inc.)
Penguin Books Ltd, 80 Strand, London WC2R 0RL, England
Penguin Ireland, 25 St. Stephen's Green, Dublin 2, Ireland
(a division of Penguin Books Ltd)
Penguin Books Australia Ltd, 250 Camberwell Road, Camberwell, Victoria 3124,
Australia (a division of Pearson Australia Group Pty Ltd)
Penguin Books India Pvt Ltd, 11 Community Centre, Panchsheel Park,
New Delhi—110 017, India
Penguin Group (NZ), Cnr Airborne and Rosedale Roads, Albany, Auckland 1310,
New Zealand (a division of Pearson New Zealand Ltd)
Penguin Books (South Africa) (Pty) Ltd, 24 Sturdee Avenue, Rosebank,
Johannesburg 2196, South Africa

Penguin Books Ltd, Registered Offices:
80 Strand, London WC2R 0RL, England

First published in 2005 by Sentinel,
a member of Penguin Group (USA) Inc.

10 9 8 7 6 5 4 3 2 1

LIBRARY OF CONGRESS CATALOGING IN PUBLICATION DATA

Peters, Ralph.
New glory : expanding America's global supremacy / Ralph Peters.
    p.   cm.
Includes index.
ISBN 1-59523-011-4
1. United States—Foreign relations—2001. 2. Terrorism—Government policy—United
States. 3. United States—Military policy. 4. War on Terrorism, 2001— I. Title.

JZ1480.P48 2005
327.73'009'00511—dc22   2005045954

Printed in the United States of America
Set in OPTI Baskerville

New GLORY

EXPANDING AMERICA'S GLOBAL SUPREMACY

RALPH PETERS

SENTINEL

To our troops

Contents

New GLORY

Introduction

A BRIEF WORLD TOUR

I n the year of our Lord 2005, the United States faces a challenge we remain reluctant to recognize in full and opportunities we fail to recognize at all. We are the greatest—and most virtuous—power in history. For now, our existence is not at stake, although the lives of many of our citizens, the degree of our freedom, and the well-being of our allies are at risk. There is no doubt that we will survive and triumph. New glory will augment the old. But the decisions we make will determine the costs our enemies extract along the way. And we *do* have enemies, old and new, merciless and uncompromising, who hate us for our success, our freedom, and our power, as well as for the global transformations we inspire.

A problem confronts us that has no historical precedent: the failure before our eyes of a once mighty civilization, that of Middle Eastern Islam. While much was made in the last decade of the "clash of civilizations," as if it were a new phenomenon, clashing is what civilizations *do*. The contest between Middle Eastern Islam and the West is thirteen hundred years old. Although it occasionally paused, it never stopped. Despite noteworthy recent progress, we will have upset the rules of history if it ends within our lifetimes.

Instead of the routine clash of civilizations we now must cope with the *crash* of a proud civilization, the stunning social, creative, intellectual, ethical, and spiritual bankruptcy of a network of cultures that once ruled half the world and now cannot rule itself adequately. The situation is aggravated into rage by the success of Islam's old antagonists and the rise of "godless" America to unprecedented power. In the gray world of policy we do not consider jealousy or dread as strategic factors. Yet faced with the Middle East's degeneracy and malevolence, statistics and academic theories falter. They cannot explain a sickness of the soul.

The convalescence of the Middle East will be long and the medicine will be bitter to those who have enjoyed monopolies of power. Nor can we know for certain if this ill-tempered invalid among civilizations will recover to our satisfaction. The free elections in Iraq and Afghanistan, followed by Lebanon's defiance of Syria, offer grounds for hope. Humanity is astonishingly resilient and capable of beating the gravest odds. A miracle cure for the Middle East just may be possible, if slower in coming about than we would like. But we cannot count on miracles. We must act.

Issues ranging from our own security and strategic needs to human rights and the healing power of democracy require our engagement in the Arab world and beyond. The United States is cast in the role of a doctor during a plague. No matter how hopeless the struggle sometimes seems, the crisis demands our courage and perseverance. The risks we take are the only hope of avoiding a greater disaster for humanity.

We would be better off by far were we able to turn away and ignore the Islamic heartlands, with their cultural squalor and contagious irresponsibility. But we cannot avoid engagement, since our enemies are determined to bring the plague of terror to our shores. Even if they cannot destroy us, they are driven to wound and humiliate us to validate themselves.

Despite the errors we have made in the Middle East, the vitriol spit in our direction by the region's inhabitants isn't really about us. It's about them. The Middle East has grown so inhumane and weak that it craves a great Satan to explain away its ineptitude. The greatest power on earth will have to do. The crisis of responsibility between the Bosporus and the Indus, the inability to accept that cherished traditions no longer work, that local choices have been wrong, and that the entire civilization's ethos simply is not competitive in either the modern or postmodern world is so devastating that hundreds of millions of Muslims have fled into a fantasy world.

We all make our own devils in our lives. And the Muslims of the Middle East require a great devil to explain why more than a thousand years of effort—often brilliantly successful—came to nothing in the end. For all its rage and appetite for cruelty, the truth is that Muslim civilization has grown feckless. It's Tobacco Road without the solace of moonshine. Until its inhabitants can begin to take responsibility for their own success or failure, to welcome change, the rule of law, hard work, individual merit, and, above all, women's rights, the Middle East will remain the world's sick civilization.

Nor can we force others to succeed. In the course of our essential and virtuous engagements in Iraq and Afghanistan we have done all that a foreign culture could do to create opportunities for damaged societies to repair themselves. We will not know the true value of our interventions for at least another decade, perhaps much longer. For all of our investment of blood and treasure, we operate at the margins. Our military efforts have been worthy and necessary, but we provide, at most, a catalyst. Success in building a future, rather than wallowing in a reimagined past, is up to the people of the Middle East. The longer they and their governments resist the necessity of reforming not only their societies but fundamental patterns of social behavior, the graver their failure will be.

Because of our efforts, Iraq may become the Middle East's beacon of liberty. Or it may end as another Arab pyre. The Iraqis, not us, will determine their ultimate fate. Their choices will shape a civilization's future.

Of course, there is much more to the world than the struggling Muslim heartlands. Europe, old and new, is in the midst of an identity crisis of its own, haunted by a brutal past and insulted by America's upstart success. The old continental powers are still far from forgiving us for supplanting them in the strategic arena—or for our generosity toward them in the last century. Had we only been as cruel as Europeans themselves in the wake of the twentieth century's great wars, we would be much better liked. The primary intellectual goal of Western European societies for the past half century has been to prove that the United States is as cruel and corrupt as they themselves have been. When your heritage is genocide, wars of aggression, or cowardly surrender, the record of the United States can be hard to bear. The old powers cannot avoid measuring themselves against us, but the disparities they discover are so great that Europe's moral delinquents cannot resist comforting themselves with lies about our naïveté, our purported clumsiness, our violence, and our crudity (without pausing to ask themselves how such pathetic mediocrities could have built the richest, most powerful, most desirable and exemplary society in history). When it comes to self-examination, the heartlands of Europe are simply the Middle East lite.

Yet Europe is likely to be good for a number of surprises—surprising not least to Europeans themselves. With our short historical memory (one American quality Germans welcome), we thoughtlessly accept that, since much of Europe appears to be pacifist now, so it shall remain. But no continent has exported as much misery and slaughter as Europe has done, and the chances are better than fair that Europe is only catching its breath after the calamities it inflicted upon itself in the last century.

We last saw widespread pacifism in Europe just before 1914 and again during the half-time break in that great European civil war that lasted until 1945 (or 1991 east of the Elbe).

Europe's current round of playing pacifist dress up was enabled by America's protection during the Cold War. We allowed our European wards to get away with a minimum number of chores. The United States did (and still does) the dirty work, seconded by our direct ancestor, Britain. Even the North Atlantic Treaty Organization (NATO) merely obscured how little was asked of Europe. For almost a century the work of freedom and global security has been handled by the great Anglolateral alliance born of a struggle against the tyranny of continental European philosophies hatched on the Rhine and Danube. Our struggle continues today—against fanaticism and terror.

It is unlikely that Europe's present pacificsm will last. Indeed, there are many different Europes. The new Europe in the east understands that freedom has a price and that security cannot be purchased with appeasement. Southern Europe is undergoing a complex second renaissance. The United Kingdom, for all its grumpy resentment of the United States, will always align with us in a severe crisis: Our mutual values are far closer than any Britain shares with France or Germany. Anglo-American sparring can be vicious, but outsiders fail to grasp that it's a family feud. And the family closes ranks against outsiders.

France and Germany are Europe's starkest problems. They wish to lead, but lack the vision, power, and generosity required to build enduring alliances. Germany and France are sick inside, having gobbled up immigrant populations they are unwilling and unable to digest. For all their fabulous criticism of American society (where their calendars stopped around 1954), the extent of the racism and bigotry in continental Europe rivals that of a long gone American South and threatens to exceed it.

Meanwhile, "Old Europe" is rapidly becoming truly *old* Europe. With aging populations, bankrupt retirement systems, arthritic economies, educational stagnation, and punitive taxation, it appears at first glance that the continent is headed for senility, for conditions under which its dwindling youth will neither be able to man the continent's already enfeebled militaries nor support the overhang of the elderly.

Don't bet on a weak, pacifist Europe doing nothing as the immigrant time bombs within explode, while demographic pressures stress its outer borders. Behind all the America scolding and empty swagger Europe is uncertain of its future. And afraid. And when Europe is uncertain and afraid, its impoverished immigrants and neighbors had best start worrying.

The most laughable predictions of the past few centuries have been those forecasting a decline of the West. The formal empires may be gone, but the Anglolateral world enjoys power, wealth, and freedom without precedent, while continental Europe has never lived so safely or so well as under the Pax Americana. The last half century has been the most peaceful and prosperous in European history and Europeans do not want the party to end. But it's long past midnight. Europe can no longer afford the lavish social welfare systems it constructed over the decades when America paid the strategic bills without demur. But Europe will not deal with its multiple looming crises by simply surrendering.

Europe will rediscover its genius, reforming itself of necessity. There will be plenty of bitterness and recriminations along the way, but Europe will accept the need to change because change will be forced upon it. The trouble with European genius, of course, is that it has a dark side. If its racist populations feel sufficiently threatened by the Muslim millions within their divided societies and by terror exported from the Islamic heartlands, Europe may respond with a cruelty unimaginable to us today. After all, Europe is the continent that mastered ethnic cleansing and genocide after a thousand years of practice. We Americans may find ourselves in the unexpected position of confronting the Europe of tomorrow as we try to restrain its barbarities toward Muslims.

Europe will manage to make its way, regardless of the cost to anyone else. Given its internal complexity, it may prove the most surprising continent of all. Except for the old Franco-German heartlands, Europe is a hopeful, evolving place. The immediate question is how much longer the self-destructive streak shared by the French and Germans will continue to plague the rest of that bloodstained continent.

Despite the proliferation of weapons of mass destruction—especially the nuclear obsessions of dictatorships desperate to preserve themselves—and strategic problems that range from water shortages to AIDS, the world beyond the Middle East and Europe is a far more hopeful place than the daily headlines and our bizarre cult of pessimism would have us believe. If we face real and immediate dangers, we also live in an age of tremendous strategic opportunity. Most of the prospects lie precisely where we are not in the habit of looking.

Although Western Europe will pull through its current malaise, it offers us little beyond unstable alliances and devious trading partners. Nor will we be able to expand our influence in Europe, new or old. We passed our high-water mark in the continent's west over a decade ago. As for our new allies to the east, we may have achieved all that we can and must aim to preserve our current healthy relations with countries such as Poland, Hungary, and Ukraine—states that fought for their freedom over centuries.

Russia is determined to be…Russia. The danger of violent confrontation has passed for now, but so has the likelihood of a close strategic relationship. We will cooperate when it serves our mutual interests, a situation vastly preferable to that which prevailed a generation ago. Russia is crawling along another of its introverted stretches, an interval of mixed reforms and reactionary retrenchment (although it stills longs to repossess Ukraine). The country may look outward again as future events entice or provoke Moscow's power brokers, but there is little potential for a handsome return on American strategic investments. Russia is finding its own way, and Russians will settle for moderate social and economic freedoms, ever willing to forgo political responsibility. Russia may be where democracy disappoints us most. Meanwhile, a weak Russia is a good Russia.

China, the bogeyman beloved of strategists in search of a conventional enemy, has become so dependent upon selling goods to the United States that it cannot afford a war that would destroy its economy. While the current state of trade is detrimental to the United States, it has had the strategic effect of addicting China. Certainly, states do *not* always act in their own self-interest—emotion has killed hundreds of millions more human beings than logic ever did—but a war between the United States and China would have to involve folly and misjudgment on both sides. History runs crimson with such mutual misapprehensions, yet the prospect of a *major* war between the United States and the People's Republic of China may be the least probable of the threats we routinely consider. On the other hand, China will not offer any potential for the expansion of American influence or hegemony. China isn't a dragon ready to attack us, but it *is* a mountain we cannot move.

Overwhelmingly, the prospects for winning strategic partnerships in the twenty-first century lie to the south. India—a nation unified by the English language and the ballot—is a natural ally of the United States. It will require the rise of a fresh political generation in New Delhi willing to discard the rhetoric of the Cold War era, but the world's two largest democracies have such a confluence of interests that only arrogance— one quality shared by our respective governments—could keep us apart in the coming decades.

Even greater possibilities lie elsewhere, but always to the south, in the direction we have conditioned ourselves to ignore.

An educated American knows more about Italy in the fifteenth century than he does about all of Latin America in the past five centuries. No country is more important to and intertwined with our present and future than Mexico. Yet who among us knows anything of the Mexican Revolution, a long and terrible struggle that prefigured the other great rebellions of the twentieth century? Which continental European state has the potential of Brazil? Yet we pay closer attention to the Netherlands. Latin America has entered a period of decisive change for the better, but we show more interest in France—that vicious

child among nations—than we do in all of the states between the Rio
Grande and Tierra del Fuego taken together. In our obsession with
yesterday's powers we've blinded ourselves to tomorrow's possibilities.

The mutually beneficial strategic alliances we could build for the
twenty-first century all lie to the south. And not only in Latin America
or India.

Africa, the continent dismissed by all, certainly is the least developed. That simply means that its development potential is great, while
investments made in the northern hemisphere pay, at best, a diminishing rate of return. Africa has so much human and material potential
that it is, literally, immeasurable. Yet, when anyone in Washington
mentions Africa, the reaction is, at its kindest, a rolling of eyes. Poverty,
AIDS, civil war, illiteracy ... isn't Africa hopeless?

No. If some tracts of Africa are grotesquely troubled—almost invariably a legacy of European misdeeds—others are far more hopeful
than the negative headlines suggest (when Africa is treated to headlines of any sort). Meanwhile, we overlook strategic developments
that will resonate globally, from the spreading frontier violence between Christianity and Islam to the epochal transformation under
way in the continent's southern cone. The Republic of South Africa is
methodically constructing a postmodern empire—similar in many
ways to that of the United States—that will make it the greatest native
power the continent has ever seen. Our response? We treat that rising
nation as Togo with vineyards.

Our engagement in the Middle East should illuminate the importance of the Indian Ocean and the rich variety of states and cultures on
its littoral. Instead, our Arab obsession narrows our focus from strategic
possibilities to parochial annoyances. This most distant and difficult
military theater, whose sea-lanes have been crucial to the rise and
maintenance of the power of the West for five centuries, is barely considered. Yet globalization is an old phenomenon, and South Africa, the
Arabian Peninsula, Iran, India, Indonesia, and all of the other states lin-
ing the Indian Ocean and adjoining seas may prove the most important theater of strategic competition in this century.

We hardly notice that a vast stretch of the planet exists. Yet, the
striving world south of the Tropic of Cancer is the last strategic frontier,
where intelligent U.S. policies, patience, and a few tokens of respect

could prove immensely beneficial to all parties. We will continue to fight in the Middle East. But we can *build* in Africa and Latin America, in India, and, perhaps, in Indonesia.

This should be the true American century, when we move at last beyond the poisonous European divisions of the world and help create a genuine "new world order"—although not one based upon the murderous nonsense of the left.

America is the most revolutionary state and culture in history. Now it's *our* turn to export revolution.

The greatest obstacle facing the world isn't terrorism, but that monstrous legacy of European colonialism, bad borders. Terrorism is a manifestation of failure, not a cause. Drawn in European capitals in the nineteenth and early twentieth centuries, the state boundaries the colonial powers forced upon so much of the world, from Africa through the Middle East to southeast Asia, remain the leading source of friction and conflict between states—and often within them. Borders demarcated to please kings, czars, and kaisers took no account of the affinities or hatreds of local populations. Now tens of millions who wish to live together are divided and hundreds of millions more who wish to live apart are forced to remain together. Perhaps the greatest tragedy of the "liberation" era was that none of the heroes or villains of the struggle could see beyond the world Europe had designed for them.

Since the end of the Cold War every conflict in which the United States has been involved has been to some degree a legacy of Europe's colonial era—including the liberation of that Frankenstein's monster of a state, Iraq. We are cleaning up the messes left by Paris, Berlin, and even London, while Europeans chide us self-righteously. We Americans may have broken from Europe politically as a result of our revolution, but we remain as miserably in thrall to European rules for diplomacy and concepts of international order as colonialism's victims do to European-imposed borders. We need a diplomatic revolution. Then we need to lead the world away from the failed European model of statecraft.

We also need to lead the world away from continental Europe's cynical approach to human rights, which consists of theatrically mourning the dead but doing nothing to protect those still alive and threatened. In the twenty-first century human rights should be one of the twin pillars of Washington's foreign policy, along with national interests. Human rights should be neither a liberal nor a conservative issue, but an *American* priority.

This does not suggest fecklessness, but moral and practical strength. Weakness never saved a human life. Support for human rights is not a "soft" issue, but as hard as the secret policeman's truncheon. We need to return to the great American tradition of standing up for the underdogs and supporting the popular will—even when that will conflicts with our own amid the turmoil of political change. Support for human rights will always be rewarded in the end, while the expedient toleration of oppressive regimes invariably comes back to haunt us.

One act of hypocrisy undercuts a hundred heroic deeds.

Nor does support for human rights mean pacifism. Pacifism is simply an abjuration of responsibility toward our fellow human beings, a stance of incomparable selfishness. It is cowardice masquerading as virtue. Fundamental human freedoms must be guaranteed by the blood of courageous men and women. The tormentors of the innocent must be destroyed for the common good, not excused by political rationalizations. In this imperfect world the forces of good must be willing to combat evil ferociously and without compromise if the good is to prevail. And no one should doubt that Americans are the greatest force for good in human history.

We have the cultural, economic, and military power to do what is necessary in these tumultuous times. But we lack the vision. It is as if Europe had its revenge after all by hypnotizing us into believing in that continent's continued power and importance. But Europe has been at least as great a danger to the world as the Middle East is today—and most of the earth's population would call it a greater one.

We live, after all, in the great age of revolutions—not those shabby, inadequate affairs led by guerrillas in berets, but the tremendous *human* revolutions of our time, each of which has been pioneered by America: women's emancipation; racial equality; the geriatric revolution in which citizens not only live longer but continue to contribute; the revolution in religious tolerance; the efficiency revolution; the information revolution; and still others. America has revolutionized everything from the quality of housing to the routines of daily social interactions.

If anything threatens traditional cultures, it's the latter. The social revolutions we've pioneered terrify those who stand to lose their precarious grip on status or political power. Nothing divides us more profoundly and irreconcilably from Islamic extremists than our society's elevation of women from men's property to men's equal partners. Even Europeans refuse to recognize the progress made so swiftly in racial, ethnic, and religious integration in our society, since they cannot bear the prospect of integrating their own darker-skinned minorities and nonnative religions.

Meanwhile, at a time when America's elder citizens decline to accept traditional passive roles and continue to work or volunteer in their communities, some European unemployment rates among youth top 20 percent, while in the developing world the proportion of the young left idle and empty of hope is fatally higher. This exclusion of hundreds of millions of young males from productive, satisfying, and tiring work is a strategic danger of the first order, since the unbridled energy of youth gallops readily into violence. Denied opportunities to "make something of themselves," young males shatter fragile societies, subscribe to extremist creeds, and kill with relish, as they've done from the Balkans to Baghdad.

No society has ever operated at the level of human efficiency attained by the United States today. No other society remotely approaches the degree of opportunity offered to each citizen or new immigrant. Much of the success and wealth our antagonists resent comes to us simply because we work harder—and believe that work is fulfilling, an attitude that is hardly universal. How can any country compete with us if their population can't or won't put their talents to work? Even Germany's unemployment rate is the highest it's been since the end of World War II.

The United States of America challenges the world. If we are wise, we will help the most promising parts of the world respond constructively to our challenges. That will mean a deep rethinking of traditional prejudices that favor Europe, of our obsession with the Middle East, and of our muddled concerns about East Asia. If we are to reach our full strategic potential, it will require a methodical reduction (not an elimination) of our commitments to the northern hemisphere, while expanding our involvement in the South.

The process of turning southward will be difficult and lengthy. All parties concerned have made errors and indulged in gratifying illusions. The partisans of the past in our midst will struggle to retain their dwindling preeminence. We will need to choose boldness and risk over comfortable habits. Our patience will be challenged and our motives misunderstood. As we seek to make new friends, we will, unavoidably, make new enemies. Yet the prospects for our expanded power and influence are literally incalculable if we turn from the overwritten texts of the North to the blank pages of the South.

For the present, we are at war and do not grasp the dimensions of the conflict.

Despite our stunning military power, there is no sphere in which we have fallen prey to wishful thinking more profoundly than in the realm of warfare, where we prattle on about "bloodless war" and worry about annoying our enemies in the course of combat. We are going to relearn the art of war—of killing boldly when killing is required—because our enemies will force the lesson upon us. In the past, America has faced more dangerous enemies than the Islamic terrorists we face today, but we have never had enemies more implacable and merciless. And if we are not resolute in our actions Allah's executioners will *become* the most dangerous of our enemies, armed with weapons of mass destruction and the mad conviction that they serve their god.

Since the end of the Cold War we Americans have stumbled forward while looking wistfully over our shoulders at the past. We need to set our eyes firmly upon the future once again, to stop trying to preserve a failed global system and force the birth of one better suited to the needs of humanity (if less congenial to Paris, Riyadh, Tehran, or Pyongyang). We need a new strategy to replace the set of outdated prejudices to which we turn for guidance in a changed and changing world.

The purpose of this book is to advance the debate over American strategy. Based upon the experience of a military career and exposure to sixty countries on six continents, its themes attempt to break free not only of the Eurocentric folly restraining us today, but of the self-limiting divisions within our own society. Addressing, in turn, the nontraditional sources of our power, our recent military endeavors, the deficiencies of our intelligence system and obsolete diplomacy, the challenges and opportunities with which the world presents us and unconventional strategies we might pursue to increase our security and well-being, this text ranges from social revolution and military reform to a plea for a grand strategic realignment. It makes no pretense of being an academic work, since academic analysis has failed us uniformly and miserably. This book is the result of service, observation, independent thought, and common sense.

It is, above all, an American book. In an age of global pessimism and fear, Americans still believe that change is not only possible, but likely to be good. Whether we wish it or not, we lead humanity. At times, we will have to lead with bayonets, but, more often, we will lead through our ideas. If we remain wise and just, as well as resolute, ever more of our fellow human beings will follow willingly.

One

MANY REVOLUTIONS

Begin with the United States of America, the greatest force for freedom and change in history. We, the American people, are humankind's pioneers. Our ancestors cultivated a natural wilderness. Americans of the twenty-first century confront a wilderness of flesh and blood in a world terrified by the virtues that we treasure, from religious tolerance to the rule of law, from the dignity of every man and woman to the rejection of hereditary power. Erupting with freedom, America challenges the world. We expose lies that justified thousands of years of tyrannies, proving that birth need not determine destiny. We demonstrate freedom's potential for all. And those we robbed of authority will not forgive us.

Each day we expand the frontiers of human possibility. Those who insist on limits are our enemies. It is their choice, not ours. The great struggle of the twenty-first century will rage between those, led by America, who believe that men and women have the right to shape their own lives, and those who believe themselves entitled to shape the lives of others. We will prevail, but the rearguard actions fought on behalf of decayed traditions and murderous beliefs will rage beyond our lifetimes.

Without the sacrifices of our forebears, most human beings—perhaps all—would live under tyranny. Without the Americans of today and our English-speaking brethren, dictators would again rise without hindrance. Because of us, freedom and the dignity of the common man and woman have become the ideal of a reordered humanity. We have lifted the weight of history from the shoulders of many millions. And we are far from finished.

Our country is a force for good without precedent. We embody the revolutionary proposition that men and women can govern themselves from below, to the benefit of all, instead of being governed from above, to the benefit of a few. Our pride does not rely upon purity of blood or religious monopoly, but upon what multiple races and creeds have built with sweat and sacrifice. Our ancestors were not children of privilege, but men and women who refused to accept the limits of the lands they left behind. The new Americans who arrive to increase our strength are the spiritual kindred of the earliest colonists. Old and new, Americans rejected the safety of submission for a chance to stride upright. And we have learned to live together without hatred, if not without passing rancor. It is an achievement few other lands can claim—and none could claim it but for our example.

Our progress has not been easy. Some of our ancestors fled chains. Others arrived in chains. Some wore chains as they lived upon our soil. Our past has been imperfect. But unlike others, we do not deny our mistakes. We do not embrace history as an excuse for continued failure. That alone sets us apart from the rest of the world.

When Americans stumble, we get back up. We do not wallow in a self-made mire and call it the will of God or the hand of fate. To err may be human, but to roll up your sleeves and fix what went wrong is American. We bear within us all the faults that humanity can manifest. But we do not surrender to those faults. While others cling to past glories, we know that our greatest days still lie ahead.

For all the complaints we must bear about America—the price of our success and the product of human jealousy—only imagine what this world would be like without us. Some may answer that proposition smugly, mocking us from foreign realms of failure. But their children line up to apply for U.S. visas. And those who complain about their American birthright rarely leave to live their lives abroad.

All men and women dream. Americans forge their dreams into reality.

We are hated not for what we have done to others, but for what we have done for ourselves. The example of our success is humiliating and bitter to all those who cling to traditions our power reveals as inadequate.

Even the American capacity for hard work excites the hostility not only of our enemies, but of fair-weather allies. Perhaps the cruelest thing European governments have done to their citizens over the past half century has been to destroy the sense that work fulfills a life. An unemployment payment is no substitute for a job, and welfare for the able robs human beings of their dignity, creating moral slaves. Most Americans, on the other hand, cannot imagine a life without work. We win the lottery, then get back behind the wheel of the delivery truck. Our passion for work and achievement is a tremendous source of strength.

As a former soldier, I see quiet heroism in the parent who labors at a grinding job, year after year, in order to raise a family, in the common citizen who will never enjoy celebrity or financial wealth, but whose steadiness and moral integrity make this country go. America has no greater reserve of strength than the honest man or woman who, instead of scheming to beat the system, keeps that system running day after day.

Few of those hardworking Americans think of themselves as revolutionaries. Yet we live in the most revolutionary society in history. We upset oppressive traditions that endured, unchallenged, for millennia. Defiantly, we created new possibilities. The average American with a social security number, a driver's license, and a mortgage is a revolutionary to a degree that reveals Karl Marx and Che Guevara as dilettantes. While revolutionaries elsewhere sought to impose arid philosophies on humankind—at the cost of hundreds of millions of innocent lives—we created a perpetual revolution of the people, by the people, and for the people.

The American revolution isn't a single event summed up by the date 1776. Our revolution began when the first colonists arrived with their backs turned to an old, limiting world and began to carve a new Jerusalem from virgin timber. Our revolution never stopped—even our Civil War was a revolutionary struggle, the only civil war ever fought to free a never enfranchised, powerless group. We have changed nearly every aspect of the social and economic orders that prevailed for centuries. And our openness to the new threatens those whose allegiance lies with the barren, dying order—even within our own population. As we pioneer change each day of our lives, those who fear and reject change yearn to stop us, whether we speak of Islamic extremists in love with a punitive god, French presidents embittered by the loss of a status for which their citizens lacked the courage to fight, or the dwindling ranks of domestic bigots.

The distance between us and the rest of the world is growing greater, not lessening.

Consider how much has changed in a half century of American life, in this great age of revolutions, and you begin to understand how threatening our society appears to those who live their lives in thrall to yesterday.

Women's Emancipation. This is the greatest revolution in history. Nothing else, not even the development of electoral democracy, comes close. The impact of the change in the status of women from men's property to men's equal partners is so great it cannot yet be measured. The energies unleashed—pent up since the earliest days of civilization—have transformed our economy and our society, making all of us richer and most of us happier. The raw power of opening workplace and educational opportunities to all, regardless of gender, creates the ultimate meritocracy. Of course, there are still glass ceilings. But another one shatters each day. Those frustrated by what they believe to be too slow a pace of change should stand back and consider that in historical terms this transformation occurred at lightning speed.

Upsetting power relationships that even a century ago appeared eternal, this change is not only practically but spiritually profound. It's a credit to the suppleness and decency of our society that we have absorbed women's emancipation with so little turmoil. Thus far, only the United States, part of the English-speaking world, and portions of Europe have been able to adjust to the shattering of gender roles. Elsewhere, the liberation of women from traditional bonds imposed by patriarchal societies is regarded with horror and even religious injunction.

Nothing divides our own society from those of the Middle East more irreconcilably than the Islamic rejection of women's equality—indeed, of a woman's humanity. Other stretches of the globe lie between the poles of justice and male tyranny. But there is one ironclad rule of which we may be certain: The easiest way to differentiate between those states and societies that will prosper or fail in the twenty-first century is to examine the roles permitted to women. Wealth and power will increase wherever women find social justice, while any culture or civilization that treats women as inferiors is doomed to remain economically uncompetitive, intellectually moribund, and culturally inert.

The math isn't hard. The economy of the United States operates on a "wartime" basis every single day, coming closer to maximizing its human potential than any other society in history. And Rosie the Riveter isn't just on the assembly line. She's in the corporate boardroom or a partner in a law firm, she's flying military jets or writing computer codes—or perhaps she's just working the graveyard shift at the local convenience store. *Every* contribution strengthens America. The creativity and economic power unleashed by the sudden introduction of the talent of half of our population into the economy has been the most important single factor in the explosion of wealth and well-being in our country over the past two generations.

Thanks to the pioneering spirit of American women we have gone from being a political and cultural democracy to becoming an economic democracy, as well.

By comparison, countries in which women are oppressed severely, such as Pakistan, Egypt, or Saudi Arabia, remain stagnant. By writing off half of their populations such societies commit developmental suicide. Islamist terror bombings may kill individual Americans, but Islamic restraints upon women drain the lifeblood from a civilization.

Worsening the matter, societies that deny women competitive opportunities invariably reject meritocracy among males as well, excluding those who lack fortunate patents of birth from educational privileges and employment advantages. Thus, at a time when the United States is operating at an unprecedented level of human efficiency, the efficiency level in Cairo, Karachi, or Khartoum is declining daily.

Where women are not free, the freedom of the male is an illusion.

We shun any consideration of psychological deformity, collective or individual, when we make our solemn lists of strategic factors. Yet, the terror of female sexuality—the fundamental cause of the oppression of women—underlies Islamic terrorism. If we could summon any dead and buried "strategist" to help us understand the Middle East's dysfunction, we wouldn't want to conjure Carl von Clausewitz. We'd need to revive the spirit of Sigmund Freud.

The War on Terror is a global struggle to decide the fate of women. It isn't really about faith but about religion perverted to satisfy male fears. The true symbols of this war are not the Twin Towers and the Kaaba in Mecca, but the chador and the woman's two-piece business suit.

The sudden breakdown of barriers to a woman's contribution to our economy, society, and culture appears to have arisen from deep currents, reaching back at least to the strong roles played by females (good *and* evil) in both the Old and New Testaments, the seminal documents of our civilization. In the Koran's phantasmagoria, women appear as minor figures, when they appear at all. Indeed, no other religious tradition spotlights so revolutionary an image as the New Testament's vignette of the women gathered fearlessly at the foot of the Cross while the male disciples hid. Our heritage of gender images includes Judith, Esther, Rebecca, Ruth, Martha, and the Marys, exemplary heroines who embody humankind's highest virtues. For the Muslim world, all women are seductresses and she-devils, Delilahs intent on cutting off more than just Samson's hair. Islam assumes that Susannah is always guilty, that the elders are always just.

Although the percolation was slow, a consequence of our anomalous heritage was that the roles of women expanded early in the West—women were not sequestered except where Islam had left its mark, as in Greece, Sicily, or the Iberian Peninsula (or in nunneries, which are, along with monasteries, among the most bizarre and backward institutions in the West). There is no Wife of Bath in *The Thousand Nights and a Night,* and Shakespeare's dazzling heroines could not have triumphed in Baghdad or Istanbul. Instead, Islam produced a strain of violent homoeroticism that reaches into al-Qaeda and beyond, as well as the celebrations of pederasty in epic histories such as the Baburnama.

Islam's great weakness is that it's afraid of the girls.

Racial Integration. Some readers may be offended that I did not list this revolution ahead of women's emancipation, but the coming of a society in which merit would replace skin color as the primary

arbiter of an individual's place was inevitable in the United States—
only a matter of time, if too long a time in coming for many who suffered. Even in the days of that first American Revolution, we were torn
over the issue. Our deeds failed to match our rhetoric, but the texts our
best souls published made a start.

For far too many years, prejudice and the demands of a plantation
economy won out. But the American Civil War *was* about slavery, despite the claims of Lost Cause apologists. Had slavery been extracted
from the American equation after 1830, there would have been plentiful sectional disagreements, but nothing would have brought North
and South to war. Nor was the struggle finished after the Confederate
defeat, despite the hopes of millions. Issues that appear simple to us today were dauntingly complex to the Americans of the past.

While it took us a painfully long time to see beyond the veil of color,
no other society has progressed as far as our own.

Women's emancipation, in comparison, was neither programmed
nor inevitable. It was as unexpected as an earthquake—and far more
world shaking. The acceptance of equality for women unlocked the
greatest prison gate in history.

In the matter of racial integration, our progress has been as swift
over the past half century as it was in gender relations. In the mid-
twentieth century neither minorities nor women enjoyed social or economic justice. Now, thanks to the courage and majesty of those who led
the struggle for civil rights, minority Americans may remain free to
fail, but they are free at last to succeed.

In addition to the valor of civil rights leaders and the many thousands who risked their lives to follow them, capitalism played an unrec-
ognized role in breaking down color barriers. Just as our economy is
now unthinkable without the participation of women in the workforce,
so, too, has the participation of minorities at all levels become indispensable. Selfishness and greed played their part in the ultimate triumph
of integration. We figured out, if ploddingly, that we generate more
wealth for ourselves when we do not exclude talent based on race—or
gender or creed. Nothing drives integration more powerfully than low
unemployment rates and a hungry job market.

Integration took time because the problem was so massive in the
United States. The numbers involved were already in the millions by

the time of our Civil War. Europe long prided itself on a lack of racial prejudice, but had so few racial minorities that no one felt threatened (on the other hand, *religious* minorities have been fair game for persecution for a millennium—and still are). Pushkin's reputed African ancestor at the court of the czar or the Harlem jazz musicians in 1920s Paris were exotic pets.

The situation changed profoundly after 1960, with the influx of foreign blue-collar workers and unemployable immigrants from North Africa and the Middle East. Today, racial prejudice in France is more pernicious than that of our bygone South. Germany rid itself of its Jews—the most creative members of German society—only to find itself host to millions of Turks no more interested in assimilation than Germans are in assimilating them. The grand multicultural experiment in the Soviet Union ended in the devastation of Chechnya, in terrorism and massacre. The casual Russian term for the people of the Caucasus or Central Asia is *chyorno zhopia:* "black asses."

There never was an idyllic earlier world in which all races were equal. A few members of a different race may have been regarded as harmless novelties in bygone societies, but once a threshold was crossed and the minority crowded the native population, even at the margins, the hatred latent in the human soul emerged. Today, Western Europe is the new Deep South, while Atlanta is a developing model for humankind's future (hopefully with better managed airports).

Real, everyday, meaningful racial integration has come further in the United States than in any previous or other contemporary civilization. Even in Latin America it's a huge event when a politician with native rather than European blood reaches high office—despite the majority non-European populations in most Latin American states.

No American institution reflects the success of racial integration better than our military—especially the U.S. Army. The first major American institution to integrate, it remains an organization in which any man or woman may rise to the highest positions on merit. When you see news clips of our soldiers serving abroad, note the human variety of both officers and enlisted troops. There is no archetypal American soldier in racial or ethnic or even gender terms. And there is no sharper contrast between the wretched bigotry of humankind's past and our future possibilities than the confrontation between the terrorists tormenting Iraq in the name of a wrathful god and our multihued soldiers struggling to help the innocent master freedom.

The Geriatric Revolution. Retirees as a source of strategic power? Absolutely. One of the several simultaneous revolutions our "strategic thinkers" ignore is the breathtaking change in what it means to age in today's America. Grandma and Grandpa aren't sitting in their rockers on the front porch. They're starting new businesses, teaching, working part-time, going back to college to learn new skills—or volunteering to help their communities, a powerful and empowering American phenomenon.

Strip away the phony romance of growing old in traditional societies. Indulging ourselves in dishonest nostalgia for those good old days that never really existed, we picture red-cheeked, white-whiskered elders sitting contentedly by the hearth, entrancing the young with stories rich in wisdom. The truth is that the aged of yesteryear were consumers of precious resources who waited in pain to die. They made few contributions to society and died at ages we consider young. And that was only fifty years ago.

At a time when Europe generates insufficient jobs for its young, when a French midlevel manager who loses his position at age fifty will not get another one, and when even university graduates remain unemployed from Brazil to India, Americans past the age of retirement continue to contribute to our society and our economy. We're also far more humane to our aging fellow citizens than are European societies, which enjoy an unfounded reputation for caring for their citizenry.

One of the greatest scandals of our time—ignored by those Americans who insist that Europe is Xanadu and Shangri-la combined—occurred during the heat wave of August 2003. Almost thirty thousand aged Europeans died, abandoned and alone, while their elected officials and even their relatives declined to interrupt their summer vacations. Fifteen thousand of the elderly perished in France alone. Can any reader imagine the outcry if such an event took place in twenty-first-century America? In Europe no government was turned out of office. No one was held responsible. As France faced the possibility of another heat wave a year later, the government's concern was limited to advising the aged to familiarize themselves with local facilities that had air-conditioning. What were those Europeans worried about at the time? The possibility that Saddam Hussein might receive the death penalty.

Burdened by unaffordable welfare systems, Europe's governments regard the elderly as expendable, as nuisances, as drains on the state budget.

When older Americans make headlines it's usually because of election-year prophesies of doom for our social security system or complaints about the soaring cost of health care. But who calculates the tremendous *contributions* these citizens make to the quality of our daily lives and to our national wealth?

Europeans agonize over double-digit unemployment rates while Americans think that Armageddon has come when unemployment breaches 5 percent. Yet European unemployment is really several points higher than those 10 to 15 percent figures suggest. Europeans retire earlier—sometimes in their mid-fifties—and their talents go to waste for a decade while Americans continue to work. And Europe has no traditions of volunteerism as robust as our own (beyond Europe, the concept hardly exists).

In terms of maximizing our human efficiency, consider the combined effects of opening our economy and society to women, to minorities, and to those who just a few generations ago would have been regarded as too old to contribute: Our humane, rewarding economy has become an irresistible juggernaut destined to roll over any competitor that restricts human contributions.

As for today's mature citizens, the most absurd statement ever made by an American not certifiably mad or sitting in Congress was F. Scott Fitzgerald's remark: "There are no second acts in American lives."

That's absolute nonsense. For Americans with the spirit to live their lives to the full, there are second, third, fourth, and fifth acts—as many acts as the longest Jacobean plays, but with far happier endings.

We are reinventing what a full life means.

The Tolerance Revolution. Europeans leap at any chance to denigrate Americans. One of their favorite images casts us as Bible-thumping bigots. Yet it's rare to find an American believer as intolerant

or as dishonest as a secular European intellectual. The haters may get the headlines, but another grand revolution in our lifetimes has been the triumph of religious tolerance in the United States.

That tolerance is a result of competition.

We accept that competition is essential to an economy and that democracy requires more than one political party. But we miss the importance the religious "marketplace" has played in making our country more tolerant and, consequently, more successful.

The Europeans are right that we remain a nation of believers. But few Americans hold religious prejudices that could compete with the European prejudice *against* religion. We've done a marvelous—indeed, a blessed—thing: We've kept our faith while setting aside the hatred.

Each of us has friends or family members who have changed denominations or even their faiths. If the church or temple in which we were raised fails to measure up to our spiritual needs, we switch to another. We may believe with all our hearts that our own faith is the best, but we don't choose our friends based solely upon creed, nor do we insist on doing business only with members of our own congregation. We befriend those whom we like and who share our interests, we shop where the prices stand in the best relation to quality without asking the faith of the owner of the store, and, increasingly, we marry whom we love, not the partner confessional loyalty dictates.

This doesn't reflect a loss of faith in God, but a gain in faith in our neighbors. We hardly give a second thought to matters of doctrine over which our ancestors slaughtered each other. Unlike our terrorist enemies who insist on a punitive god, we have opened ourselves to God's mercy.

Meanwhile, we must cope with a world in which religious monopolies still prevail—and monopolies are *always* bad. The West could not take off until its own internal religious monopoly was shattered, opening the door to the pursuit of science. Today, one of the many causes of the sickness of the Middle East is the monopoly position of Islam, whether the Sunni form in one state or the Shia in another. Yes, small Christian and other minorities exist in the region, vestiges of the past. But functionally, Islam holds a monopoly. The penalty for changing one's creed would be great, even fatal, under many regimes. Today's Middle Eastern Islam is a locked-down faith as closed and ignorant as medieval Christianity. A religion once unrivaled in its intellectual vitality has shut itself off from the possibility of change, clinging to antique opinions that were subject to vigorous debate in the days of their authors and pretending that sour, aged males hold a monopoly on wisdom. There is no strong alternative voice to call the hate-filled mullahs to account.

A monopoly on religion invariably means a monopoly on hatred. The absence of a single church or synagogue in Saudi Arabia also means the absence of a future. It is not a matter of the virtues of one creed over another but of the self-examination forced upon any religion when its adherents have choices. If power corrupts, absolute religious power corrupts religious leaders absolutely.

Even India, a country of great promise, suffers from attempts to create a Hindu religious monopoly. The will to assert the dominance of a single faith is a tragic impulse as old as humankind. All religious monopolies restrict human possibility in spheres far removed from the rituals of faith, whether we speak of the Catholicism that crippled Latin America for centuries or the Islam that ravages already weak education systems in Saudi Arabia or Pakistan. It is not a matter of which faith has the monopoly but of monopoly itself. Those who would argue a Protestant exceptionalism, pointing back to the flourishing ports of northern Europe in the seventeenth century, forget that both the Calvinist and Lutheran churches grew strong because of their life-or-death competition with Catholic southern Europe—and with each other.

Those of us who need doctrine may resist the argument, but God thrives best on earth when no single clergy is authorized to define Him for an entire population. Americans have been building that "city on a hill" all along. The surprise is that it has any number of different spires.

And minarets, too.

The Family Revolution. What institution has been more maligned than the modern American family? Were we to believe Hollywood, the American nuclear family is a realm of horror trapped within four walls. The only instance in which filmmakers or writers allow us a fleeting glimpse of family happiness is to set up a tragic event or a cruel betrayal that will "expose" the concealed hollowness of our family life.

Nor is the denigration of the contemporary American family only a sport for the left's vacuous artists. The family as an endangered species is an image cherished equally by hard-liners on the right. Our Pharisees warn us that every new social development is going to jump-start the final destruction of the family and, of course, of all America.

Oh, thou of little faith!

While dysfunctional families date to the days of myth—Adam and Eve were the first failed parents and the House of Atreus wasn't exactly happy—the American family is doing just fine, thank you. The institution has adapted to social upheavals with an elasticity and perseverance that frustrates every prophet of doom and decline. The too-hip-to-live crowd from the Hollywood Hills forget that men and women have a blessed knack for loving each other, having children, then loving their kids. Divorce rates rise and fall, but the family endures.

Its shape has changed, though. The new American family is streamlined. Another criticism we hear, to attendant wails, is that the old extended family has broken down. Well, it has. And good riddance. Extended families, clans, and tribes are a blight upon the world, holding back individuals and entire societies. Find a state or region where the extended family or clan remains the basic building block of society and you'll find it lags badly in development and justice. Extended families foster corruption, prevent the rise of a meritocracy, and inhibit the development of trust beyond blood ties—the latter essential to even an industrial-age level of modernity. Consistently, societies in which blood ties count the least in the public sphere have been the most successful and advanced.

The American nuclear family, by contrast, is a ferocious economic tool, enhancing our country's human efficiency mightily. Extended families keep their members on a leash, pulling them back whenever the family patriarchs or matriarchs sense that freedom has become too seductive. A man who moves away to seek opportunity in defiance of the clan is regarded as a traitor to his kind, and a disobedient woman may be lucky to escape with her life. The extended family or clan provides a measure of safety, but it's the safety of the cage.

The modern American family is as loving as any family in history. The parents of the adult members are still respected and loved, as are siblings and other relatives, but we have escaped the tyranny of proximity. We return enthusiastically to holiday family reunions and stay in touch by telephone or e-mail, but we are not slaves to a human system that regards itself as locked in combat with the rest of the world.

If a family lives in suburban Philadelphia and one of the parents receives a splendid job offer that demands a move to Denver, the family moves. One spouse may remain behind until the end of the school year for the children's sake, then the family reassembles in Colorado.

This ability of our economy to geographically reallocate skills and talent further increases our collective human efficiency—and it's a very American quality. We were always a people on the move, a nation of Huck Finns. But the mobility revolution that followed World War II enabled the constant and dramatic redeployment of labor. Today, the least successful Americans tend to be those who refuse to leave their birthplace.

Because we do not rely on blood ties for our friendships or business relationships, we've become adept at rebuilding communities wherever we find ourselves; most American communities welcome newcomers, while traditional societies are distrustful of outsiders. Even the dreaded "homogenization" of our cultural landscape, though much exaggerated, aids in the reintegration of the family at a new location. As a result, our economy is able to shift skilled human resources as effectively as a superb general maneuvers troops on a battlefield.

In Europe, the educated young are displaying a mobility unprecedented in the Old World, flocking especially to English-speaking European capitals. But yesterday's economic powers on the continent, such as Germany and France, face enduring problems with workers who do not want to move, who cling to what they know with a tenacity now rare in the American workforce. The executive class may be willing to relocate (having no choice), but Hans and Pierre not only want their six weeks of vacation, plentiful sick days, a thirty-five-hour workweek, early retirement, and a generous pension, they don't want to leave Bavaria or Lorraine. This workforce immobility, combined with Europe's overregulation and punitive tax laws, makes it remarkable that the continent does as well economically as it manages to, although it's weakening under the smothering hand of the European Union. Today's Europe is a bureaucracy masquerading as a civilization.

Only a tiny fraction of those Americans who take this book in hand will read it in the town where they were born. Many will have moved across states lines several times. And each move that sought to improve a family's well-being strengthened America.

Many Revolutions. Other vital revolutions have been occurring simultaneously, from an efficiency revolution that expands the possibilities in our daily lives to the suburban revolution that, despite a half century of wailing from intellectuals, has given Americans the most humane, safest, healthiest, spacious, and desirable housing in the world (my mother's family lived twelve to a two-bedroom company house—Levittown, too, was a "city on a hill").

Sparked by the G.I. Bill, we've enjoyed a strategically vital education revolution that continues to strengthen after six decades. Not only do we have the best educated population in the world, with the highest percentage of college graduates, we also have the finest institutions of higher learning, magnets for global talent. And our quality universities are not limited to a handful of select schools—opportunity has cascaded downward through state universities to community colleges, rendering advanced education accessible to citizens of every age and economic station.

Excellence is everywhere in America.

We are so successful, so powerful, so wealthy—and so humane—that our very existence humiliates the failed and failing around the world. Every improvement we make to our society horrifies someone. And the gaps in development, material and moral, are nowhere diminishing—except, again, between us and our sister states where the English language, English law, and an English respect for individual dignity shaped the cultures.

English isn't merely the language of global business. It's the language of global justice.

Jealousy may prove to be the key strategic dynamic of this century. And our enemies have much of which to be jealous. The multiple

American revolutions of our time were built upon firm foundations, from the rule of law to social mobility, that prepared us for the takeoff of the past few decades. Despite occasional lulls as our economy catches its breath after winning yet another race, we will continue to grow wealthier and more powerful. We are programmed for success. And the failures hate it.

Two

BLOODLESS WARS, THE FAILED REVOLUTION

The single American-led revolution that fell short on its promises has been the Revolution in Military Affairs (known in Washington circles simply as the RMA). Its dishonest claims were concocted by theoreticians unburdened by practical experience and by defense contractors whose greed can never be satisfied. The RMA claimed to substitute technology for flesh and blood on the battlefield, replacing the soldier with the satellite. It was not only going to change the nature of warfare fundamentally, but would lead us into bloodless wars so swift they would be painless. The gory hand of man would give way to precision weapons, robotics, and, eventually, non-lethal weapons to inaugurate a military version of the Age of Aquarius.

The claims were not merely lies. They were among the most expensive lies in history.

The nature of warfare *never* changes, only its superficial manifestations. Joshua and David, Hector and Achilles would recognize the combat our soldiers and Marines have waged in the alleys of Somalia and Iraq. The uniforms evolve, bronze gives way to titanium, arrows may be replaced by laser-guided bombs, but the heart of the matter is still killing your enemies until any survivors surrender and do your will.

Warfare is not about carefully modulated gradations. It is about winning. The absurdities of the RMA long obscured this eternal truth—which our political leaders continue to resist even now. Our losses in Iraq, slight as they have been in historical terms, were gifts to an enemy our civilian leadership lacked the will to defeat promptly and thoroughly.

Warfare is an irremediably human endeavor. Advanced weaponry changes the sound-and-light effects and, wisely employed, can aid us in our battles and campaigns. But as we should have realized by now, we remain far from the day when technology alone can win wars. Indeed, a paradox of this great age of technological innovation is that the challenges we face abroad are crudely human—crises of the individual soul and of collective identities. And human problems still demand human solutions. Our soldiers must stand upon the ground to convince our enemies that they have lost and have no hope of winning in the future. In this era of digital wonders, our wars are knife fights.

When General William Tecumseh Sherman remarked that war is hell and cannot be refined he simply stated the truth. Attempts to prettify war, to strip it of consequences—not only for ourselves but for our enemies—only prevent victory. During Operation Iraqi Freedom, our lightning campaign in Iraq, we made a grave error that undermined our battlefield success and encouraged our opponents to extend their resistance as terrorists and guerrillas: Our leaders strained so hard to limit death and destruction among our enemies that many never felt that they were beaten, as if our conquest of Baghdad was only a trick that savagery in the streets might soon undo. We tried to wage war primly, and paid dearly.

The enemy who has no need to fear has no incentive to surrender. We wish to wage war with tweezers, but combat remains the province of the ax. Hi-tech weapons certainly have their place. Used well, they can help keep our troops alive while making enemy leaders pay a price they hoped would be paid by their privates. Precision weapons can disrupt the enemy's infrastructure and even destroy individual tanks and guns. But the lesson of our recent wars is that attempts to wage war surgically only postpone—and aggravate—the butchery. The great failing of precision weapons is that they lack sufficient force to convince an enemy of his defeat—whether we speak of individual leaders or of a hostile population. War must have penalties, and those penalties must be painful. War's destruction must be sufficiently graphic to convince the enemy that further resistance is futile.

The greatest lie told in the last fifty years is that the world has changed so that victory is no longer possible. Victory is *always* possible. But it does not come to the irresolute. Time and again, from Mogadishu to the First Battle of Fallujah, the valor of our troops was undone by the cowardice of our political leaders. We had to fight the Second Battle of Fallujah in November 2004 to redeem the folly of stopping short the previous April.

If we do not mean to fight to win, we should not fight at all.

Meant to persuade the services and, especially, Congress to buy yet another outrageously expensive weapon system to replace the last hyperexpensive system that never lived up to its promise, the cynical claims of the RMA have been especially seductive to armchair generals, pundits, and politicians. The armchair generals can imagine war as a great video game in which they, too, could play a heroic role at a computer keyboard were they called upon to serve. The pundits can pretend to military knowledge they do not and will not possess. No chubby former congressman who learned about war from books can imagine himself as an Airborne Ranger, but he can fantasize all he wants about defeating America's enemies with a toggle switch. Make no mistake: Exploiting the fantasies of sedentary men has played a greater role in the RMA con than even its fiercest critics have yet realized.

Likewise, Congress—or presidents—can be lured by the lie that precision weapons mean no friendly casualties. Major defense contractors, for whom "vampires" is much too kind an epithet, play shamelessly on the myth that the American people won't accept casualties. But the American people are sensible and brave. They know that some things not only remain worth fighting for, but *must* be fought for in this troubled world. No one wishes to lose his son or daughter in battle, but all we Americans ask of our leaders is that our children's lives should not be wasted—and wars we do not fight to win waste lives. When the cause is just or when we are provoked, the American people will accept the necessary cost in lives—as we have proven time and again, even as recently as in our Iraq engagement, when the stoicism of the American people consistently disappointed commentators determined to declare defeat.

The problem lies in Washington, where sensible men and women from both parties succumb rapidly to a groupthink divorced from the human reality of our country. The myth that Americans cannot tolerate casualties under any circumstances abides even now, despite abundant evidence to the contrary. We have made progress, but there is still a bipartisan reluctance to accept that war means killing and that the killing cannot be measured in teaspoons. While we should not engage in wanton destruction, we must be willing to do all that might be necessary to bring a conflict to a clear end; the American people will accept bloodshed, but, as the Vietnam War demonstrated, they don't like a muddle that drags on without resolution.

As a result of their uncritical acceptance of the views of miniature urban elites on casualties, our political leaders try to wage war temperately, complicating combat with long lists of rules and, God help us, with lawyers present at the commander's elbow.

Reality will force us to our senses…eventually. The carnage of 9/11 began the process of sobering our leaders. Subsequent military engagements helped as well. But we are still far from recognizing that attempts to fight war halfway end by doubling the costs—and setting us up for political defeat.

We have the finest military in the world. But all its skill and courage mean little if our political leaders lack the will to win.

In 2005, we are still learning war's reality from our enemies. They are only too glad to teach us.

Our most resilient enemies are rooted within our borders. I do not mean our Muslim fellow citizens, who are or will become Americans as proud as any others. Nor do I speak of either political party. The most pernicious enemies of our national defense are our largest defense contractors. President Eisenhower was right in 1960: The military-industrial complex cripples our national defense.

We could have beaten the Soviet military. We could beat the Chinese were we ever forced to fight. The North Koreans could never defeat us militarily. We're whipping the terrorists, although the struggle will be a long one. We can beat insurgencies, ragtag bands of thugs, and presidents-for-life. But we can't beat Lockheed Martin, Boeing, or Northrop Grumman.

Far from being the staunch pillars of our defense that their full-page newspaper advertisements proclaim, big-money defense contractors divert billions upon billions of defense dollars that are desperately needed to support our troops. Infamous for sweeping aside (or devouring) small, innovative competitors who could provide superior military tools more cheaply, Lockheed Martin has entrenched itself so deeply within the revolving-door cult of our capital that no matter how bad, overbudget, underperforming, or unnecessary its offerings may be, the programs cannot be killed by either the armed services or by that minority of senators and representatives who retain some shreds of integrity.

Consider the most appalling current example, the F-22 "Raptor" (disingenuously redesignated the F/A-22, which implies a ground attack role for which it was not designed and remains ill suited). Conceived and first designed in the 1980s, during the final years of the Cold War, the F-22 fighter was intended to employ stealth capabilities and advanced avionics to surprise and then overpower the best the Soviet air force had to offer. The F-22 was designed for extravagant dogfights. But few air forces intend to engage in aerial duels with the United States military in the twenty-first century—and the aircraft we presently have are superior to any others in the world and will remain so.

Lockheed Martin's approach to the disappearance of an air-to-air combat requirement was to jerry-rig a ground-attack capability that degrades the aircraft's vaunted stealth characteristics. The F-22 carries only a small payload. Planes we already have can deliver more bombs more efficiently. While I have been warned personally by Air Force generals that we "need" the F-22 to overcome the latest generation of air-defense missiles, they were hard pressed to identify specific countries that would possess sufficient numbers of such weapons to interfere with our strategic designs (unless we are going to declare war on Russia, after all).

The F-22 is a Lamborghini at a time when we need more pickup trucks. Yet even that might be overlooked if the F-22's price tag had not swelled to three hundred million dollars per aircraft, after all the costs are factored in—including those one-hundred-thousand-dollar apiece Lockheed Martin newspaper ads subsidized by the helpless American taxpayer.

The standard, self-righteous howl from Lockheed Martin's lobbyists and their servants in Congress is that "nothing is too good for our military." That's true. The problem is that the F-22 is not good enough for our military. It is irrelevant to the actual threats we face today and to those we will meet in the future. Although nothing is too good for our troops, some extravagances are too expensive while we're at war. Despite their swelling size, defense budgets have limits.

Some of those limits already have been exceeded, thanks to the inept political conduct of our occupation of Iraq—a situation redeemed only by our military. Yet with real and pressing battlefield needs facing our troops, the rear-guard actions fought by the RMA's proponents mean that, for now, we will see at best a reduction of the F-22 buy from 277 aircraft to 180 (at least 60 already have been delivered; they sit unused and unusable while our country is at war). Only an empty Pentagon cash drawer has managed to annoy the program to this degree, and preserving the F-22 purchase remains a higher priority for the Rumsfeld Pentagon than saving our soldiers' lives or defeating terrorists.

As he began his tenure as secretary of defense, Donald Rumsfeld declared that he was going to transform our military. It was a lie. Transformation would have had to begin with the outright cancellation of platinum-plated Cold War-era systems such as the F-22 or Virginia-class nuclear submarines designed to fight a nonexistent Soviet Navy. But among the other grave faults of this worst Secretary of Defense in our history, Rumsfeld declined to cancel a single big-ticket weapons system. His only cut was the relatively minor Crusader, an Army artillery piece excellent in itself but too cumbersome for the swift strategic deployments twenty-first-century warfare requires. Despite his self-congratulatory rhetoric, the secretary of defense revealed himself as the Secretary of Defense Industry.

To its credit, the U.S. Army itself canceled the Comanche attack helicopter as unaffordable. The Comanche was a superb system, but not as essential as more mundane matériel had become. The Army leadership behaved responsibly and wisely. For their part, the Marines have always been excellent stewards of our tax dollars and the Coast Guard does more with less than any comparable organization in history. Deprived of its comfortable Soviet enemy, the Navy faces questions of purpose and doctrine it is struggling to resolve. But, regrettably, our Air Force has become the greatest abettor of the waste the defense industry celebrates at the expense of those in uniform (and of every citizen who files a tax return).

In Donald Rumsfeld's Pentagon, Air Force misbehavior reached a new low. An attempt to push through a leasing deal with Boeing for a new generation of refueling aircraft was based on outright fraud. Imprisoned as of this writing, a senior civilian official on the Air Force staff, Darlene Druyun, sweetened the already inflated contract by several billion dollars for the promise of a $250,000-a-year retirement job, along with jobs for her relatives. Secretary of the Air Force James Roche, who later found it prudent to resign, broke with approved procurement practices and internal regulations to favor Boeing over competitors, crushing internal dissent and directing efforts to mislead Congress (the Air Force continues to refuse to turn over all the documents requested by the Hill). One Boeing executive, Michael M. Sears, went to prison for his own role in the scandal and, as the investigation into further procurement irregularities expands, we need not be surprised if other defense executives find themselves facing prosecution.

The tanker aircraft in question were not needed as urgently as the Air Force secretariat insisted. The real purpose of the deal was to allow Boeing to keep an unprofitable assembly line open—while scoring enormous unearned profits. Internal attempts by midlevel Pentagon officials to shed light on the potential for fraud or to argue for a standard cost-benefit analysis were crushed by Secretary Roche and his deputies. Only dogged resistance to the deal from a handful of legislators led by Senator John McCain (perhaps the greatest senator in American history) prevented Druyun, Roche, and Boeing from ramming the deal through Congress, since three out of the four congressional committees involved had given it rubber-stamp approval before McCain dug in his heels.

Despite intense lobbying from Boeing and the Air Force, Senators McCain, Phil Gramm, John Warner, Joseph Lieberman, and a few incorruptible others defended our military and the American taxpayer, eventually grounding the disgraceful tanker deal. Along the way, they prevented Rumsfeld from moving Secretary Roche from the Air Force to become the Secretary of the Army (a position Rumsfeld since has filled with a pliable nonentity with no military service and no experience of military affairs). Rumsfeld's consistent practice has been to break the will of the service staffs until they docilely serve the defense industry and a reckless ideology of privatization.

Atop all else, Rumsfeld and Roche presided over the worst series of sex scandals in the Air Force's history, reaching from multiple rapes at the Air Force Academy to the demotion to colonel and cashiering of Major General Thomas J. Fiscus, the service's top lawyer in uniform, for a series of sexual shenanigans that, to say the least, prejudiced good order and discipline. Conduct unbecoming began to seem the norm on the Air Force side of the Pentagon. Political appointees and generals alike operated in a moral vacuum.

Is this the way our troops should be served by their senior leaders? Should we allow the miserably corrupt Air Force to become a model for the other services, where ethics still prevail?

We need a strong Air Force. We have a craven one. Conscientious pilots realize that the tanker scandal is only one indicator of the decay at the upper echelons of their service. Even at reduced numbers, the F-22 is a destructive purchase that would result in fewer operational aircraft available to us at a time when we need more. Real defense needs go ignored while follies are pursued. Yet the Air Force leadership, civilian and military, consistently defends the program.

In 2004, the cynicism and subterfuge spread from the Office of the Secretary of the Air Force down through the uniformed ranks.

Early in the year, the U.S. Air Force engaged in war games with the Indian Air Force. Our blue-suiters went into the exercise full of hubris. Our attitude was arrogant, our planning was inadequate, and our pilot performance was poor, added to which we turned off part of the electronics suite on each of our fighters to protect classified capabilities. By studying our tactics and developing innovative responses, the Indians handed our Air Force humiliating defeats—fortunately only in mock combat.

The problem was not the quality of our equipment, but human failure. Our Air Force committed the beginner's error of underestimating the opponent.

The result? With breathtaking shamelessness the Air Force insisted that the loss to the Indians proved the need for the F-22. No matter that the Indians won through tactics, imagination, and numbers, or that Air Force intelligence officers, planners, and pilots let America down. The answer, as always, was to buy a new airplane.

Our Air Force has real needs, including twenty-first-century transport aircraft, a new generation of ground-attack aircraft to replace the stellar (and cheap) A-10 Thunderbolt, improved aerial refueling capabilities, *affordable* new bombers to begin to replace fifty-year-old B-52s—still the workhorses of our strategic air campaigns—and the continued development of unmanned aerial vehicles. We need *more* aircraft, not fewer. And yes, we need larger Air Force budgets, not smaller ones, once we have digested the costs of liberating Iraq.

But we don't need the F-22. Its purchase is one of the greatest outrages in the history of congressional pork, crowning the long tradition of buying ever-costlier aircraft of diminishing utility, from the claptrap B-1 bomber (the solid-gold jalopy of the skies) through the billion-dollar-plus B-2 stealth bomber, whose cost leaves the Air Force terrified of using it in dangerous situations, to the vulnerable and unnecessary—but profitable—F-117, a distinctly unstealthy "stealth" fighter bomber that couldn't evade antique Serbian air defenses. Consistently, our most successful combat aircraft have been those, such as the A-10 ground-attack aircraft or the F-15, F-16, and F-18 multirole fighters whose design was straightforward and whose cost was rational.

The uniformed Air Force leadership has allowed itself to be corrupted intellectually and ethically, identifying more with the interests of the defense industry than with our national defense (of course, the defense industry is always glad to employ retired generals at splendid salaries or to award them lucrative do-nothing seats on corporate boards—a perfectly legal practice). One of the most appalling moments I have experienced in dealing with our military came during a question-and-answer session after a lecture I gave at the Air War College, where the Air Force trains its best and brightest for promotion to the senior ranks. The Kosovo campaign had just concluded and I criticized the pilots present—to their faces, not behind their backs—for their refusal to fly low enough to strike ground targets effectively or to tell the difference between real tanks and crude decoys.

A pilot responded that if he had flown below twenty-five thousand feet his aircraft would have been endangered. I was stunned. I responded by asking him how he would feel if the Infantry insisted on staying thirty miles from the battlefield, outside of artillery range.

The purpose of our military is to *fight*. Mission accomplishment comes before all else. But that pilot had been conditioned not to put his expensive aircraft at risk, even if flying outside of the enemy's air defense envelope meant compromising the mission. Such functional cowardice would be unthinkable in the Army or Marines.

This problem has been evident in each of our recent conflicts. We now have so few aircraft, and each aircraft is so expensive, that Air Force planners are afraid to lose any. The advent of hi-tech weaponry compounded this, creating the illusion that all missions might be accomplished outside of the range of the enemy's missiles. Contrast that with the heroism of the Army Air Corps in World War II, or of the Air Force in Korea or over Indochina. Or with the unbroken courage of Navy and Marine pilots whose mission it is to support ground combat and who never lose sight of their purpose.

Certainly, our Air Force has many brave and richly skilled pilots. Air National Guard aviators flew low and slow in their aging A-10s during Operation Iraqi Freedom, doing the tough ground-attack work their active-duty counterparts disdained. Some pilots flew through dangerous weather conditions, including sandstorms, to help our soldiers and Marines reach Baghdad. The problem isn't the spunky young jet jockeys, but the careerists and the generals.

The culture of our Air Force is broken—the RMA has shattered it. And buying three-hundred-million-dollar F-22s that we don't need and can't afford won't fix it. We're not going to dogfight Soviet ghosts. Most of our air missions will be to support ground combat. Buying aircraft so expensive that the Air Force feels it can't afford to risk them in battle does nothing for our national defense. It's merely a gift to the defense industry. And Congress wraps it with a new blue ribbon every year.

And it's all legal. Our laws have been rewritten to protect the fraudulent practices of the defense industry. There is no meaningful penalty for failure if your corporation is big enough. Contracts are nearly impossible to terminate. Outrageous cost overruns are forgiven. And when a weapon system flops, the response is to buy a new one from the same contractor. Our forces get far less than we pay for. Everybody knows. And few in Washington care.

We must thank God for the men and women who wear our country's uniforms. With Congress unwilling to stop the legalized fraud in defense procurement, and politicians in both parties unwilling to take war seriously, only the skill, dedication, and valor of our troops prevents disaster.

And the military's recent civilian leadership begged for disaster. Conveniently forgotten now by the RMA's apostles, Operation Iraqi Freedom was supposed to prove that ground forces were obsolete. While Rumsfeld reserved even low-level tactical decisions for himself (crippling our military's preparations for war), he turned essential aspects of planning over to two of the most arrogant and inept political hacks ever to have stepped inside the Pentagon: Neither Undersecretary of Defense for Policy Douglas J. Feith nor Undersecretary of Defense for Intelligence Stephen A. Cambone had served in the military (they were far too important, of course), and they treated those in uniform as janitors whose views were as unimportant as their lives.

The only qualifications Rumsfeld's acolytes had for their posts were the temperament of Bolshevik commissars, political connections, and a handful of cracked-brain theories about how to win wars for five cents on the dollar in order to shovel the savings into the defense industry. Privatization was expected to turn soldierly lead into corporate gold. Rumsfeld, Feith, Cambone, and the other alchemists in their coven convinced themselves that a campaign of "shock and awe," employing hi-tech weapons, would stun Saddam Hussein into surrender overnight. Our soldiers would simply drive to Baghdad and direct traffic until the dust settled.

Refusing to give a hearing to military leaders who tried to warn them, the RMA fanatics at one point insisted that the war could be waged with less than ten thousand ground troops. Airpower alone would do the job. The Office of the Secretary of Defense intended to use the war's results as a rationale for *cutting* the Army and Marine Corps to free up still more funds for the defense industry.

Rumsfeld and his sorcerer's apprentices were stunningly out of touch with reality. As haughty as Saddam Hussein, Rumsfeld's gang not only believed that they knew how to fight and win wars painlessly and cheaply, but that postwar Iraq would take care of itself. When former Army Chief of Staff General Eric Shinseki stated that an orderly occupation of Iraq could require hundreds of thousands of troops, he was mocked as yesterday's man, out of touch with the glittering new truth revealed to those whose knowledge of war came only from the campus or the think tank. Military commanders and planners had to fight for every last platoon that composed the force that eventually fought the war.

Operation Iraqi Freedom began with a hi-tech sound-and-light show that achieved nothing. Unable to locate the Iraqi leadership, despite the billions spent on target acquisition technology, the Air Force bombed empty buildings—and not many of them, at that. We wanted to win a war without breaking windows.

The overhyped shock-and-awe campaign fizzled overnight. Among other things, it had failed to take into account the psychology of the enemy. A mere display of our technological prowess was supposed to persuade Saddam Hussein and his regime to surrender. But the Iraqi leadership had no incentive to sue for peace. They knew it would mean the loss of everything they had stolen from their country, as well as the end of their prestige, power, and personal freedom—if not their lives. The war was an all-or-nothing struggle to the enemy leadership. They weren't impressed by a few small-yield, guided bombs creating a fireworks display on the Baghdad skyline.

The war had to be fought and won the old way, with ground troops engaging in close-range combat in sandstorms. Faced with the failure of its initial gambit, the Air Force's emphasis shifted toward providing more battlefield support to the Army and Marines. Suddenly, as our services began to work together, the effectiveness of each of the parts increased. Airpower was able to make a striking difference by focusing on the destruction of enemy combat capability instead of blowing up filing cabinets in Baghdad. The Marines and Army could move even faster with airpower paving the way. A great national team came together to win one of the most lopsided victories in history.

We won because our troops and our combat leaders made up for the deficiencies in the plan. But the effort was far riskier than it had to be. Because Donald Rumsfeld personally refused to send more troops, we lacked cavalry regiments to guard our lengthening supply lines, which led to resupply disruptions and deadly ambushes. Fatefully, we got to Baghdad with insufficient numbers of troops to inundate the Sunni Triangle, the regime's bastion of support. In the cities that later became hotbeds of the insurgency—Fallujah, Ramadi, Samarra, Baquba, and others—the Coalition could not establish a robust, convincing presence.

Towns and villages in the Sunni heartland did not see an American soldier for months—or may have glimpsed a convoy racing by, stirring up dust for a minute or two. A hostile population was never forced to comprehend its defeat.

Warfare still requires adequate numbers of ground troops. Twenty-first-century warfare, with its very human enemies, requires far more than we presently have in the ranks. But it's not only the battlefield that demands sufficient troop strength. As we have learned yet again, occupations cannot be staged on the cheap. Especially in conflicts waged between asymmetrical cultures, sheer human presence—in uniform—is essential if we want to extract long-term benefits from our battlefield victories.

There certainly is a place for technology, and plenty of it, in our military. Modern communications gear, unmanned aerial vehicles, and small-ticket items such as laser designators or night-vision devices give our grunts a powerful advantage. But we must learn to avoid the trap of allowing weapons systems to dictate strategy, instead of developing weapons to support our strategy. Employed in support of a well-wrought campaign plan, hi-tech weapons can bring us enormous advantages. But the campaign plan must never be written to justify the weapons.

Do we want the best military technologies? Of course. But the best doesn't always mean the most expensive. The weapons and support systems we buy have to be appropriate, affordable technologies that genuinely help our troops instead of deluding decision makers into imagining that war can be waged antiseptically.

History takes a special delight in frustrating human vanity and exposing mortal folly. Operation Iraqi Freedom, which was supposed to be the first war won by technology alone, proved, instead, the enduring need for strong land forces. Instead of cutting two to three Army divisions to fund the purchase of more defense-industry pork—as he desired to do—Rumsfeld found himself fighting efforts by Congress to *increase* the size of the Army and Marines. And the manpower demands of the occupation of Iraq, for which Rumsfeld and his deputies refused to plan, had to be met by extensive reserve-component call-ups, mandated enlistment extensions, cruelly delayed retirements—and every form of denial and subterfuge in which Rumsfeld's pack of amateurs could engage.

Rumsfeld and his bench of incompetents set out to do the right thing by deposing Saddam Hussein. But they did it very, very badly. Their ambitions were rescued only by the Infantrymen they disdained. Convinced that they were smarter regarding military affairs than those who had dedicated their lives to uniformed service, the Rummycrats humiliated generals and colonels in front of their subordinates, dismissing them as fools. Notorious bullies, Rumsfeld's apparatchiks knew full well that those in uniform were forbidden by military codes of conduct and by law from answering back. They wielded their power with the vanity and pique of Chinese court eunuchs. When things went wrong they proved themselves as cowardly and inept as their apparent role models.

We all have known people who appeared invincibly strong while life was going their way, but who collapsed abruptly when confronted with adversity. Like all inbred cabals, from the acquaintances of Timothy McVeigh to Osama bin Laden's inner circle, the insular Rumsfeld ideologues talked themselves into an alternative reality, listening only to those rare outsiders who reinforced their vision (including at least one convicted criminal, Ahmad Chalabi, who allegedly betrayed the United States to Iran). McVeigh and his tiny circle convinced themselves that one dramatic blow would ignite a nationwide revolution. Likewise, bin Laden believed that the 9/11 attacks would force the United States to retreat from the world. Rumsfeld's commissars convinced themselves, in accordance with their dogma, that the various peoples of Iraq would instantly unite to form a peaceful, rule-of-law democracy the moment they were rid of Saddam Hussein. There was no need to consult the military on the requirements of an occupation. Even the word "occupation" was avoided as long as possible.

This wasn't just denial. It was delusion.

As soon as the postwar looting began in Baghdad, Rumsfeld, Feith, Cambone, and their accomplices lost their nerve. They had not planned for trouble, and they refused to begin planning. They improvised from day to day, hoping that things would magically go right. Throwing money at the problem, they didn't even know how to do that effectively. All the while our troops bore the burden, paying with their blood. Our policies killed our soldiers, as surely as the terrorists and insurgents did.

One lesson we should take from Operation Iraqi Freedom is that we need well-balanced armed forces in adequate numbers. Every service has its role to play, but no service, no matter the lurid claims made by defense contractors, can win a war alone.

The lesson we must take from the occupation of Iraq is that, if war really is too important to be left to the generals, the subsequent peace is far too complex to be left to political hacks. Or to defense contractors, no matter how well connected they may be politically.

Our engagement in Iraq showed the world that we have the finest military in history, and thanks to those in uniform Iraq's long-term prospects are encouraging. But our experience should have warned us that our troops need adequate support, and that their expert leaders deserve respect. An amateur would not presume to tell a neurosurgeon how to operate, yet military affairs are far more complex than even the most arcane surgery. Nonetheless, every junior staffer in Washington knows better than the generals.

Had Rumsfeld and his underlings listened to General Shinseki, or to the many other military officers, diplomats, and intelligence hands who sought to talk sense to them, our occupation of Iraq would have gone far more smoothly, far fewer of our troops would have died or suffered wounds in the war's aftermath, and the people of Iraq would have had to endure far less chaos, confusion, and bloodshed on the road to freedom.

Instead, we learned that, in the pell-mell rush of successive Democratic and Republican administrations to pander to defense contractors, we had bought nearly useless, shockingly expensive weaponry, but neglected to provide our combat troops with sufficient sets of body armor.

Why? Because there isn't much of a profit margin in body armor. Or in the other scraps of gear that combat troops really need. Soldiers were forced to buy their own goggles, hi-tech water packs (critical in the desert heat), and even Global Positioning System (GPS) handsets for the war. The perverse logic of defense acquisition is that the more expensive a piece of military hardware, the more advocates it finds. Virtually no one in Congress or in the military-industrial complex against which President Eisenhower warned us takes an interest in equipment that is useful, robust, and cheap.

We lacked sufficient armor plating for our vehicles. Ammunition ran gravely low in multiple categories. Precision weapons not only failed to win the war, but were so expensive that our reserve stocks proved dangerously thin.

Precision-strike capabilities are fine for targeting terrorist safe houses. But in warfare you need abundant supplies of every form of ammunition you mean to use. Between defense contractors and civilian defense "experts," we had been persuaded to rely on precision weapons to prevent "collateral damage." But the "smart bombs" were so few and so weak that they failed to inflict the *necessary* damage—and our troops were running out of several categories of basic munitions by the time we reached Baghdad.

Had we faced a more determined, more capable enemy, a significant portion of our airpower would have been grounded for lack of armaments. Even the hi-tech intelligence network that was supposed to enable precision warfare failed us; not only couldn't it locate the enemy leadership, it missed the mass shift of Saddam's *fidayeen,* his private thugs, to the cities and towns along our lines of advance.

Worse, the mantra of privatization—an excuse for tossing still more money into the laps of contractors—meant that our battlefield supply system no longer had the robust qualities that helped us win previous wars. Units in battle were running out of bullets, fuel, food, and water. The contractors who were supposed to pick up the slack in the rear were nowhere to be seen. Only truly heroic efforts by Army and Marine logistics personnel kept the attack moving forward.

The failures of Rumsfeld's phony defense reforms have been hidden behind assertions of greater efficiency. But war isn't about efficiency. It's about effectiveness. The concept of just-in-time spare parts may work down at the local auto dealership (in fact, it doesn't—it saves money at the expense of the customer's convenience), but the approach doesn't work on the battlefield. An Infantry battalion can't wait for FedEx to deliver its machine-gun ammunition.

Our military leaders themselves have failed us on this count. They've never had the courage to stand up before Congress and the American people to explain that some amount of wastage, in peacetime and in war, is part of freedom's price tag. You can't go to war with insufficient supplies in the warehouse—and warehousing supplies means that some spoil, at which point the media launch yet another self-righteous "exposé." We don't need F-22s, but we damned well need enough rifle ammunition. And extra boots. And body armor.

Nor does employing insider organizations like Halliburton save us money. Many of the tasks that the last several administrations—from both parties—have contracted out to their campaign contributors belong in the military services. Friends of mine in uniform were furious in the early days of the occupation when the contractors who were supposed to deliver supplies and even the soldiers' mail refused to do the jobs for which they were being paid so generously. Iraq was a dangerous place, you see. You can order Private Snuffy to drive his truck into a combat zone, but civilian contractors ignore you.

Contractors do a fine job of supplying meals in garrison (where they can be monitored for fraud) and even in supporting benign peacekeeping operations with temporary housing or showers. But the essential tasks of warfare—and occupations—belong within the military services. We have stripped our military services to the bone so defense-industry executives can buy bigger vacation homes in Aspen.

In times of conflict or during election campaigns politicians wrap themselves in the flag and promise those in uniform the sun, the moon, and the stars. Then they lavish money on the defense industry while soldiers buy their own body armor from their austere salaries. And still our troops go out and win our wars.

––––––––––––

We must break free of the myth of bloodless, hi-tech war, as well as from the thrall of defense contractors, with their private armies of lobbyists and lawyers. We must find a way to hold Congress to account, as difficult as that may be when the common citizen so often must choose the lesser of two evils at the polls. And we need to give our troops what they need, not what corporate thieves prefer to foist upon them.

The Revolution in Military Affairs was the only American revolution that failed to deliver on its promises. It was also the only revolution that attempted to ignore the human factor. Even the information technology revolution remembered that it had to serve a customer. And nothing makes greater demands on flesh and blood than warfare. No machine will ever replace that flesh and blood entirely. By lying to ourselves about the essence of war, we not only make war more likely, but more deadly in the end.

Our troops know how to fight. But our leaders forgot how to win. The resolution belatedly displayed by President Bush in the postelection Second Battle of Fallujah suggests that we have begun to come to our senses. But we will never lack for voices insisting that, if only we heed the wisdom of the defense industry, technology by itself can bring us victory, or that military victory is meaningless, or that we should stop short of destroying our own—and humankind's—enemies.

If we wish to conquer our enemies, we must conquer our own delusions.

Three
THE MEDIA AS A COMBATANT

In this age of microchips and blood our obsession with technology nearly rivals the passion of our enemies for vindictive religion and a punitive god. One dream is postmodern, the other vision premodern, but both are attempts to master the complexity of humankind, to simplify the world in order to attain an impossible perfection. Both are frustrated by the human element.

Which factors *will* shape our conflicts? How must we fight in order to win when our enemies rarely confront us with armies, preferring the fluid affinities of hatred? How can we advance the cause of freedom, human rights, and individual dignity in a world where oppression delights not only our violent opponents but their many passive supporters? How is it that so many human beings welcome the limits placed upon their lives, *preferring* the embrace of tyranny over the risks of liberty? Is it habit, fear of the unknown, or the fault of culture? Is it biology? Why are the Lincolns and Washingtons so rare, the Robespierres, Hitlers, and Osama bin Ladens so common?

Much ink already has been spilled to describe our struggle with terror as a war of ideas, but the truth is grimmer than that. Our enemy has only the flimsiest ideas—but his *visions* are powerful and enthralling to those who have failed in every other sphere of human endeavor. We are at war with devils, ghosts, and dreams, with the spirits that have haunted humankind down the ages. All we can do is to kill them whenever they take the form of flesh and blood.

Before they kill us.

———————

The most profound shift in warfare does, indeed, rest upon a techno-logical foundation—but not upon our ballyhooed military technology. The greatest single challenge our forces face when they must fight is the power of the global media.

The media can no longer sustain their pretenses of being aloof, ob-jective observers dispassionately recording events. The media are com-batants. Their cameras may not slay directly, but their reporting now can change the outcome of battles and alter the course of campaigns. In the Middle East and elsewhere the media are often no more than prop-aganda outlets explicitly hostile to the United States, the West, and any attempts to foster democracy or liberty. Our own media's capacity to damage our struggle for freedom and security lies in their appetite for sensation, their lack of context, and their partisanship. The better ele-ments within our media try to report the truth, but even the finest me-dia outlets rarely report *all* of the truth. The herd behavior of media organizations and individual journalists leads to a selectivity in re-portage that is sometimes calculated, but frequently witless. Warfare is far from the only field of human behavior in which repetitious broad-cast coverage of an isolated incident creates an unjustified sense of cri-sis, hopelessness, or defeat, but it *is* the area in which misapprehensions fostered by the media can have the most fateful consequences.

Overseas, the problem is far worse. Much of the media are reflex-ively anti-American. We shall not be forgiven for winning the Cold War and exposing the bankrupt lies of leftist theory, nor for the many social revolutions we have led and sustained, nor for our abundant success as a state and a society. Having failed on its own, much of the world needs to find us at fault. We cannot change this with "public diplomacy" or ap-peasement. The world *needs* a "great Satan America" as desperately as the Arabs need Israel to blame for their self-inflicted misery.

We have been slow to understand the power of the media (al-though advertisers have not). Our military fumbles in front of the mi-crophones—this was never part of their job before—and officers brave in battle grow timid and terse when the cameras take their aim. Our political leaders are irresolute, even cowardly, when it comes to chal-lenging outright propaganda. And much of what is broadcast about our military operations abroad is nothing but propaganda, from the spiteful leftist nostalgia of the BBC to al-Jazeera's infectious lies.

We agonize over how to make the world love us while much of that world is preoccupied with hating us more effectively. Propaganda is far more powerful today, in the age of multiplying media outlets, than ever it was before, and disinformation campaigns will only grow more powerful in the future. Hostile reporting already has defeated our forces on battlefields where we were winning militarily, most notably in Iraq. In the First Battle of Fallujah, in April 2004, our enemies could not withstand the military prowess of the U.S. Marine Corps, but our civilian leaders could not withstand the assault of calculated propaganda.

Unwilling or unable to come to grips with a defiant reality, our civilian representatives in Baghdad, as well as our national leadership, refused to accept that the nature of the Middle East's broadcast media was irreconcilably malevolent. They convinced themselves that Arab government–sanctioned advocates for hatred, such as the television networks al-Jazeera and al-Arabiya (to be fair, the latter has attempted some reforms), were forces for freedom and free speech in the Middle East. As our media enemies openly did all they could to undermine first our destruction of Saddam Hussein's regime and then our reconstruction of Iraq, American journalists insisted that the only issue that mattered was freedom of the press. As al-Jazeera and al-Arabiya broadcast fabricated stories of atrocities and provided platforms for professional haters, our journalists, more concerned with the spook of censorship than with terrorism or atrocities, defended their unscrupulous brethren without reservation. Our leaders and editors alike forgot that freedom of the press is founded upon a sense of responsibility and a steady insistence on facts.

Our own media view themselves as members of a lofty global collective, and thus they mistake the character of their Middle Eastern counterparts. Our journalists are no more of the same breed as Arab propagandists than our soldiers are identical to Islamic terrorists. Our insistence that all media, everywhere, deserve unquestioned freedom is lunatic. That logic would justify the Nazi propaganda ministry.

If foreign journalists are unwilling to report the truth, we are not obligated to facilitate their lies.

Yet we do. The most insidious enemy we faced in Iraq was never Saddam Hussein's military or his security services, nor was it international terrorists or criminal insurgents. It was al-Jazeera and the global media.

Shortly after the handover of authority to an interim Iraqi government at the end of June 2004, the Iraqis themselves did what our own leaders had been afraid to do: They suspended al-Jazeera's press privileges. The Iraqis knew full well how al-Jazeera had poisoned the Middle East against every step their country took toward the rule of law or democracy. Staffed by aging pan-Arabists (the last of the Nasserites), embittered exiles, and bright young bigots, al-Jazeera's coverage was a torrent of lies about purported American attacks on hospitals and schools, invented massacres and mass rapes, and violations of mosques by American troops.

The lies worked.

The maturity of the media as a combatant came in the spring of 2004, when al-Jazeera won the First Battle of Fallujah. Previously, the media had never truly decided a battle or stopped a war. America's military involvement in Indochina did not end because of the pontificating of journalists. It dragged on until the American people realized for themselves that the halfhearted war was unwinnable as our leaders chose to wage it.

Nor did the media force the American withdrawals from Lebanon or Somalia. In both cases presidents panicked under the misapprehension—a legacy of Vietnam—that Americans would no longer accept casualties. The retreat from Mogadishu was especially disheartening, since it followed a powerful battlefield victory. Certainly, both presidents involved in these events worried about the effect media images would have on the electorate. But our media, while influential, was not decisive.

The destruction of the Taliban regime in Afghanistan went too quickly for the international media to react with its usual anti-American venom—and the shadow of the Twin Towers still stretched around the globe. But by the time the United States and our allies went to the Arab heartlands with a program of liberation, democratization, and reform the America haters had regained their footing. Middle Eastern journalists were—and are—prepared to sacrifice the hopes, the welfare, and even the lives of tens of millions of their fellow Muslims to frustrate America. During the Iraq crisis Arabs and their regional brethren committed yet another act of civilizational suicide out of wounded vanity and spite.

Arabist and Islamist propaganda has had an indisputable effect. Our failed initial effort to subdue Fallujah offers the perfect example of how this new form of warfare functions, simultaneously handing terrorists and fascist dead-enders their first victory in Iraq and inspiring the Arab media to even more ambitious propaganda. Although American casualties were few, that first fight in Fallujah may have been the most serious American battlefield defeat since the retreat from the Yalu during the Korean War. The American aura of invincibility was shattered, albeit not through military means. Terrorists gained new reasons to hope, and America's enemies felt a renewal of confidence after their shock at the ease with which our forces conducted Operation Iraqi Freedom. We shall have to wait and see how much lost ground we have regained as a result of our subsequent success in the Second Battle of Fallujah.

I was in Iraq during "First Fallujah." Night after night I sat with Kurdish friends, watching the spectacle unfold on al-Jazeera. The Kurds have an excellent intelligence network and we were receiving reports from their agents in the city. After my own military career I could put the things I saw and heard into perspective, interpreting our combat moves and enemy claims.

The U.S. Marines were fighting methodically, in accordance with the urban warfare doctrine the Corps had been refining for nearly a decade. They were winning, hands down. The terrorists who were not being killed were coming out hands up.

But the Marine operations in Fallujah were destined to fail. They were just too slow for the media age.

The American military places a great deal of emphasis on disciplined speed, on a high battle tempo. The exception long has been urban combat, where a deliberate approach was deemed essential. The unspoken rule for the First Battle of Fallujah was "Be Careful!"

This flaw in our doctrine (which is now being revised in the field) had understandable justifications. Urban combat notoriously produces high casualties. Not only are ranges reduced, while the enemy can hide in three dimensions, but the environment itself causes injuries. Civilians crowd the urban battlefield. Terrorists and other irregular forces think nothing of using the innocent as human shields. Intelligence work is more difficult; despite all of our technological whistles and bells, you often locate your enemy for the first time when he shoots at you—if then. Extensive destruction is not only costly in economic terms, but creates visual effects that play into the hands of propagandists.

In a classic city fight you gnaw your way through. Teams clear houses methodically, working forward block by block. And when you face an enemy who refuses to wear a uniform, you may not know the difference between an innocent man and an enemy combatant until one raises a gun or detonates a bomb.

Prevailing military logic argued for step-by-step urban campaigns that minimized friendly casualties, while doing as little harm as possible to the civilian population or the infrastructure.

That logic proved wrong. We can no longer win urban battles by fighting slowly and carefully. We have to speed the kill and bear the cost.

Fortunately, our military demonstrated its ability to fix its problems on the move after the politically imposed retreat from Fallujah in April 2004. The Marines and the Army studied the problem of postmodern city combat, experimenting with new approaches in subsequent urban operations, from Najaf to Samarra. By the time the order was given to return to Fallujah and eliminate it as a terrorist base our commanders had drawn the essential lessons: Speed is as vital in urban operations as in every other form of combat; skill and technology still can't substitute for adequate numbers of troops; the enemy must be overwhelmed on multiple axes; you cannot shy from necessary destruction; and combined arms and joint operations are as valuable in city fighting as in mounted armored warfare in the desert.

Our commanders realized that they had to "operate within the media cycle," to get the job done rapidly, before hostile propaganda could rescue our enemies. As a result, a sophisticated plan employed feints, multiple lines of attack, simultaneous armored and dismounted assaults, irresistible firepower, and fifteen thousand troops instead of the two thousand engaged in First Fallujah. A ferocious tempo of operations concluded the major fighting in less than a week. It was a textbook case for future urban operations.

But we will need other models, too, since every combat environment has unique qualities. We had significant advantages in the Second Battle of Fallujah: The civilian population had abandoned the city, allowing us to employ firepower more freely; the terrorist leadership had fled, leaving the fight to undertrained subordinates; we had had plenty of time to study the city and its defenses; we had been able to "prepare the battlefield" with air strikes and special-operations raids for months before our assault; hostile journalists had enjoyed only restricted access to the city; and we had strong backing from the host government. The need to launch a short-notice attack on a fully inhabited city would present both tougher military challenges and greater ethical dilemmas. Finally, Fallujah was a minor city, with a peacetime population of three hundred thousand, while many of the megacities in the troubled regions of the world have populations of several million or more.

Still, Second Fallujah was a brilliant achievement, superbly planned and skillfully executed. We not only beat the terrorists and insurgents handily, with friendly casualties reduced by almost 90 percent from historical standards for urban assaults, but we showed that, given resolute leadership at the national level, we could beat the global media, too.

Nonetheless, the victory closed with our own media delightedly broadcasting a tape of a Marine shooting a wounded Iraqi prisoner—with few attempts to place the event in the infernal context of combat. Instead of reporting our remarkable military achievement, our own media and their global counterparts leaped on the clip of that young Marine pulling the trigger, broadcasting it over and over again for a week, while refusing to show the videotaped execution by the terrorists of Margaret Hassan, a selfless aid worker whose dismembered body was tossed into the street. If the media couldn't defeat us in Fallujah the second time around, they were determined to spoil any satisfaction the American public might take from our victory.

As with the media's self-righteous amplification of the abuses in Abu Ghraib prison, the American people shrugged off the morbid glee of the journalists with typical common sense. The real damage done was in the Middle East, where the irresponsible release of that footage of the young Marine allowed the regional media to spark another wave of anger toward the United States (al-Jazeera broadcast the clip with the Marine shooting the prisoner over and over again, but refused to show the simultaneously released video of Islamic terrorists shooting an innocent woman in the head).

The media's default position is that "the public has a right to know." But do the media honor their own claim? Should it be acceptable for many of our media outlets to portray only the side of a story that shows our country in an unfavorable light? When our government behaves in a selective fashion, the media howl for blood. But the media close ranks against external criticism. Journalists are the self-appointed saints of our society, but it's the public that goes to the stake.

In the Second Battle of Fallujah the U.S. military beat the media (as President Bush had done earlier the same month). And the media didn't like it one bit. Just as we learned from our initial defeat, our enemies, foreign and domestic, will learn from theirs. Our troops will never again face a single opponent in our military encounters. We will face the enemy with the gun—plus that untouchable third party to the conflict, the enemy with the camera.

In the Middle East the cliché proves true: The enemy of my enemy is my friend. The greatest perversity about al-Jazeera's (or the BBC's) lionizing of the terrorists is that, were they ever to come to power, the Islamic assassins the Marines flushed out of Fallujah would imprison, torture, and execute the journalists and staff from al-Jazeera and any similar Arab networks. Even their slight degree of independence (to say nothing of the female news anchors) would be vastly too much for fundamentalist extremists to tolerate. The Taliban didn't rush to found a free media. Terrorists who ban even folk music aren't about to let others air their political opinions.

Nonetheless, the pan-Arabists from al-Jazeera put all of their energies to work to support the terrorists and insurgents in Fallujah in 2004. While Second Fallujah is the best model we have for how to execute urban operations, First Fallujah is the case we need to study to understand the strategic power of the media. Night after night al-Jazeera broadcast utterly unfounded claims that American forces were targeting mosques, hospitals, and schools, killing hundreds of innocent civilians. The "casualty" clips did not bear scrutiny. The indoor shots of a single wounded child and wailing mother could have been archival footage—or even generated by the terrorists. The footage I saw was cleverly intermixed with shots of the Fallujah city-scape, but nothing convincingly tied the few actual images of the wounded to the ongoing battle or the city itself.

Al-Jazeera created an alternative reality.

Even though the film clips from April 2004 showed no mass carnage and no destroyed mosques or hospitals, the reporters and anchors repeated over and over that Americans were massacring women and children by the hundreds, that our bombing was indiscriminate. They never criticized a single terrorist action and celebrated any hint of American losses. And they consistently cut from images of U.S. troops to footage of Israelis engaging Palestinians.

It was the most transparent propaganda I have seen in my lifetime. And it worked.

Not only did the other Middle Eastern media follow al-Jazeera's lead, even European networks—still furious that our troops had not suffered a bloodbath on their way to Baghdad—jumped on board.

While our Marines were methodically and successfully clearing one district of Fallujah after another of the terrorists, taking great pains to minimize civilian casualties and limit destruction in the city—doing everything right doctrinally—they were losing the battle at the strategic level.

How did the process work? In the wake of his steadfast support for freedom during Iraq's liberation, British Prime Minister Tony Blair was in political trouble. Incensed that the world was moving on without them, the British media sold anti-Americanism as political Viagra. Long a leader of vision and courage, Blair feared he would go the way of another valiant European, Spain's recently defeated prime minister, José María Aznar, who lost an election to al-Qaeda after the Madrid train bombings.

In Blair's case, it wasn't terrorist bombings that threatened to send him packing, but the British media's fantastic claims, bought wholesale from al-Jazeera, that his American allies were slaughtering innocent Arabs. The BBC portrayed the First Battle of Fallujah as the bombings of Rotterdam, Coventry, London, and Dresden combined, with Hiroshima looming.

Long brave, Blair folded. He threatened to leave the Coalition unless we ceased fire in Fallujah (another source claims that the Italian government made a similar threat).

Bush gave in. He personally had grasped the need for retaliation after the public dismemberment of four American contractors in Fallujah and had pressed the military for results, but he couldn't face the prospect of the Coalition disintegrating.

The Marines were ordered to withdraw. A disastrous deal was made for a pro-Saddam militia to take control of the city. Former Baathist military officers swore they would root out the terrorists themselves. Instead, they cooperated with them. Fallujah was left as a city-state of terror, a refuge for all the violent actors opposing us and an encouragement to terrorists and insurgents elsewhere to resist until propaganda delivered victory. An uprising reignited in the Shia cities of southern Iraq and in the Shia slums of Baghdad, led by a renegade cleric, Moqtada al-Sadr. The Sunni Muslims had won in Fallujah; now the Shia had to match the achievement.

Al-Jazeera won the First Battle of Najaf, too, by countering our operations with lies that excited Iraq's political factions. American forces had to go back into Najaf again. And again. Ultimately, a canny U.S. military operation, the resolve of Iraq's interim prime minister, and some ruthless horse-trading among the Shias pacified the city. But central Najaf was badly battered, the thug cleric Moqtada al-Sadr remained free, and what might have been an easy win for our troops turned into a protracted struggle.

We have to repeat it to ourselves until we get it: If we are not willing to fight to win, we should not fight at all. A near victory is a defeat. And when we stop short of victory, for any reason, we have wasted the life of every soldier lost. We relearned that lesson over the course of 2004, from Fallujah to Najaf to Samarra and, at last, back to Fallujah. Our military will not soon forget it. Whether our elected and appointed officials will remember it is open to question.

Both Bush and Blair drew the correct conclusions from watching Fallujah become the world capital of terror after our disengagement. The second time around they not only supported each other without wavering, but cooperated on operational matters such as redeploying British troops to permit American units to bolster the Fallujah attack formations. Neither man backed away from the combat intensity required to finish the job. But that is no guarantee of future behavior.

For their part, our armed forces must continue to devise additional techniques to win quickly on the urban battlefield—the combat environment of the future. In the media age speed has acquired a new dimension of importance—the operation that bogs down is likely doomed. Plodding military operations in urban terrain, no matter their virtuous intentions, *always* favor our enemies, both those who shoot bullets and those who fire words and images. We must win urban battles so swiftly that the president can present the world—and even our allies—with a fait accompli. This will be our primary tactical and operational challenge in the coming decades.

Fallujah, one small city in Iraq, was a rehearsal for the American wars of the future.

We not only must learn to fight faster, to kill our enemies with digital speed in a digital age, but we need to rethink our approach to media coverage of conflict. We need a two-track approach that recognizes the difference between legitimate journalism and enemy propaganda.

Were we only to apply common sense to the media problem, we would find it far simpler to solve than alarmists fear. During the Second World War we did not feel compelled to grant the Nazi media access to our military operations. Imagine if German Propaganda Ministry cameramen had been on Omaha Beach filming that D-Day bloodbath, with our troops forbidden to interfere in the name of media freedom. The situation today is even more absurd. It's as if the Allied media had taken German propaganda at face value.

Irresponsible members of our own media will claim that the heavens are collapsing and the earth is yawning to suck us down to hell, but we have to distinguish between journalism and propaganda, between honest reporting errors and cynical lies.

Legitimate media outlets should be given the fullest access to our military operations commensurate with security needs. And security requirements should not be exaggerated to exclude the press when their presence might be an inconvenience or even an embarrassment. But we also have a right to expect fair treatment from journalists and should not hesitate to restrict the access of those who have demonstrated a propagandistic agenda. Our military should never use censorship to cover up mistakes, but it *is* legitimate to demand that news organizations withhold specific pieces of information until a battle or even a campaign is over.

America's media, for all their problems, form a cornerstone of our freedom. While most journalists are herd animals who engage in groupthink, the mavericks redeem the profession. For its part, the Internet has been a mighty tool for spreading hatred, but it also has made it harder for governments, businesses, or prominent individuals to cover up much of anything. Web sites and blogs are not going to replace the print media, television, or radio, but they do augment them meaningfully. Some of the best reporting from Iraq wasn't from any news organization, but from soldiers and Marines who used the Internet to share their combat observations with comrades back home. The Internet has also become a first-rate tool for keeping journalists honest, as CBS learned during the 2004 election campaign, when it attempted to foist forged documents about President Bush's National Guard service upon America's voters.

Our media are also plagued with jealousy. In part, this is simply human nature in a competitive environment. But the broadcast media, especially, inflate egos. During Operation Iraqi Freedom it was fascinating to watch our media divide into opposing camps.

In a stroke of public relations genius the Pentagon allowed reporters who had sufficient fortitude to embed themselves with combat units liberating Iraq. It had finally dawned on a new generation in uniform that the press versus the military hostility was far from consistent, that many in the media did want to get the story right, and that it was often the military, not the media, that was responsible for keeping old resentments alive.

Our soldiers impressed the journalists, who naturally filed admiring, if not entirely uncritical, stories from the battlefield. Viewed up close our soldiers and Marines are magnificent, not only in their skills, but in their decency (and, not least, in their politically incorrect sense of humor). The "embeds" produced some of the best war reporting ever printed, rivaling the finest coverage from World War II or Vietnam.

This time, there was no hostility from the military. The anger came from the colleagues of the embedded journalists. While reporters long had been in the habit of complaining about a lack of access to military operations, when the armed services suddenly offered a seat in an infantry fighting vehicle en route to combat to any credible journalist who wanted to sign up, plenty of reporters found innumerable reasons to avoid the risks of battle. We long have seen brave journalists in wartime, many of whom died to tell a battle's tale. They continue to die today. But others had grown comfortable with a culture of complaint about military restrictions. After posing a few cynical questions at a rear-area headquarters they were accustomed to fleeing back to their luxury hotels, filing what they could glean from briefings and snippets cajoled out of harried staff officers.

Suddenly, there were riveting, real-time stories pouring in from the battlefield. And the journalists who had chosen to stay behind to wage war from the Ritz-Carlton weren't getting on the air. The jealousy they displayed toward their comrades who had chosen to go unarmed into combat was one of the least attractive aspects of the media's war.

The embeds were accused of being soft on our troops, of having been co-opted by the military. Of course, when a platoon of Marines is fighting like the devil to keep you alive in a firefight during a sandstorm, it may suggest that our troops possess some virtues. But for the journalists who hid in the rear while the bullets were flying downrange the positive coverage of our men and women in uniform was beneath contempt.

The stay behinds were far more critical of their colleagues at risk in combat than they were of al-Jazeera's deadly lies.

Something's just plain wrong when a substantial part of our media gives the benefit of the doubt to anti-American propaganda while criticizing any positive coverage of our own troops.

We don't need endless adulation of our military or unrestrained celebration of our policies. But the assumption that America is always wrong is unacceptable. Just as our military has to adjust to a changed and changing world, so too our major news organizations need to go back to Ethics 101. A bit more common sense, combined with less intellectual conformity to the prejudices of the herd, wouldn't hurt, either. But, above all, it's a matter of integrity.

It was wrenching to read the *New York Times* or *The New Yorker* during Operation Iraqi Freedom. They all but cheered any hint of an American reverse. The same publications rooted for our occupation to fail from the moment Saddam Hussein's statue crashed to the ground. Our engagement in Iraq has brought some of America's most venerable publications to new low points, revealing the emptiness of their claims to be media of record. They called every combat development wrong because they were determined to see a presidential administration embarrassed, and they were so far removed from the flesh-and-blood reality of our troops that they reported friendly casualties with barely disguised glee.

For all that, we are far better served by our media than any other society is by its own. The sins of an arrogant minority sully the reputation of the rest. If only the media would be slightly more self-critical, their intermittent misbehavior and petty ambitions would be easier to bear. Meanwhile, the brave and forthright redeem the rest.

But when we are engaged in military operations overseas we not only have the right to decide which foreign media outlets we will permit to cover our forces, we have the duty to exercise that right diligently. We are no more obliged to give known enemies access to our combat operations or to headquarters briefings than the Marines on Iwo Jima were obliged to give interviews to Tokyo Rose.

We cannot stop propaganda organs from lying. But we can stop assisting them.

In the coming decades the propaganda war may become so ferocious that we will have to declare hostile journalists as full combatants and legitimate targets. A camera or a microphone cannot be allowed to protect hate speech when the diatribes and lies kill American troops and frustrate our purposes. Americans should never fear the truth, but deadly liars must learn to fear America. And when, as we have seen in Iraq, hostile journalists throw in their lot with our enemies so completely that they accompany them on terrorist ambushes or bombings, the "journalists" become legitimate targets.

Propaganda isn't free speech. It's the enemy of free speech.

One of the myths of the War on Terror is that "public diplomacy"—artfully concocted programs, pronouncements, broadcasts, and pamphlets—will make our enemies and the populations that sympathize with them love us. While it is certainly worth taking pains to make our case, the best for which we can hope is a slight effect on the margins of Middle Eastern societies. Reform is ultimately a do-it-yourself project.

Public diplomacy will not and cannot have the great effect that advocates of "soft power" claim for it. Those who think that all we have to do is to frame the argument properly to counter the appeal of terror are the soft-power counterparts of those RMA advocates who insist that buying one more expensive weapons system will neutralize the hatred in the human heart and arrest the decay of violent civilizations.

We must stop casting about for easy solutions to the world's distemper. There are none. We are in a multidimensional war that will last at least until our grandchildren are old enough to wage it—and perhaps much longer. This war will have its deceptive lulls, but until the Muslim world makes peace with itself, overcomes its addiction to blaming others, and reinvents itself from top to bottom terrorists will strive to do us harm. When they succeed tens of millions of their coreligionists will be gratified.

The weakness of our public diplomacy abroad isn't due to underfunding or even to American naïveté or a lack of talent, although each of those factors plays a part in our failure. The problem is far more basic. When a society plunges into crisis—as every society in the Middle East has to one degree or another—people grow susceptible to demagogues who tell them comforting lies. They will not turn away from their homegrown media and their favorite preachers of hatred to believe American broadcasts or presidential declarations. Radio Liberty and Radio Free Europe succeeded against the Soviet Empire because Moscow's victims yearned for freedom. But not all of the populations of the Middle East yearn for liberty. Many want revenge.

We can only hope that our experiment in forcing freedom on the peoples of Iraq will work over the long term. Political oppression and punitive religion have a long head start, and both have many acolytes. It's far too soon to tell, but we may find that rule of law democracy as we know it doesn't transplant to the soil of some cultures without the risk of hideous mutations. At present, there is room for sober optimism, but the Middle East remains an experiment, not an accomplishment.

The notion that everyone on this planet wants freedom more than anything else is absurd. Freedom is one of many things people want. Some people want it more than others. Even in Europe, hundreds of millions of Westerners willingly accept attentuated freedoms in return for different forms of security. Freedom may be virtuous and good, but not all human beings find virtue or goodness especially appealing. Personal or clan advantage may prove far more powerful than democracy, and we may find, over the coming decades, that what other civilizations desire isn't American-style freedom but simply more tolerable forms of oppression.

Our struggle to increase global opportunities for freedom and democracy remains worthwhile. We have no choice but to fight for our values in a world where our self-appointed enemies are determined to fight to the death for theirs. But we may have to be glad of partial successes. Some of the time we may fail utterly. Entire populations may continue to cling to familiar traditions, no matter how cruel and limiting. Yet every expansion of political and social freedom benefits America and humanity. We must remain true to our ideals, but we must pursue those ideals as realists. Ideology may get you into Baghdad, but it won't get you out again. We must face humanity in all its complex reality before we can hope to develop its taste for freedom—which will be an acquired taste for many millions.

Platitudes do not advance our cause. We must demonstrate freedom's benefits.

We will fight where we must and win where we can. But we should not expect to convince others that all they cherish is wrong—even when it *is* wrong. To be effective at all public diplomacy must leave behind its obsession with what we desire and work from within the desires of our enemies. What America thinks is good doesn't matter to an impoverished Pakistani whose only scraps of education came from a rural religious school that taught him how to read haltingly and how to hate passionately. If we do not take account of his dreams and desires our efforts to reach him will be entirely wasted. And his path to freedom may prove to be far longer and more difficult than we like.

We want to change the mind of a world we decline to understand. Meanwhile, the populations that breed terror are watching al-Jazeera. Or listening raptly to a mullah tell them that Americans are devils.

We cannot believe that *they* can be so gullible. But why should we expect them to trust us? After dictators we coddled told them all their lives that America was to blame when they had nothing to eat or their

children had no schools? Or when their ruling families, in between de-
bauches in Paris or London, funded religious fanatics who preached
a holy war against the West?

Would anyone reading this page trust a Middle Eastern news outlet above our own media? Human beings trust the familiar until it be-
trays them so obviously that it loses all credibility—as happened in the
Soviet Union and its satellites. But defeating Communism was relatively easy. It was a foreign philosophy shoved down the throats of the
suffocating. Communism didn't have centuries of tradition, and its
mortal gods all proved to have feet of clay.

Now we are trying to persuade at least a half-billion people that
what they have made of their religion over the centuries doesn't work
in the twenty-first century, that their elementary values must change,
from their treatment of women to their views on education, from their
work ethic to their intolerance.

In the First Battle of Fallujah Western leaders worried about losing
the public relations battle. But we had already lost it. Nor can public
diplomacy save the day. In the Second Battle of Fallujah our leaders
did what they were convinced was right, gave our military a free hand,
and ignored the criticism. The negative consequences were far less
than those produced by their earlier irresolute behavior.

We need to fight to win, no matter what it costs or whom it angers.
In the end, the price we pay will be far lower if we emulate Henry V
than if we carry on like Hamlet. War in the media age increasingly will
be war *with* the media. Before we agonize over winning hearts and
minds we had better be certain that we win on the battlefield.

That means fighting fast, and devil take the hindmost. We must
win the Fallujahs of the future before the world can react, before
broadcast lies can create so much international unrest that our allies
panic and our national leadership wavers. Once the president orders a
military operation our troops must accomplish it so swiftly that it's finished before the world can raise a complaint.

By the time the hostile camera crews arrive our enemies must be
corpses. Propaganda doesn't help the dead.

Four

THE ENEMY WITHIN

If the media's power to influence combat outcomes is the most pernicious obstacle to success on the contemporary battlefield, twenty-first-century warfare confronts us with plenty of other challenges as well. The first requirement for the American military and those who send it overseas to fight is to strip away most of the intellectual baggage accumulated over the past half century. While American society has been embracing constructive revolutions, each interacting with the others, our strategists and our national leadership, Democrat or Republican, have wandered off to Never-Never Land in regard to war.

We have spent decades convincing ourselves that war is what we wish it to be rather than what it is. With our fantasies of minimizing even enemy casualties en route to the achievement of bloodless war we have constructed a theoretical house of cards. But war is a fist that delights in smashing flimsy intellectual architecture.

Crucial to the proliferation of nonsensical theories of warfare has been the rise, in the wake of World War II, of "defense intellectuals," creatures who wish to prescribe, from the safety of think tanks and campuses, how the general should command and the infantryman fight. From the games theory shenanigans of Herman Kahn down to the antics of Newt Gingrich (from Polonius to Pandarus) we have been plagued by adult children who want to play Army without doing a push-up.

Although our think tanks harbor some quality minds—men of integrity such as Michael Ignatieff, P. W. Singer, Michael O'Hanlon, Thomas Donnelly, Michael P. Noonan and others—their contributions are diluted and finally overwhelmed by the awesome volume of nonsense produced by those welfare agencies for intellectuals. Ranging from the unbearable pretentiousness of the Carnegie Endowment for International Peace to the hucksterism of the RAND Corporation, these parasites consume much and contribute nothing.

The RAND Corporation (once satirized acutely as the "Bland Corporation") is by far the worst offender in the sphere of national security. A self-licking ice cream cone, RAND hires influential inside-the-Beltway figures to assure the organization of continued favor with Congress (a practice aped by many another think tank). During my tenure as an officer on the Army Staff I never saw a single RAND product of the slightest utility. Yet we in the Office of the Deputy Chief of Staff for Intelligence had to continue to commission studies from them—knowing we would get nothing of value—because the funding mechanism provided that RAND would be paid whether we tasked it or not.

It was a disgraceful scam, and I once got a (light) slap on the wrist for confronting a RAND briefing team in our secure facility in the Pentagon. After a presentation startlingly devoid of content one of the RAND representatives told me, in front of my comrades, that RAND might have a job for me if I decided to retire. My verbatim response cannot be printed in these wholesome pages, but it involved a graphic act and a herd of elephants. The RAND dignitaries scurried off to lodge a protest with the chain of command. When he later had to "discipline" me my boss could barely keep a straight face. We all knew what the RAND reps were doing, but it was beyond our power to call them to account.

Think tanks parade their nonprofit status, but many are funded by loathsome interest groups. Their executives do not starve. Most Washington think tanks are no more than holding pens for politicians temporarily out of a job and nests for flocks of intellectuals whose featherweight ideas would never survive the turbulent skies of the marketplace. I defy any reader of this book to name a single Washington civilian think-tank product from the past quarter century that has had a significant positive effect upon our national security. The only such organizations that contribute to our national defense are the meagerly funded, hardworking think tanks inside or closely affiliated with our military and staffed by former or active-duty officers, men and women who have firsthand experience of the armed services and the world beyond our shores.

Were every civilian think tank in Washington swept away tomorrow the functioning of our military and of our government would be improved, not hindered. Republicans, especially, should be critical of this welfare culture, which only serves to provide off-campus sinecures to those who cannot endure capitalist competition.

If any idea, in any sphere, has merit it will hold its ground in the marketplace. Any text that must rely on a Washington think tank to subsidize its printing is not worth reading. There are no exceptions.

No enemy could have designed a scheme more subversive to common sense or military effectiveness than the rise of the defense intellectual without military experience. The result has been the overintellectualization of warfare, a pretense that a classroom calculus can discipline and dominate this intensely physical, emotional, and spiritual form of human conduct. It creates delusions that kill.

Charts, checklists, and formulas don't win battles. Soldiers do. Elaborate theories, even when backed by trillions of dollars of technology, do not win wars. Indeed, the startling flaw in virtually every theory of warfare generated by defense intellectuals in the past six decades has been an unwillingness to take the enemy into account. Not the phony enemy encapsulated by comparisons of warhead yields and missile counts during the Cold War, nor the "enemy as customer to be persuaded" tomfoolery that voided our military power in Indochina, nor the naive assumptions that mortal enemies might be dazzled into submission by a *son et lumière* display over Baghdad, but a human enemy of fears and desires, ambitions, courage, and, sometimes, genius.

As a former soldier, I have no doubt that the warning to "know thine enemy" antedates Suntzu and the other military prophets of antiquity. What warning is more timeless, or more sensible? Yet that is the theme too often slighted in the deluge of think-tank studies about conflict (many of which exist only to justify the purchase of a particular weapon system). Designed to pander to our prejudices and acquisition programs, even our war games pay far less attention to an enemy's complexity than common sense would dictate. We have tried to demote warfare to the status of an academic discipline, although it is the least academic mass endeavor imaginable.

When those who never served themselves propose theories for fighting our nation's wars, we have virgins writing sex manuals.

What are the practical effects of all these decades of impostors playing army behind a desk? We first saw the bloody results during the Vietnam war, when American lives were "invested" in perverse attempts to achieve never quite specified goals against an enemy willing to go to any length to win—while we attempted to capture war in algebra. But when you attempt to wage war on the cheap, you end up paying a far higher price for worse results than resolute behavior would have gained in the beginning.

Did our political establishment learn from Vietnam? Did our nation's leaders turn away from the failed apostles of "managing" the battlefield or the ideologues for whom warfare is less a solemn act of policy than a tool of partisan politics?

We refused to learn a thing. The amateurs remained in the ascendant, lauded until even military officers began to hang on to their prophecies.

We saw how little we had learned in 2003, during Operation Iraqi Freedom. Despite austere numbers and civilian interference that attempted to corrupt the ability of our ground forces to fight effectively, our dirty-boots military performed brilliantly in combat along the road to Baghdad. But they did it their own way, after all the grand theories promising victory through technology alone collapsed in the war's first seventy-two hours. Once again we saw the blight of the theorists evidenced by our civilian leadership's determination to make war as painless as possible even to our enemies. We did all we could to minimize the *enemy* body count, to spare entire Iraqi military formations and to avoid "unnecessary" damage to the country's infrastructure—to say nothing of our obsession with avoiding civilian casualties.

The result was a dazzling battlefield triumph but a hollow strategic victory. Despite the magnificent performance of our troops, we never convinced the Iraqi hard-liners, international terrorists, or even the general population between the Kuwaiti border and Kurdistan that Iraq had been conquered fair and square. It all seemed a trick to our enemies, some sort of betrayal, but not a lasting defeat. In the "Sunni Triangle" west and north of Baghdad, the fountainhead of the old regime's support, the effects of war were so slight that there was no convincing sense of failure. Iraq's Sunni Arab population never really felt the war. As a consequence they did not feel defeated.

It is not enough to win a war on technical points. You must devastate your enemy psychologically, destroying the last shred of his hope for success. And you must do it whatever the price in blood and destruction. If you do not do so your enemy will recover from his initial shock and continue the struggle. An enemy who has not suffered an *agonizing* loss will see no reason why he should cease his resistance. War is about punishment, not friendly persuasion. You may hope for a swift resolution with minimal destruction, but you must be ready to prove your victory by planting your flag in your dead enemy's eye socket.

The apparatchiks in the Rumsfeld Pentagon, whose arrogance quickly proved no substitute for competence, had refused to allocate sufficient forces to mount a convincing occupation throughout Iraq. Their venture was intended to prove, among other things, the neoconservative cult belief that democracy is so universally appealing that regime change can be accomplished at a discount. Timeless laws of conflict were ignored. But we cannot alter the nature of war with wishful thinking or even our sense of humanity.

In warfare, if you are unwilling to pay the butcher's bill up front, you will pay it with compound interest in the end. The primary advantage of a superpower is … super power. By attempting to minimize our military commitment Rumsfeld and his cabal guaranteed that our involvement would turn out to be longer, more expensive, deadlier, and far more demanding on our forces than it had to be.

The principles involved are simple and timeless: Do it right the first time. And don't start something you don't have the guts to finish.

War is not an experiment waged to prove academic or commercial theories. War is a terrible endeavor for a great purpose—and if the purpose is not great, we should not go to war. In Iraq, the purpose was powerful, but the ends the Bush administration hoped to achieve required more extensive means than decision makers were willing to deploy. The tragedy is that we *had* the means. We could have sent more forces initially, done more detailed planning, and prepared ourselves for the worst-case scenario—as the military always does when political hacks don't interfere. But Rumsfeld's paladins prevented our military from executing its standard war-gaming and -planning procedures while playing havoc with complex deployment processes, afraid that revelations of a potentially higher cost for removing Saddam Hussein might deprive them of their longed-for war.

Rumsfeld's henchmen were ideologues who elevated theory above human experience. They more closely resembled the early Bolsheviks than any predecessors in the American grain.

We Americans are at our worst when we behave like Europeans, embracing theories instead of behaving pragmatically. America's (and Britain's and Australia's) great strength has been its refusal to sign up for intellectual schemes for the "betterment" of humankind. We just want to know what works and what doesn't. It gives us a great advantage over the rest of the world.

The political appointees who had Rumsfeld's ear never considered the enemy's psychology or the culture of the country they intended to reinvent as the proof of their wisdom. They convinced themselves that religion, ethnicity, tribe, and tradition would all evaporate when an uneducated population, schooled in hatred, was invited to try democracy without the least preparation. They convinced themselves that our senior military officers, our intelligence agents and analysts, and our Middle East experts knew nothing about Iraq or war or democracy's magical appeal. The result was a great thing—the liberation of Iraq—done very, very badly.

When our military goes to war in the future the civilian theorists who have burrowed into the flesh of our defense establishment will be the first enemies with whom we have to contend. If only we could draft those "experts" and make them face the same dangers as our troops, one suspects there would be a great deal less civilian pontificating on military affairs. But we do not draft them. We reward them for pandering to the prejudices first of this administration, then of that one. Indeed, were integrity a requirement for residence in Washington, "downsizing government" would be an instant reality.

While military service is not, and should not be, a prerequisite for election to our nation's highest offices, we are undeniably paying a price for the rise of an apparatchik class, nursed in think tanks and on university faculties, who disdain military service and lack military experience, but who are quick to resort to the military tool in fits of political pique, whether that tool is appropriate or not. There certainly are differences between our two political parties when it comes to employ-ing our military, but both sides of the aisle do our country and our troops a disservice: Democrats prefer brief, ineffective interventions that make them feel better, while Republicans prefer grander campaigns, fought on the cheap, that make them feel stronger. Both parties have in com-mon their willful ignorance of military reality and the tendency to use our forces to suit their prejudices rather than our country's needs. In our dismally incestuous national capital the problem isn't merely that infamous revolving door. The truth is that the door is shut ever tighter against those with practical experience of the world.

In the United States of America our civilian leaders should always decide if and when and where we will go to war. But our military lead-ers must be allowed to decide the technical details of how to fight. We have the most loyal, obedient armed forces in history, but that is no rea-son for our elected officials to abuse our military establishment or risk the lives of our troops unnecessarily. If an issue is so vital that we decide we must go to war or otherwise intervene with military forces, we must have the common sense and decency to let our soldiers win.

———————————

One of the few negative developments in American life over the past half century has been the loss of the ideals of service among the most privileged. An insider's path in our government, punctuated by spells in think tanks or in temporary professorships, is not one of genuine ser-vice, but of self-service. One of the few actual—as opposed to mythic—legacies of Vietnam has been the abdication by the most fortunate Americans of their responsibility to serve in uniform. Our nation's fa-vored young took their opposition to one war as a license to turn their backs on our military permanently. As a result, those likeliest to rise to high office lack not only a sense of war's complexity and vagaries, but of the human beings inside our country's uniforms.

Another consequence has been liberal complaints that we have a politically conservative military. Of course, if liberals wish to be repre-sented in the ranks, they only have to join—which they no longer con-descend to do. There is nothing cheaper than complaining about a problem you are unwilling to help fix. Military service would convert many a starry-eyed young leftist into a rational creature; there's nothing like contact with reality to dispel campus fantasies. Some might even find their service ennobling while they earn a new respect for the less privileged.

In the course of their political campaigns politicians of every persuasion assure Americans that they revere our troops. Yet, once in office, both Republicans and Democrats increasingly view our military as an international janitorial service with guns whose primary purpose is to clean up the messes made by Clintonian irresponsibility or right-wing arrogance. I have little time for the lies of Michael Moore, but he was right on target in his film *Fahrenheit 9/11* when he queried legislators as to whether their children served in the military they were so anxious to send to war.

For its part, our military has done a poor job in explaining what war means to those who will never face its complexity firsthand. Our generals and admirals are wonderfully adept at testifying in defense of the weapons systems they wish to buy, but far less interested in educating our leaders or our country about the essence of war. Above all, our military has not summoned the wherewithal to drive home the fundamental truths—and to drive them home again and again and again—that war means death and destruction, that bloodless war is worse than a myth, and that we must be ready to do whatever it takes to convince an enemy of his defeat.

In 1945, convincing our enemies that they had lost irrevocably meant, in the first case, destroying enemy cities by the dozen, then fighting through his heartland; in the second case, it meant dropping two atomic bombs. Since then we have persuaded ourselves that a light spanking is an adequate substitute for an artillery barrage.

We all hope that we shall never have to use a nuclear weapon. But faced with implacable enemies determined to destroy us, inadequate conventional measures increase the likelihood that we will eventually need to resort to weapons of mass destruction ourselves. The use of such weapons seems unthinkable today, but sufficient destruction wreaked against our homeland could bring about a rapid change of heart. We value our sense of humanity, but we, too, will do whatever it takes to survive. In a world of nuclear proliferation—which neither of our political parties, nor our closest allies, have demonstrated the strength of will to stop—the chance that we will live out our lives without witnessing at least a regional nuclear exchange is far lower than any one of us might like.

Weapons of mass destruction are ideal for enemies intent upon mass destruction. At least some of our current and future enemies—Islamist fanatics—seek nothing less than the elimination of our country and the destruction of our civilization. They do not, and will not, have the strength to achieve their goal, but they are likely to gain the capability to inflict losses on our society and economy far more painful than those of 9/11.

If we lack the fortitude to do whatever it takes to win we may be certain that our enemies do not share our reticence. Despite the terrible dangers of the Cold War, the truth is that America and its allies have lived through a golden age of safety. That age is now at an end. Despite our best efforts to secure our homeland, we live in an age of vulnerability unprecedented since our frontier days. And the only enduring means to reduce that vulnerability isn't frisking Grandma at the airport. We must carry the struggle relentlessly to our enemies, as we have done with broad success since 9/11.

We *can* win the War on Terror. Or any other war. But only if we are willing to fight without reluctance and reservations—and if we are willing to fight for a long time to come.

The losers in the War on Terror will be those who first despair. Our fanatical enemies cannot defeat us. But we can defeat ourselves through a failure of will.

————————

The nonsense that "victory isn't possible today" is an absurdity foisted upon us by academics and pundits. Victory is *always* possible. *If* we're willing to pay the price. And if we are not we should not engage in military adventures that only worsen the plight of a broken world.

To do great good with the military you often must begin by doing great harm to the enemies of the good. Sparing our enemies is not an act of virtue. Nor does it mean that they will choose to spare us.

It is essential that our military help civilian decision makers escape the cancerous lies concocted by think tanks and university faculties about war. The military's first domestic mission is education: to help civilian decision makers unlearn the nonsense they have been taught throughout their careers. If our uniformed leaders neglect this educational mission they will have no right to complain when their advice is ignored in a crisis, when our troops are misused, and when the nation's leaders leave our military holding the (body) bag after things go wrong.

Warfare is a bath of blood in a pool of horror. Any imagined alternative is not war.

The observations offered above sound cruel. But warfare is not kind. If we are unwilling to accept that it is not enough to defeat an enemy technically, but that he must be convinced of his defeat, we will continue to falter. The shock of an attack by our military in a general war should be so overwhelming—so deadly, graphically destructive, and uncompromising—that the enemy, faced with unbearable losses, loses his will to fight. When we face particularly tenacious enemies whose resolve to resist does not waver we must be willing to destroy them.

If we shrink from the acts of destruction necessary to defeat an enemy thoroughly we will find ourselves suffering unnecessary casualties in a needlessly protracted struggle.

Even in comparatively benign peacekeeping operations we always should display overwhelming force. No potential enemy should be allowed to calculate a chance of success for himself. In operations short of war the appearance of irresistible strength can sometimes obviate the need to use that strength. But when we allow ourselves to appear diffident we only compound our problems. Many strategic lessons come from the schoolyard—no bully respects weakness, for example.

Our ambition to do everything military cleanly, quickly, and cheaply in political terms has brought us to the point where we are often better at encouraging our enemies than we are at defeating them. Only strength is respected in the world beyond our shores. Not kindness, not wisdom, not the philosophical constructs so impressive to graduate students, but *strength*. A strong state that allows itself to appear weak will be challenged by weak states hoping to appear strong.

There is no substitute for being feared.

Paradoxically, we are undermined by our own capabilities. As we saw in Iraq, even when stripped to a bare minimum of forces our military is so skilled that it can wage campaigns and win conventional wars with breathtaking speed. But a swift war without attendant devastation inflicts no pain on the enemy population—and often too little on the enemy's combatants. It is not enough to win fast, although speed is increasingly essential. The victory must be devastating. Under different circumstances and against different opponents the amount of physical destruction required will vary widely. But while we may wish to minimize friendly casualties, it's a counterproductive absurdity to go to outlandish lengths to spare our enemies.

We must get rid of the notion that we can make our enemies love us.

This sounds harsh to American ears. But many of us will live to see our enemies commit such horrendous acts of brutality that the fiercest observations offered here will become second nature to us. Once enough of our fellow citizens have been slaughtered because of our fecklessness we will learn to kill with relish once again.

This isn't barbarism. It's the human condition.

Five

THE WARS WE WILL FIGHT

I n the decades looming before us, our military will engage in a range of operations and campaigns whose detailed description would require a separate book. We will continue to be drawn into peacekeeping operations when, as in the Balkans, our allies prove so timid and partisan that only American involvement convinces the sparring sides to cease tormenting one another. At home and abroad we will participate in disaster-relief operations, which are *not* a waste of our military capability (relief operations are not only morally requisite but build crucial goodwill and penetrate diplomatic barriers, as illustrated by our engagement in the wake of the December 26, 2004, tsunami). We will provide logistics support to small-scale interventions by our allies or those sponsored by that most disappointing organization, the United Nations. We will conduct counterterror operations around the globe.

Our armed services, including the underappreciated and underfunded Coast Guard, will engage in homeland defense, counterdrug, counter–human trafficking, antipiracy, and rescue operations. Our forces will keep the world's sea-lanes and airspace free for peaceful commerce and travel. We will train the forces of weak but promising states, engage in shows of force to deter foreign folly, and conduct clandestine operations to eliminate deadly enemies when the light of day is an inconvenience. And, if we are both unlucky and inattentive, we may find ourselves on the periphery or even in the midst of a nuclear exchange.

This is but a partial list of the myriad challenges facing our military. Except for the prospect of nuclear use, about which our denial verges on superstition, each of the above activities has been written about exhaustively and many have been written about well. The purpose here is to consider those forms of military operations that we have failed to investigate adequately or at all, either because we find doing so uncomfortable or because we have not mentally entered the grave, new world of the twenty-first century.

When it comes to the prospect of future war we are like children unwilling to leave the broken-down crib they know but have outgrown. We take comfort in the familiar, however miserable it may be, and fear change in the spheres of war and diplomacy. But change is upon us, and we no longer fit within the crib—or coffin—of the past. If we are to break our tradition, now more than a half century old, of avoiding victory, we shall have to abandon our military childhood and enter the deadly, adult world of our enemies.

We made a start with our *preemptive war* against Saddam Hussein's regime. Despite the botched forecasting of the requirements and results, and even though weapons of mass destruction proved elusive, the war set a crucial precedent, putting dictators and rogue regimes on notice that they no longer can count upon American passivity until we are attacked directly. Going to war in Iraq in defiance of the dictator-ridden UN was an essential step away from past models of warfare that favored tyrants and aggressive regimes.

Since our transformation of Iraq became more difficult than its sponsors predicted, we have been assured by the effort's opponents that preemptive war is now a discredited concept, practically and morally. That's nonsense. The next time a preemptive strike becomes desirable, it will be easier for us, not harder. The old rules have been shattered, and good riddance. Preemptive wars and other preventive exercises of military power now constitute one more useful option for a president and Congress faced with mortal threats.

This does not mean that preemptive war will always be our preference. More often we will wander down the traditional, confused paths to the outbreak of hostilities. But the precedent established in Iraq signals that we no longer feel obliged to allow a known enemy to strike first or a tyrant to escape justice as long as he butchers selectively.

In an age of weapons of mass destruction, long-range-missile proliferation, global terrorism, shifting alliances, and international mobility,

retaining the option of preemptive war is common sense. If a man
threatens me with a knife I am not obliged to allow him to cut into my
flesh before responding. Nor am I therefore inclined to attack a man
who has not brandished a knife. The rhetorical trickery of those who
oppose *any* use of the U.S. military implies that once we have embraced
the right of preemptive action we will not know when to stop, but will
go on to invade Switzerland. But our problem has been the opposite in
the recent past: We have stood by while mass murderers worked their
will upon the innocent, while oppressive regimes harbored and abet-
ted terrorists, and while entire countries were ravaged by presidents-
for-life. Americans know when to stop. But we also must recognize
when to start before it grows too late.

Nor have the tragic, avoidable blunders of Rumsfeld and his accomplices discredited *wars of liberation* waged by the United States
and like-minded allies. In the great twenty-first-century struggle between progress and reaction, between a humane future and a brute,
oppressive past, ideas often will prove inadequate to remove entrenched dictators. Nor do the difficulties the Iraqis have faced in overcoming their legacy of servitude "prove" that wars of liberation do
not work. Whether Iraq is having a good day or a bad one as you read
this page—even if it is torn by civil strife—we are far from knowing the
ultimate results of our intervention. Ten years from now we may
begin to see the emergence of the deeper, enduring effects of our
Baghdad sojourn. The results may be disappointingly negative, but
the odds remain good that Iraq will emerge as a far better place than
it was under the Baathist regime. Indeed, at present our challenge is
to avoid premature euphoria, but that is far from the worst problem
we might have.

Even should Iraq break apart, the result may prove beneficial.
Deep currents are in play and no person, whether in North America,
Europe, or the Middle East, can forecast where the tides will take Iraq
and its neighbors. The only certainty was that the status quo in the
Middle East was intolerable, an oppressive stasis that generated hatred,
delusions, fanaticism, and terror. And now, thanks to us, that status quo
is crumbling.

Changing the strategic (and human) landscape takes decades.

Anyone who expects instantaneous results, or who prematurely declares success or failure for our efforts in Iraq, Afghanistan, or the
greater Middle East is a fool. We cannot change the world between
quarterly earnings reports. But do our best to foster change we must.
The alternative is to grant our enemies a free hand amid a civilization
in decay.

Along with military prowess, we must cultivate the art of patience.

The phony "crisis" about losing the support of our allies over Operation Iraqi Freedom provided a necessary catharsis. Our alliance with
the bleak, selfish heart of continental Europe was moribund. A hag-
gard Circe, Europe dulled our senses and fooled us into believing in
her attractions. But the dugs are dry in Germany and France. They
deluded us into prolonging the affair long after our attentions should
have turned to more important states such as India, South Africa, and
Brazil.

Multiple Europes exist today, with the cracks between them thinly
plastered over by the European Union, an extravagant, crypto-fascist
bureaucracy. France and Germany, the moral ghettos of Europe, are
not only the most repellent but the least useful of our European "allies." Even had France or Germany seen fit to cast off their shared affection for dictatorships and the profits such romances bring, their
participation in Operation Iraqi Freedom would have been detrimental, not helpful, both on the battlefield and in the Coalition's attempt to
guide Iraq toward democracy.

With the French, especially, military participation would have created friction during combat operations and would have allowed Paris
to demand a greater voice in Iraqi affairs than justified by the paltry
military contribution of which France is capable. The French and Germans did not defeat us through their defiance. They defeated themselves. By limiting their strategic vocabularies to "*Non!*" and "*Nein!*"
they helped us maintain internal cohesion in the coalition for the war's
duration and kept the international friction safely away from Baghdad.
To their astonishment, the French and Germans found that they were
neither needed nor heeded, diminishing their stature among all but

the most desperate and backward regimes in the developing world (and, of course, among America-haters from Cambridge to Cairo).

As long as they remained nominal allies of the United States France and Germany were able to claim greater roles on the world stage than their strategic resources justified. The French had been employing strategic sleight of hand since World War II, when the Anglo-American allies made a terrible mistake—second only to the division of Europe at Yalta—by letting Charles de Gaulle pretend that the French played a significant role in their own liberation. We then compounded the problem by allowing France, a bankrupt, savage colonizer, a seat on the Security Council of the new United Nations.

As a result of the ineptitude and hucksterism of President Jacques Chirac and his then foreign minister, Dominique de Villepin, the Gaullist legacy that had maintained a facade of French importance collapsed. Now all that is left to Paris is the craven pursuit of Arab favor even as France oppresses the seven million Muslims on its soil. France is weaker now (apart from the Vichy interlude) than it has been since the turmoil of the late sixteenth century, able to demonstrate its "power" only by the occasional dispatch of mercenary thugs to Africa to murder blacks in the name of *liberté, égalité, et fraternité*.

For far too long we had been unable to free ourselves of Europe's antique thrall. Thankfully, the French and Germans did it for us with their support of Saddam Hussein. As a result, we are—belatedly—withdrawing most of our military forces from Germany, where they had become a mere cash cow for the welfare state on the Rhine. Instead of increasing our influence, the presence of our troops in Germany had exaggerated Berlin's importance, allowing third-rate party hacks to imagine themselves as *Meisterpolitiker*. Now Germany has been revealed as a disembodied voice, able to shriek like a harpy but lacking the muscle to influence world events. With a blighted economy, stifling laws, a welfare mentality, and a shriveled, incompetent military that is no more than an employment agency for uniformed bureaucrats, Germany, like France, is in decline. And states in decline never make good allies—they consume resources and energy, while giving little or nothing in return.

As we draw away, at last, from yesterday's Europe we free ourselves to work more closely with the Europes of the future—in the East, South, and, as ever, in the West, where the English-speaking world began and begins.

Although our preemptive war in Mesopotamia was waged with an alliance that included most of the anglophone states that defeated totalitarianism in the twentieth century, the pundits warned us solemnly that we must not ever again go to war "without allies." But it would be wiser to go to war alone than with false allies at our backs. If you cannot trust those on whom your life may depend, you had best learn self-reliance.

Treaties do not make allies, nor do presidential visits, handshakes, or joint press conferences. It takes the willingness to bleed beside one another. When we liberated Iraq we also liberated ourselves from the prison of empty alliances.

Certainly, it is desirable to share burdens. But we must be careful to avoid the trap into which we fell so often in the past, that of adding to our own burdens in the name of "burden sharing." NATO has been a feast provided for Europe at American expense. When fighting is necessary it would be a grand thing to have stalwart European companions beside us—no soldier would dispute that. But if European forces are too small to help, too immobile to deploy without our airlift, too blind to be able to operate without our intelligence support, too primitive to be able to keep up with our own forces, too burdened with political restrictions to be able to fight, and, on top of all else, about as dependable as a "Rolex" bought from a Bangkok street vendor, we had better be prepared to stick with the Anglolateral alliance that so enrages the French. (Who speaks French today but waiters and dictators?)

There may be times when we must stand entirely alone, as Britain did in 1940, against the forces of evil. To insist that we must await the permission of Belgium before defending ourselves is as foolish as expecting the United Nations to depose a tyrant.

It is wiser to wage a just war without allies, and to accept the world's chagrin, than it is to let evil flourish.

Preemptive or not, future military commitments will be diverse. Counterterror operations will include tactical *raids* of strategic consequence, some involving special operations forces, others executed by standoff weaponry (but used aggressively, not timidly), and those greatest in scale deploying multiple services and putting boots on the ground long enough to purge a targeted area. The art of the raid will be an essential study for the rising generation of soldiers. Especially where we have no abiding interests, or where local hostility is especially pronounced, we will need to strike hard and then leave before becoming entangled: global reach, local strikes, strategic results.

There is no formula for strategic raids, except the rule that it is better to employ too much force than too little. Harebrained schemes for "proportional response" must be rejected if we are to make any progress at all. War is not a game of tit-for-tat. The correct proportional response to any attack on the United States or its interests is to strike back with such devastating force that even friendly nations are shocked. Failed strategic raids, such as the Clinton administration's popgun attacks on al-Qaeda training camps in Afghanistan, only increase an enemy's confidence. We should never use our military impulsively, but when other methods are unsuitable to achieve our ends, the use of military force must be decisive.

Especially in counterterror and irregular operations anything short of our complete success is a victory for our enemies. The lone terrorist who survives to strike another day will, indeed, strike another day—after rebuilding his cadres. Fighting terrorists or extremist guerrillas is a zero-sum game. If your enemy believes that his god is whispering in his ear and commanding him to kill you, he is unlikely to be intimidated by failed cruise-missile strikes. In fact, the employment of expensive military technology, if the attack is unsuccessful, is particularly encouraging to asymmetrical opponents. They comfort themselves that all of America's scientific prowess counts for nothing against the strength of their convictions.

Attacks launched as political gestures to placate a domestic electorate are especially unwise. The gesture will not be understood by our enemies but will inflate their self-confidence and ease their recruiting efforts. Every military attack, great or small, undertaken by the United States must be resolute and supported by sufficient reserves to redeem unexpected reverses. Our enemies can afford to lose ninety-nine engagements if they appear to win one. We, on the other hand, can never afford to lose. Even if the tangible stakes seem slight, once our military is committed it must appear invincible to real and potential enemies.

If you think you need a nail file, bring a chain saw.

We need to relearn the usefulness of *punitive expeditions* for circumstances under which a raid will not suffice. Since the Second World War we have conditioned ourselves to believe, in words attributed to former secretary of state Colin Powell, that "you break it, you own it." We have convinced ourselves of the preposterous fallacy that, having subdued a hostile regime, we are obliged to remain and rebuild the country that Dictator X has ruined. Certainly, there will be times, as in Afghanistan and Iraq, when an extended American presence may be required by our ambitions or our fears. But there also will be instances when, faced not only with an oppressive regime responsible for American deaths, but with a population that broadly supports its bloody-handed government, we simply will need to send in our military on a punitive expedition to exact a price that discourages further attacks on our homeland or on our interests, and then leave with our guns still smoking.

We need to get over the dangerous belief that all of humankind can be won over to our way of thinking if only we discover the right formula. Some populations will be so deeply imbued with hatred toward us—because they have been convinced that our success is the reason for their failure—that an American occupation would be a waste of blood, treasure, and effort. We are not obliged to make killers love us before we send them to their deaths. Nor can we expect to repair the broken soul of a failed civilization. Our enemies need to learn that there will be consequences for their misbehavior without expecting that we will stay to bind their wounds after attacking them.

Punishment is terribly underrated in our "you're going to get a time-out, young man!" society. In a hate-filled world we will sometimes need to take an old-fashioned strap to the foreign progeny of hatred. And the world will be better for it.

Punitive expeditions are not described anywhere in our current military doctrine. This isn't proof of our moral enlightenment but of the benighted state of our strategic thinking. We hear, again and again, that we are an empire, if in a new, postmodern guise. We possess, like it or not, a vast economic and cultural imperium—with global security demands. And even we do not enjoy unlimited resources. We are foolish if we do not study the lessons learned by the empires of the past, especially those of Rome and Britain, the two that most closely resemble our own as empires of law, language, learning, culture, and commerce protected by small, professional military forces.

The Romans and the British ultimately realized that not every region could be occupied successfully, that not every tribe could be usefully subdued. All the oratory of Cicero or Gladstone could not persuade foreign renegades bent on massacre and destruction that they should desist from the only pursuits at which they could boast competence. Similarly, the terrorists we face today will not be convinced to cease their campaigns by civil arguments, nor by the compromises so alluring to diplomats, nor by appeasement. Now and again, we will simply have to go to their lairs, dig them out, and kill them.

Sometimes those "lairs" will be hostile states in which terrorists find respite, succor, and encouragement. Or they may be refuges in the underdeveloped hinterlands of weak states lacking the power to enforce the rule of law throughout their own territory. Hostile states are, of course, more dangerous than lawless mountain ranges or unpoliced jungles, but in either case we shall have to send troops in pursuit of our deadly enemies. And we often will find that there is no advantage in remaining on the scene.

The British learned this painfully, not least in Afghanistan (where we have a welcome, while the British did not). When challenged by tracts of hostile territory impossible or too costly to occupy, punitive campaigns are the history-proven answer, from the ford of the Kabul River to the shores of Tripoli. With a military establishment as small, comparatively, as our own is today, the British realized that no empire, not even one that enjoys great economic wealth and cultural authority, can do everything everywhere to the fullest measure. The Romans shifted their few legions like fire brigades, but they rarely failed to use those legions forcefully. Impact matters more than numbers—and when you lack numbers, you had better have plenty of impact.

Our military speaks of "economy-of-force operations." On the battlefield this usually means that in order to concentrate overwhelming combat power at the point of decision the commander accepts a measure of risk elsewhere, allocating minimal forces on a flank or along a supporting axis of advance (perhaps only enough troops to provide an early warning should the enemy appear unexpectedly). The underlying maxim is that he who tries to be strong everywhere is unlikely to prove sufficiently strong anywhere—and far too weak at the critical point. Warfare is always about choices and risks, but warfare in the service of an empire, formal or postmodern, demands especially bold decisions. The one thing that we cannot afford is weakness of conduct or character. Our strength of will must be invincible.

Punitive expeditions, although they may involve large numbers of troops, are strategic economy-of-force operations. The concept accepts that an enemy must be chastised, but that an attempted occupation of the territory in question is not to our advantage. It is not only a sensible technique, but for twenty-first-century America, with its global responsibilities, it's a necessary one.

Our punitive expeditions will not aim at burning down towns and villages but at searing dread into the souls of our enemies. A punitive expedition that functions as a strategic raid, striking our enemies a catastrophic blow then swiftly withdrawing, is much more apt to inspire respect for our capabilities and will than a muddled occupation that allows the enemy to regroup and strike us at will on the home ground he knows far better than we ever could. Occupations, although sometimes necessary, also send entirely the wrong signal to much of the world: that America wants to control country Y or its resources in some neo-colonial fashion. A great American strength has been our reluctance to colonize foreign parts (admittedly, with exceptions). Even in the depths of the Cold War we were never viewed seriously as colonizers. We would be foolish to allow ourselves to appear as colonizers now.

Strike hard, then leave. Even if we are so worried about our strategic table manners that we avoid the actual term "punitive expedition" we must relearn the concept. "Relearn" because we staged successful punitive expeditions even before we declared our independence. From innumerable operations on our Indian frontier or the punishment of the Barbary pirates, to the suppression of the Boxer Rebellion in China or the defeat of the Moros, our history includes numerous examples of effective punitive expeditions. We are not breaking new ground, but returning, after the deformations of our long European involvement, to a core American military tradition. Some will bluster and call such actions immoral, preferring great defeats to small successes, but losing a war is never a moral act for the United States. Much of the world may disagree, but when we lose a war, humanity loses.

We are not obliged to rehabilitate every enemy we face. Often our responsibility will end with defeating them.

Yet there also will be times, as in Iraq, when the stakes are so high and the potential for long-term strategic advantage is so great that a full-fledged military occupation is worth the costs. In preparation for those full-scale interventions in foreign cultures we need to take to heart the lessons provided by the Bush administration's blundering in Iraq—in the wake of the battlefield victory delivered by our troops. While each occupation will have its own unique requirements and frustrations, due to eccentricities of local culture, traditions, beliefs, and economic conditions, there are a number of fundamental "rules for military occupations" that consistently apply.

Setting the right conditions from the outset is essential. And if there is one firm maxim on which we may depend, it is that there is no such thing as "occupation lite" (a lesson underscored by the travesty of our initial laissez-faire behavior in Iraq). You cannot do occupations on the cheap, as recent events should have taught us. When you try, the price in deaths and difficulties ultimately proves higher than a sound initial investment would have cost. There is no easy way to stage a military occupation, but there are sensible techniques that dramatically increase the occupier's likelihood of success.

Know Your Enemy. The greatest practical difficulty Americans face during military operations is ignorance of our enemies. Despite possessing an intelligence system whose forty-billion-dollar annual budget dwarfs the gross domestic products of half the world's states we go to war blithely assuming that our enemies think as we do, assign a similar value to human life, and share our aspirations—even if they have not yet realized it. While the next chapter will address our intelligence community and its weaknesses, the stipulation is worth making here that he who does not know his enemy increases his enemy's strength. Whether you wish to win a man over or kill him, it is far easier to reach your goal if you grasp his fears and dreams.

In disappointing ways our intelligence system and our military's attitude reflect our nation as a whole, with our lack of curiosity about foreign cultures. Perhaps this prejudice has deep roots, stemming from the fact that most of our ancestors fled their homelands, cutting old ties to begin a new, American life. Most of us are happy to be Americans in America, regarding our passports as necessary evils to get us to our Caribbean playgrounds. Still, our ignorance of the greater world is inexcusably slothful—and expensive.

Of course, Americans are far from the worst offenders. Most of the world knows far less of our reality than we know of theirs, elitist propaganda notwithstanding. One difference between the average American and the average European is that while the American will admit he knows little about Europe, the European, with no greater depth of knowledge, insists that he knows everything about America. But comparing ourselves to others is no excuse. *We* comprise the power that must cope with the entire world. Others can afford some degree of parochialism. We are obliged to know the quality of life in rural China and the level of corruption in Moldova.

Contrary to the myths of our enemies, foreign and domestic, Americans are fully capable of grasping the crucial nuances of foreign cultures. After all, we possess the bloodlines of all the world. In the past we have conducted successful occupations based on a sound understanding of our enemies. In Germany we did have great advantages, from the insight of recent émigrés to citizens of German heritage who kept the culture and even the language alive, but Japan was another matter.

Our small Japanese-American population was excluded from occupation planning (and, for far too long, from justice as well). Still, we had plenty of officers who had served in the Pacific during their careers and who had spent decades thinking about Japan. General Douglas MacArthur, for all his many faults, demonstrated a grasp of Japanese psychology and values that fairly may be called genius. Although our complex alliances contributed to the problems we faced in Europe, the surprising thing is that we made fewer mistakes in the occupation of

Japan than we did in Germany—despite such advantages as having German refugees in U.S. Army uniforms (the young Henry Kissinger, for example). Of course, as we learned again in Iraq, refugees and émigrés may have their own agendas.

What matters is that both occupations were conducted forcefully and intelligently, after thorough planning and with a realistic grasp of what was possible. If anything, we underestimated the speed with which German and Japanese societies and their economies could recover—but it is *always* better to err on the side of pessimism in planning an occupation.

Another crucial advantage at play in both Japan and Germany was that the populations knew, beyond any doubt, that they had lost the war. Despite the leftist cult of Hiroshima and Nagasaki that seeks to put the United States on a level with the aggressors who started the conflict, Japan's remarkable success in reinventing itself could not have come without the shock of those two atomic bombs. There was no question of liberating Japan; the population did not view itself as oppressed but as a willing partner of Tokyo's militarism. But through an unexpected quirk of fate the power of the atom liberated the Japanese from centuries of destructive traditions. Those crude atomic devices may not have made war unthinkable—despite immediate proclamations to that effect—but they did make the triumph of the samurai unthinkable.

We knew how to do occupations. So why did we make so many beginner's errors in Iraq?

Part of the answer is not just ignorance but *willful* ignorance of the various cultures at play along the Tigris and Euphrates. The political operatives who conceived the liberation of Iraq—in itself a noble idea—needed to believe that the country's disparate peoples could not wait to be reborn as the Middle East's first Americans. Factions within the Bush administration wanted a war. To their credit, they wanted the right war. But they refused to accept that their war—and the subsequent occupation—needed to be conducted the right way. They closed their ears and minds to information that contradicted their prejudices. Iraq was going to be a "cakewalk." Democracy alone would provide the magic to make all things right.

But democracy, although glorious, is not magic. It relies on so many cultural and societal factors to work as we believe it should that the jury remains out as to whether it will transplant from the soil where it was nursed down difficult centuries even as far as continental Europe (the states of the European mainland have already ceded a worrisome degree of power to unelected bureaucrats in Brussels). Democracy may be desirable to us, but it often appears less desirable to others. Nor is democracy nearly as robust and reliable as we like to pretend. Nor is it quite synonomous with freedom. Elections, too, can be a path to tyranny—especially under conditions in which a majority ethnic group or confession votes as a block to subjugate a weaker group or faith.

Above all, the civilian proponents of Iraq's liberation did not want to be deflected by unpleasant facts. Thus, they ignored the advice of those who knew the region firsthand, who had studied the language and culture, and many of whom not only had served in the Middle East and fought the Iraqis in our first Gulf War, but who had worked with the Kurds in the country's mountainous north. Data was readily available on the woeful state of Iraq's infrastructure, as well as on the society's complexity and conflicts.

The problem for the administration was that serious military planning for an occupation would have revealed the complexity of the challenge and the resources likely to be necessary. Having been warned publicly by one general that an occupation might require hundreds of thousands of troops—leaving the war's partisans aghast—the endeavor's advocates in the Pentagon and in the White House were not going to chance losing the public relations battle before they got their war. The consequence was the confusion and incompetence that plagued our it-isn't-really-an-occupation occupation policy for months—while our enemies recovered from the shock of defeat and rallied.

If there is even a remote chance that a military endeavor will require an occupation in its wake we must plan early, honestly, and thoroughly. Almost every problem the United States military faced in Iraq, from terrorism and an insurgency to the prisoner abuse scandal at Abu Ghraib, could have been avoided had each of the staffs in our relevant commands been allowed to prepare for a full-scale occupation. We made our fate.

———————————

What are the indispensable rules of an occupation? Beyond knowing your enemy as well as you can and planning as thoroughly as possible?

First, every occupation, no matter how welcome it may be to the local populace, must begin with an immediate declaration of martial law. This doesn't mean that our soldiers need to shoot every dog that approaches a fire hydrant. Martial law serves humane, logical purposes. It reassures the population that despite the shocking upheaval they have witnessed the world remains orderly, with clear rules. Imagine how much destruction and ill will would have been prevented had our forces been allowed to impose martial law the day they reached downtown Baghdad. Instead, our troops were left uncertain of the extent of their authority. Looters and other criminals ran wild, not only harming Iraq and its citizens while getting liberation off to an execrable start, but creating a global public relations disaster that undercut the positive effects of our swift military victory.

Martial law does not mean that the innocent will suffer. It means that criminals or terrorists enjoy far less freedom to make the innocent suffer. Life is regulated through the imposition of essential laws and restrictions, such as curfews, antiexploitation measures, and, when necessary, the rationing of goods and services. Those who obey the rules have nothing to fear. While this may sound oppressive to lifelong residents of the faculty lounge, the truth is that when all they know has collapsed around them, human beings need basic security before they can meet the challenges of freedom. The Iraqis *expected* us to declare martial law, as did the world. It would have created few, if any, problems, while preventing countless difficulties.

The Rumsfeld cabal envisioned *The Lord of the Rings* and delivered *Lord of the Flies*.

If you impose martial law and then find its weight unnecessary you can easily lift it (it's usually best to do so in stages, giving the population a sense of rewards for good behavior). But you cannot recover from an initial reluctance to wield authority. A military occupation is similar to the situation facing a new teacher on the first day of class. It's wise to begin strictly, letting students earn greater liberties. The teacher who appears lax at the outset may never establish discipline.

In times of crisis people want clear rules. Martial law provides them. It also avoids the trap of relinquishing war's authority too quickly. The

moment peace is declared the world expects that hostile acts against occupation forces will be treated as criminal matters. Under martial law
you shoot terrorists dead. You need not read kidnappers their rights.
And looters find the price of their stolen goods forbiddingly high.

If martial law sounds harsh ask yourself if its conditions would not
have been more humane than allowing Iraqis to spend month after
month in fear of the very men from whom we claimed to have liberated
them. The American tendency to confuse kindness and weakness blinds
us to what less fortunate populations desire.

Democracy cannot exist without order. Order cannot exist without
law. And in the wake of war and the absence of a government martial
law is the only kind of authority that will serve. Declare martial law,
then ease up on its provisions, and the population will thank you for
your generosity. Allow anarchy to reign and you give the very people
you wish to help a reason to hate you.

What war does not take away from the common man and woman
criminals and corruption will seize in the absence of firm laws. It takes
only a fraction of 1 percent of a population, armed and determined, to
destroy a fragile or convalescent society.

Our military gave us an inexpensive war. Political charlatans gave
us a costly peace.

———————

Because he hoped to prove that soldiers were obsolete and to minimize
political costs at home by limiting Reserve and National Guard call-
ups, Secretary Rumsfeld refused to deploy the hundreds of thousands
of troops necessary for Operation Iraqi Freedom's comprehensive
success—not just to win on the battlefield, but to occupy the country
successfully. This ideologically driven parsimony created needless
risks during the war, but the real price was paid afterward.

An occupation is manpower intensive. You must send troops in
numbers that may initially seem extravagant. There is no alternative
that works (our foray into Afghanistan was an intervention, not a true
occupation). No matter how benign you anticipate the postwar environment will be, your only insurance is to put soldiers on every street
corner. Physical presence matters. Nothing else conveys psychological
as well as physical mastery. If recently defeated enemies or common

criminals do not see you they will not fear you. Troops must be on display constantly, standing guard, patrolling, driving past, and flying overhead. The population must feel that resistance has no chance, that our military power is so great, so omnipresent and omnipotent that there is no alternative to good behavior.

This is not hard to grasp. Unless our errors encourage the spread of violence, as was the case in Iraq, an occupation *is* much like police work. And the police officer has to be seen walking his beat. No urban police department in the United States would imagine that it could maintain order merely by guarding its precinct headquarters while flying aircraft overhead and occasionally sending a convoy from one police station to another. Cops and troops need to be visible. And, sometimes, intrusive.

You must permeate the occupied territory with men and women in uniform as swiftly as possible. In the early days of an occupation the presence of our troops *should* be an inconvenience to the population. Without needless abuse the people must be made to feel powerless, to be reduced to a childlike state in which they feel the need to ask permission before they act. Once their dominance is established our soldiers can behave charitably, reassuring the locals with their decency. But you cannot drive into a hostile village, smile and wave, toss out a few bags of rice, and then drive away again. The initial occupation presence has to feel like a shadow following every individual. The fearful welcome mercy. But if we offer nothing but mercy from the beginning, we will soon be the ones who need to fear.

American troops are very good at interacting with occupied populations. They're smart, they're humane, they have uncanny instincts, and they aren't afraid to seize the initiative. Frequently, a junior enlisted man will see through a problem while his officers are still complicating the matter. If something doesn't work the way it's supposed to our soldiers find a way to make it work. But numbers matter. Soldiers have to get to know their occupation "beats" the way cops do. And although it will be hard on our soldiers and their families, we must break ourselves of the habit of rotating troops in and out of occupations for brief stints. Occupation troops should expect to remain deployed for at least two years. If improved conditions allow an earlier troop reduction, that's fine. But we cannot afford to lose the institutional memory and our hard-won tactile feel for the operational environment through constant unit or individual rotations. A rueful observation from our past is that the U.S. Army didn't have ten years' experience in Vietnam, but one year of experience ten times.

If we enter a country for the purpose of occupying it our troops need to stay long enough to penetrate the culture.

And it bears repeating that numbers always matter. *Any* form of military operation that forces false economies in troop strength throws away our superpower advantage, increases the likelihood of higher casualties, and raises the odds of failure. In a crisis we may be forced to react swiftly with the forces on hand, but when we have time to plan and prepare methodically—as we certainly did in Iraq—denying our troops and their leaders the numbers they may need to achieve success is not only a false economy, it's treason.

Study the enemy. Plan thoroughly. Employ mass. Impose martial law the moment the firing stops. Flood the occupied territory with troops. These are timeless rules that our military leaders knew and were prevented from following. But the occupation of Iraq made a new rule necessary: *Don't treat an occupation as a bonanza for American contractors. Hire locals.*

As disgraceful as it was counterproductive, the reverse looting orgy that politically connected American contractors enjoyed in Iraq did far more damage than our government has yet realized. By hurling money at greedy, often incompetent contractors the Rumsfeld Pentagon not only betrayed the elementary trust placed in our officials by the American taxpayer, but crippled the occupation.

The trumpeted promises of American largesse inflated Iraqi expectations of what we could do for their country. Those expectations were already irrationally high, based upon a conviction that America is so rich and powerful it can do anything and everything, from instantly fixing an antiquated electrical grid to creating immediate prosperity for one and all. We handed the terrorists and insurgents a gift by promising far more than we could deliver—while delivering many of the wrong things.

Underdeveloped countries do *not* need state-of-the-art infrastructure. Even if it is provided to them they cannot afford to maintain it. Countries such as Iraq need robust, simple, affordable systems, not more advanced technologies than our own population enjoys. The domestic critics who complained that tens of billions of dollars of development money were going to Iraq when we had needs at home had an even better case than they realized. It wasn't only that the insider contracts were written generously, but that they gave Iraqis the wrong support.

The decision to stamp the reconstruction effort "made in America" *delayed* Iraq's economic recovery. We needed to hire Iraqis to do everything they could possibly do for themselves. Our payroll should have included not just Iraqi laborers but Iraqi contractors, engineers, manufacturers, builders, and surveyors. Not only would this have been far less costly to the American taxpayer, it would instantly have given hundreds of thousands if not millions of Iraqis a stake in the reconstruction process. And it would have put the burden of accomplishment on Iraqis rather than on us. The work done would have been less sophisticated, but it would have been appropriate to the country's needs and capabilities.

Had we contracted directly with Iraqi companies to do the work we would have seen no end of petty corruption. But might that not have been preferable to the debacle of handing out multibillion-dollar contracts to American corporate entities that failed to deliver the promised goods and services? Yes, Iraqi-run reconstruction would have been less efficient on the ground. That would have been an advantage: Iraqi reconstruction efforts would have been more labor intensive, reducing the mass unemployment that provided a recruiting pool for terrorists, insurgent leaders, and criminal gangs.

The Iraqis know their own country. Would they have tried to wheel and deal and beat the system? Of course. But the cost to us would have been far lower, many aspects of reconstruction would have gone faster, and the Iraqis could have been proud of their rebuilt infrastructure—instead of doing their best to blow it up.

If there is even the slightest chance that a future military operation might turn into an occupation, *uniformed* contracting officers, with clear orders and priorities but local freedom of action, should follow behind our combat units just outside of hand-grenade range to identify local businessmen who can help in any rebuilding we intend to do. Money converts more opponents than speeches ever will. Immediately give local authority figures and businessmen a financial stake in your presence and you will have a far greater chance of a successful, peaceful occupation than you will achieve by bringing in brigades of American contractors who when not counting their money are counting the days until they can go home.

Local contractors are imperfect in many ways. But the advantage gained by shifting reconstruction responsibilities from American shoulders to local shoulders outweighs the many frustrations. Let the locals blame the guy down the street when the power remains in short supply instead of creating expectations of Disney World in the sand.

There is always profiteering in wartime. War draws out both the valorous and the vile, and Daddy Warbucks is alive and well (although considerably less charitable toward orphans these days). But our occupation of Iraq was the first time an American government *celebrated* profiteering. We not only wasted billions of tax dollars but undercut our own professed intentions. The combination of an austere military commitment and lavish contracts for American firms faltered from the start. Only the spirit of our troops and Iraqi ingenuity saved the occupation from outright failure.

Were we wise we would create a permanent U.S. Occupation Command as part of our ongoing military reforms. Staffed lightly—but competently—in peacetime, it would be responsible for planning relevant contingencies, for the design of military governments (traditionally far more effective than the abysmally inept and now defunct Coalition Provisional Authority), for identifying the key personnel needed for any given occupation, for contracting in support of an occupation, and for running any such operations that become necessary. We are sufficiently likely to find ourselves staging future occupations to make such a permanent headquarters a necessity, not a luxury.

And officers assigned to that headquarters should be forbidden, by law, from working for defense contractors upon their retirement from the military.

Austerity inspires, while largesse corrupts. We should have learned that lesson in Vietnam.

Walk Softly, and Carry a Big Stick. Presidential administrations, whether Republican or Democrat, have developed a deadly case of big-mouth disease. The affliction is extremely contagious and it's spreading to our military leaders. It is a plague that kills.

Yet another basic rule in warfare is that you do not tell your enemies what you intend to do. Surprise—and the accompanying shock—may be the most important single factor in battle. Surprise does not necessarily win wars, but it can defeat entire armies. We seem increasingly determined to squander that advantage for minor political gains at home, for the self-gratification of a sound bite, or simply to vent. But presidents and generals are not salaried to throw tantrums or to pose, but to guarantee our power and to win our nation's wars. When our leaders, whether in business suits or in battle dress, publicly promise to subdue a terrorist stronghold then quit short of the goal, they not only suffer a loss of credibility but increase the enemy's prestige. In the peculiar conflicts already scarring this new century—wars of perception as well as of flesh and blood—it is crucial not to issue threats that we might not fulfill.

By the spring of 2004 we had struck a low point at which swagger trumped strategy. Faced with the terrorist stronghold of Fallujah the Bush administration, echoed by generals in Iraq, declared to the world that we would cleanse the city of our enemies. Those declarations only strengthened the enemy's will to resist. Once America had stated its intent so vaingloriously all the enemy had to do to win a victory in the eyes of their admirers was to outlast us, to hold on to just a few city blocks to prove their defiance of the last remaining superpower. As a result, the First Battle of Fallujah was a public relations catastrophe for Washington.

The classic approach—and a far wiser one—would have been to keep our mouths shut and *act,* to finish the job, and then let the results speak for themselves. If election-campaign crowing still seemed necessary the cawing might more wisely have been restrained until after we had gained a victory.

We were slow to learn from our error. Shortly after the debacle of First Fallujah our civilian leadership and a few generals repeated their behavior in Najaf, declaring that we would eliminate any threat from Moqtada al-Sadr, an upstart thug in clerical robes. Then we backed down. Faced with another, larger scale uprising led by the same figure in the same city a few months later we again told the world that we were going to put an end to the threat from al-Sadr and his Mahdi Army. We moved too slowly, and our efforts were trumped by Iraq's leading Shia cleric.

Since the summer of 2004 we have had a number of notable military successes. But our enemies and the world celebrate our all too public failures. Raging like Lear on the heath that we will do "such things" is political and military idiocy. Our leaders must wean themselves from the microphone when the issue is deadly combat. The best way to gain a long-term public diplomacy victory is to *win* the battles we fight in the short term. Rhetoric doesn't help—especially when the ringing words are empty. Teddy Roosevelt's advice to "walk softly, and carry a big stick" sounds even wiser today, in the age of real-time media coverage, than it could have a hundred years ago. We cannot afford to brag about victories before we win them.

Every time that we promise to do something militarily only to fail to do it—usually for ephemeral political reasons—we suffer a defeat far more serious than those who focus only on domestic opinion polls realize. By blustering, and then revealing ourselves as weak willed, we tarnish the image of irresistible American strength.

This is a bipartisan problem. President Clinton bragged that he would bring terrorists to justice but did nothing to fulfill his public promise. Next, President Bush announced that he would bring terrorists to justice. For a time, he did, in Afghanistan, Iraq, and around the globe. Then he let his reelection campaign take precedence over a military campaign in which American troops were dying. For most of a fateful year—2004—the administration rarely fought to win. The loss of time cost us the blood of thousands killed and wounded, and after the presidential election our troops had to fight ferociously to regain the initiative. (I should state that I voted for President Bush in the election of 2004, since a leader willing to make decisions, however flawed, is preferable to one who cannot make up his mind.)

Partial victories are not really victories. Wars are not necessarily won by the best equipped, or the best trained, or the biggest armies. They are won by those who persevere, whose leaders do not waver, who realize that today's "catastrophe" will look less fearsome by morning, and who are determined to win no matter what it takes, or how long it takes, or what accusations a restive press raises against them.

Our enemies lack much. But they do not lack strength of will. Nor are they fools. When we offer them an opportunity to embarrass us, they seize it.

We need to relearn the old American virtue of quiet courage. It's not just a question of doing what we say we're going to do but of having the discipline and common sense not to say it at all until we have done it.

Instead of telling the outlaws that the sheriff is on the way we need to appear suddenly and unexpectedly at the bandits' hideout. Nor can we allow meandering diplomacy or domestic opinion polls to delay necessary decisions. Leaders must lead. When they look too long and hard for support for unpopular but essential actions they betray the trust placed in them by our citizens.

If fighting is required, we need to shut up and fight. A dead enemy is worth countless sound bites. No war was ever won by a government press release.

Six

BUREAUCRACY VERSUS INTELLIGENCE

Whenever our country is surprised or politicians make willful foreign policy blunders the automatic cry is "intelligence failure!" Our intelligence community has been blamed for the consequences of poor budgetary decisions, for developments abroad that we cannot control, and for the inattention of our leaders to the world beyond our shores. Pundits who have never worked in intelligence and political operatives intent on damage control thunder about the incompetence in our intelligence agencies. Journalists, as always, assume the worst.

I worked in our intelligence system for two decades, from the grinding tactical level at which intel meant a radio and a map to levels of access whose existence is classified. I have no ax to grind beyond desiring the sharpest possible blade for our country. And I can assure anyone reading this book that we do not have a *bad* intelligence system. We simply have a mediocre one, its practical value less than the sum of its very expensive parts (over forty billion dollars per year at present).

The problem is not that the intelligence community performs ineptly. It doesn't. Our intelligence bureaucracy—and it is, above all, a bureaucracy—delivers dependable competence in routine matters. True intelligence failure in the sense the critics mean it is reassuringly rare. But *excellence* in analysis, the ability to understand the threats to our country with breathtaking acuteness, is rarer still.

Nor is every intelligence failure avoidable. No intelligence system, no matter how vast and intrusive, could identify every threat our nation will ever face. This is not an excuse for laxity but a recognition of reality. A talented enemy will always be good for a surprise or two. We must and can do far better than we have done in the past—but perfection is the province of God, not man.

Unfortunately, the odds remain slight that our intelligence system will reach the notably higher levels of performance required by the threats we face. We have been assured that intelligence reforms are under way, a result of the findings and recommendations contained in the *9/11 Commission Report* issued in 2004. Yet, those top-heavy, superficial reforms are unlikely to make the pervasive difference the times demand.

The *9/11 Commission Report* was remarkable in several regards: Bipartisan, the research was thorough and the writing stunningly readable for a document associated with our government. But the report's fateful weakness lay in its recommendations—especially in those our government has been anxious to apply. Despite its quality in other respects, the report was naïve and elitist where it counted most. Betraying the prejudices of its sponsors, Democrat and Republican, the document demanded a director of national intelligence, an overseer with the power to better integrate and forcefully direct the multiple agencies and departments that contribute to our national intelligence effort.

Washington blinds its powerful sons and daughters. Instinctively, they assume that the solution to any problem is to further empower one of their own kind, that the need is always for a champion from their ranks, whether the issue is drug use in our streets or intelligence analysis beyond combination-lock doors. But the battles our intelligence system must fight will not be won by adding another general. An intel czar, adequately empowered, may make a useful difference but will not solve the crippling systemic problems that stifle creativity and dissent.

In intelligence, as on the battlefield, the generals may issue any orders they like, but the fight has to be won by the infantry. And the foot soldiers of our intel system are treated shabbily, with slight respect, low salaries, and little support for even the finest analysis if its conclusions are politically unpalatable or simply apt to raise eyebrows among the powerful. Intelligence executives do not want to be challenged by subordinates or called on the carpet by their superiors in the White House. So they play it safe, dressing up bland work with a string of classifications and caveats, with charts and satellite photos.

Instead of the uncomfortable truth on one page, decision makers are provided with handsome documents constructed to appear authoritative but containing the intellectual depth of a sales brochure.

The essential problem with our intelligence system is that it is, above all, a bureaucracy. In some respects bureaucracies have acquired an unfairly bad name. They do some useful things quite well, from insuring that Social Security payments go out on time to keeping adequate toilet paper on hand to resupply government restrooms. Bureaucracies provide dependable competence at mundane chores. Bureaucrats may not offer daring, incisive intelligence estimates, but they will be certain to reproduce, staple, and circulate their neutered estimates on time.

Bureaucracies are friends to routine but enemies of excellence. They do not take risks, and sophisticated risk taking is crucial to good intelligence work, whether we speak of CIA operatives in the field or analysts asked to prepare background papers for the White House. Bureaucracies produce and promote cautious managers. But when intelligence officials worry most about securing their own careers our country is less secure. The most insincere phrase in circulation in Washington, D.C., is "think outside the box." In Washington, when a superior tells you to think outside the box he or she wants you to come back with fresh reasons why the in-house position was right all along.

We have been doing intelligence work so dully for so long that even when an agency makes a sincere effort to unleash its brainpower or to profit from outside talent the practice is to hold a seminar, speak with reasonable candor, take notes, pat oneself on the back, and go back to doing business the same old way. No bureaucrat has bad intentions, nor do government employees go to work in the morning asking themselves "How can I do a poor job for the American people?" But habit is a killing trait. And we are in the habit of confusing the volume of raw data we collect with quality intelligence, of qualifying our analysis until it becomes meaningless, and of tempering our judgment according to the body language of the boss's boss.

A system that does not demand excellence will not get it. In the intelligence world the general attitude is "How can we make this requirement go away?" The implicit message is "What's the minimum we can do to meet the suspense date?" And, of course, far more time is spent in preparing sleek presentations than on rigorous thought.

Our intelligence system has suffered from inertia for so long that it no longer recognizes when its work is inadequate. As in any bureaucracy, uniformity is treasured and eccentricity feared. But great intelligence work is, by its nature, eccentric. Traditional thinking provides traditional answers. Such answers are inadequate to the times.

When political expedience adds its weight to the natural bureaucratic tendency to produce mild, readily defensible, noncontroversial intelligence products, the result—as I myself often have seen—is useless babble.

Regarding political influence on intelligence, the best we can hope for is to minimize it. It is humanly impossible to eliminate it entirely. Few analysts or managers in the intelligence system consciously skew analysis to make a presidential administration happy, but as we saw in the weapons of mass destruction miscalls in the buildup to our engagement in Iraq, there is a natural human desire to please and an equally human tendency toward groupthink (especially in conformist Washington, the only city in America where young men can't wait to sprout their first gray hairs). Political influence isn't a matter of ordering analysts to come to a desired conclusion. It's more subtle. Inside the Beltway everyone develops a sense of what an administration wants to hear. White House biases are no secret. Most human beings instinctively lean in the direction those gale-force presidential winds are blowing.

Still, the greatest problem is the timidity of intelligence bureaucrats at every level. Time and again I personally encountered resistance to new ideas that threatened the standard way of doing business or prevalent beliefs. It was almost impossible to excite any interest in the rise of unconventional or "asymmetrical" threats, in faith-fueled terrorism, or even in the importance of cultural factors to violent conflict. The technocrats and the dreary conventional minds dominated. For the gatekeepers who decided which information would reach the executive level the goal was not necessarily to get things right but to avoid being demonstrably wrong.

The result was the relentless pursuit of consensus among the various agencies. If everyone agreed on a common position, no matter how inadequate that position might be, heads were unlikely to roll. The CIA, DIA, NSA, the armed services intelligence staffs, the Department of State intelligence specialists, and all of the other players on our bench could point to each other when things went awry, saying, "The CIA agreed...NSA took the same position...State signed off..."

When one of my areas of responsibility was involved I would drive up the Potomac from the Pentagon to the CIA's headquarters and work through the dreary security layers to participate in National Intelligence Council working-group sessions. Every relevant agency would be represented. The ostensible goal was to find a community position on topic X. The sessions often lasted all day, beginning with the bolder analysts actually saying something, but only to get it off their chests. As the morning droned into afternoon, punctuated by a poor cafeteria lunch, and as rush-hour traffic thickened, we invariably reached a lowest common denominator position that would do no harm to us—but would be of precious little help to the president or his subordinates. Technically, any agency's representative was allowed to "take a footnote" disagreeing with the group's position, but the practice was, to say the least, discouraged.

The sessions were so worthless that I began doing what I could to dispatch other officers—the sort who were glad to get out of the office for any reason—while I concentrated on work I believed might have some worth. Thinking back on those meetings it angers me still to think how little good we did for our nation's leaders or the American people. There was deep, genuine talent in the system. But the system didn't want it.

Nor were those NIC sessions exceptional in their addiction to conformity. Some of us recognized the threat from asymmetrical enemies well over a decade ago. Officers and agents who actually had been out in the world, observing its harsh realities and the tumult in the wake of the Soviet collapse, could not mistake the growing dangers from religious fundamentalism or from nationalism collapsed into madness. From the Caucasus to the Andean Ridge, from the Balkans to Pakistan, I personally enjoyed an up-close look at cracking worlds. Others saw more than I did.

We shared our insights with anyone who would listen. We briefed. We wrote. We ambushed our superiors in hallways. But it was impossible to draw more than passing interest from a Pentagon obsessed with preserving Cold War–era weapons deals. The National Security Agency was determined to pretend that the Russians were coming back, while the CIA was casting about desperately for anybody who might replace the Soviets as a huge but manageable enemy. After the Clinton administration arrived it was taboo to hint at a threat from religious extremists (unless they were domestic Christians, of course). As I personally experienced, "Islamic fundamentalism" and "Muslim terrorists" were unacceptable terms in the Clinton years. Diversity was good, even when it was deadly.

It was all a shambles. Anyone looking for the roots of 9/11 must look far deeper than an FBI error here or lax airport security there. The Clinton administration's determination to ignore terrorism until it went away on its own, and its politically correct bigotry in favor of America's enemies, permeated Washington. Astute generals hoping for another star wanted no part of religious hatred as a cause of violence. Pretending that the Chinese were coming was safe and palatable to congressmen and lobbyists alike. There was money in it. But facing up to the threats from ethnic thugs and Allah's butchers was simply too uncomfortable. Reality didn't match the administration's philosophy, so reality went begging.

Time after time we made excuses for the ugly new world erupting around us; even as our "leading thinkers" insisted that democracy was coming overnight around the world. Mogadishu was an exception, we wouldn't make that mistake again. Then we found ourselves in Bosnia, but that was a one-off. A shrinking, shrieking Yugoslavia sucked us into Kosovo. That was the limit, and the Clinton administration really meant it this time. No more foreign adventures…the world was coming together.

Embassies were bombed in Africa. Troop dormitories were struck in Saudi Arabia. An American warship was crippled by suicide bombers. All of those blows were "isolated events." Al-Qaeda was a minor problem. All you had to do was to hurl a few cruise missiles at empty huts and terror would vanish.

Our enemies were shouting their intentions at us, then emerging from the shadows to kill us. *They* lived up to their rhetoric. Nothing could have been plainer. But admitting that such threats were real would have been more than an inconvenience requiring action. It threatened to destroy the belief system the Clintonites had carted into office from Ivy League graduate seminars and debates in Oxford or Cambridge during the Vietnam War. Anyone seeking a textbook case of denial need look no further than the Clinton White House.

The rest of Washington took its cue from Clinton's commissars. Just as the city later harmonized with the Bush administration ideologues. And both the Clinton and Bush administrations savaged any critics who dared to point out that they were not entirely perfect. The response of the intelligence community was to give each president the replies that he demanded. There were dissenters—there *is* genuine courage in our intelligence system—but they rarely made it past the lower gatekeepers.

In Hollywood movies a brilliant but lowly analyst is ushered into the Oval Office just in time to save us from nuclear disaster or a terrorist attack. The reality is different. It's rare for even a senior intelligence analyst to make it into the White House. Political appointees brief the president and his key subordinates from staff papers, sometimes bringing along a senior executive from the bureaucracy. But that bureaucracy waters down or completely removes any extreme positions long before the briefing papers cross the river into the District of Columbia.

Those who brief the president are generally far removed from firsthand expertise on any given subject. They're talking dogs in suits. They know how to speak in the earnest, no-nonsense tones executives value, but they rarely have the depth of knowledge that might make a difference. They know very well how Washington works. They just don't know how our enemies work.

The result is the Washington version of the parlor game in which people sit in a row and pass on a whisper—but in this game each next listener calculates the political cost of saying something the ultimate listener does not want to hear. The result is not merely a muddle, but a sanitized, useless muddle.

Even the finest intelligence system could not guarantee the prevention of all terrorist attacks (to be fair, we *do* stymie much incipient terrorism). But better intelligence work would have *prepared* us for an occurrence such as 9/11. We would have been looking harder—perhaps in the right places. At a minimum we would have taken Osama bin Laden seriously when he told us he intended to kill Americans in America.

What are we to make of successive administrations, Democrat and Republican, that ignored our mortal enemies—though those enemies told us in advance what they intended to do?

The threat was inconvenient. So we marched with eyes closed toward 9/11.

If we stand back and consider the long series of warnings our enemies broadcast as their attacks grew ever more audacious it's clear that our country could have been better prepared. Even the targets were not hard to identify. Alert analysts spotted them: In *Parameters,* the unclassified journal of the U.S. Army War College, an officer considered the effects of a terrorist attack on lower Manhattan. A Justice Department attorney analyzed how passenger aircraft could be employed as weapons. The information wasn't hidden away; it was on the street. But giving it credence would have upset the system.

Yes, 9/11 was an intelligence failure to some degree. But the warnings were there that a major attack was coming. The far deeper failure was a leadership failure—for eight years under William J. Clinton and for eight months under George W. Bush. When it gently chided both administrations that 9/11 commission report maintained its bipartisan loyalty to our Washington elite. The tragedy was blamed upon intelligence. Executive wrists were barely slapped. We were advised to move on.

The truth is that our government had been negligent. At the top. Through one administration after another. Poor intelligence was a convenient scapegoat.

Even had our intelligence system been superhuman in its predictions the odds are good that any president would have vacillated when warned that al-Qaeda was about to strike America with multiple passenger aircraft employed as flying bombs. He would have demanded proof, hesitating to disrupt air travel and commerce, wary of alienating the business community and depressing the stock market. Now the view from the Oval Office has shifted. But 9/11 should be a warning for all presidents to come: If we do not have leaders of vision and courage all the good intelligence in the world will not prevent disaster.

We can and must do better. While changes under way should be given a fair chance, and we all should seek to avoid the instant judgments so popular on talk shows, it's hard to believe that the further centralization of authority over our disparate intelligence agencies will solve our problems. In fact, there's legitimate cause for concern that we're adding yet another layer of insulation between the genuine experts and the president, isolating him like an oriental despot.

Time will tell. Meanwhile, adding weight to the top of the pyramid does little to fix the cracks in the foundation.

I can assure the American people of one thing: We have hundreds of superb intelligence professionals spread across the system, men and women supremely dedicated to our national security. We have thousands more who are solidly competent professionals. But we do not have enough of those top-of-the-game analysts and agents to achieve critical mass. Those in the ranks are dispersed across a complex system with enduring communications problems. Worse, the street-level grit that the best analysts can offer us *never* makes it up the chain unfiltered. At every level the expertise is less acute, the knowledge more general, and the breath of political reality colder on the back of the neck. So we have two core intelligence problems: attracting and developing more top performers, and re-creating the system so innovative work isn't crushed by bureaucracy.

Even if an intelligence analyst were to call the "next 9/11" dead-on, the odds that his or her analysis would make it to the president's desk remain slight. Much that appears painfully clear in retrospect seems downright crazy before the event occurs. And no intelligence executive wants to risk the president's derision.

Humanity as a whole is far more creative and infinitely more vicious than the individual mind can comprehend. Even now we cannot quite explain the Holocaust. Prior to 9/11, persuading our nation's leaders that Islamic terrorists (*if* we were allowed to use the term) would attempt to slaughter tens of thousands of American civilians in cold blood and would succeed in killing three thousand of them in one morning would have been a very tough sell. We're vigilant today. But the dead are dead.

Of course, we must avoid the other extreme, as well. We can't go to a high alert level every time an intelligence officer gets an itch. Sorting out the plausible (if extreme) from the impossible is one of the greatest challenges in high-stakes intel work. Too often, the wrong people—the bureaucrats—make the call.

As with warfare in the twenty-first century, intelligence work ultimately comes down to people. We have magnificent collection technologies. We can spot tiny objects from space, listen in on multiple forms of communication, pinpoint targets, and crack hypercomplex codes. But none of this means much if a human being can't make sense of the resulting data. We are so deluged by the volume of information we collect each day that it's far too easy to overlook that one essential scrap. Getting it right takes talented people in adequate numbers—and luck. No computer program is a substitute.

Overwhelmingly, the money in our massive intelligence budgets goes into technology. Those who counter that billions also go into people fail to whittle down the numbers. Once the bureaucratic overhead and the support staff is whittled away, the number of analysts, linguists, and agents remaining, while it may appear large as an aggregate, is simply inadequate to our present requirements. We are so under-strength in those key areas that specialists are swapped madly between offices to meet the demands of one crisis after another. The best analyst we have on Brazil may find himself or herself detailed to spend months working on Iran. Some of the skills transfer, but the lack of personnel depth means that during our lengthy crises vast stretches of the globe receive scant attention.

We're playing the highest stakes game there is with a shallow bench. Recent hiring efforts at the CIA will help somewhat, but the numbers involved are still too small. Furthermore, it takes many years to develop a first-rate analyst. You can't just lure them off the street, no matter what their educational credentials. And identifying the right men and women, then recruiting, developing, and retaining them, is tough in a system that favors management over expertise.

Our solution long has been to turn to science and technology. It's the American way. Except that in intelligence, technical collection means remain woefully inadequate to solve the riddles of the soul—the arch problems of our time. Our satellites and computers certainly have great value, but taken altogether I do not believe they offer us as much in the War on Terror as one analyst of genius could do. And we have a fair number of analysts of genius. But they make the management very, very nervous.

Just as the apostles of the Revolution in Military Affairs insisted that machines would make the soldier obsolete so, too, intelligence bureaucrats continue to hope that the next wave of technology will limit the need to rely on the unstable human factor. We use computers to fish tidbits from vast seas of information, we attempt to program patterns, and long have toyed with "perfecting" machine translations to make up for our paucity of linguists. But the human factor endures as the most important element in intelligence.

It would bore the reader to death were I to list the innumerable occasions upon which officers and officials, neck-deep in gee-whiz technologies, assured me that some new "system of systems" would solve our intelligence problems. Sad to say, my own service, the U.S. Army, was particularly guilty of this sin. Repeatedly, Military Intelligence bought expensive junk that didn't work, insisted it *had* to work, then wasted our scarce human resources in years of pretending it worked. We failed in the duties we were assigned but, by God, all that technology kept us busy.

Satellites can locate ships or tanks. Computers can detect a terrorist on a cell phone. But we do not yet possess a device that can peer into the enemy's mind. Machines are the ephemera of war. The human being is the constant. No matter how many terrorist training camps our imaging systems identify, if we cannot get inside the thoughts, longings, beliefs, prejudices, and even the madness of our enemies, we will never be as effective as we need to be in defending our citizens and our country.

Only humans can understand other humans. They cannot always do so, but flesh and blood remains our only hope. And the best intelligence analysts are uncannily good. Managers prefer safe, linear analysis, but human beings do not behave in a linear fashion in times of stress and conflict. The analyst's incisive call, based on instinct honed by long experience, will often sound absurd to the bureaucrat safe behind his desk. Our machines churn out swamps of data every day, providing us with an appearance of productivity, while a great analyst may be stymied for months, an apparent drag on the system, before he or she achieves a useful insight. And bureaucracies value predictability. They like things they can measure, indices of productivity that continue to rise each quarter. But a talented human being trying to decipher the future behavior of another individual continents away is anything but predictable.

The amazing thing is how accurate analytical calls can be. An intel hand at the top of the game may predict an enemy's actions before the enemy himself has made a decision. This sounds incredible, but it's based on a pattern we all have experienced: A friend or relative approached us to ask for "advice" about a romantic partner. From our remove we could see clearly that the intended bride or groom was a disastrous choice—while the person directly involved remained oblivious. Fanatics, especially, can be oblivious to their own patterns and behaviors. Sometimes an outsider can define an enemy's predicament and likely course of action more clearly than the enemy himself. Even when the enemy is a genius—and Osama bin Laden displayed at least a streak of that quality—genius itself can be predictable once the analyst cracks the subject's emotional codes.

Our intelligence machines operate within astonishing parameters. But not one approaches the complexity of the human mind.

———————————

Cut the share of the intelligence budget that goes to technology and divert the money into hiring more people—and rewarding them. It's impossible to specify dollar amounts, since our national intelligence budget remains classified and its breakdown is opaque. Certain programs within the budget are invisible to all but a handful of decision makers, overseers, and members of Congress. But an arbitrary cut in the portion of the budget that goes to contractors and technology would reverse the enfeebling current situation in which the technocrats always get their way while those on the human side of the intel equation are forced to make hard choices—or have no choice at all.

We need to bring some discipline to the blank checks contractors have enjoyed behind the wall of secrecy. By forcing the program managers to make sharp choices between the various systems they wish to purchase we would be far more likely to improve our intelligence capabilities than to harm them. Force the moneycrats to decide which systems are most vital to our nation. And legislate much tougher penalties for technology purchases that do not live up to the promises their builders make for them.

On the human side, we need *more*. More analysts. More agents. More linguists. More interrogators. More counterintelligence specialists. And we need to concentrate more intensely on the quality of those whom we're recruiting. At present, we focus on formal education. That matters to a limited extent, but a Ph.D. is no guarantee of the ability to understand other human beings or even of basic competence to connect the analytical dots. Some of the weakest performers I've known in government proudly hang their Ivy League diplomas behind their desks.

We need to study ways to identify the unique talents that make for extraordinary levels of performance in the intelligence field. And since those skills range from a tactile sense of how to question a prisoner to the instincts to know what an enemy has in mind, no current battery of tests or rounds of interviews will suffice.

Our government, from our military to our intelligence agencies, still has an industrial-age mentality and an assembly-line approach to processes. The prevailing attitude is that while some workers obviously perform better than others in the end they're all interchangeable.

But they're not. We accept that it takes special gifts to become a concert violinist or a major league quarterback. Yet we assume that any intelligent person with a degree in the right discipline can fathom the deepest secrets of the human heart and soul. In intel work instincts are more important than IQ. Time and again I've seen how one analyst could make calls so prescient they were uncanny, while those surrounding him not only could not replicate his performance, but had no understanding of how he did it.

It's not a matter of spells and incantations, but simply of peculiar human talents. Some human beings are born with abilities—which still must be developed over years—that give them an edge in forecasting behaviors. It's not a consistent or a uniform talent, but it works.

We'll always need solid professionals, as well. But we must accept that special requirements demand special gifts. Not mumbo jumbo or fortune-telling. Just a different skill set. Some human beings run faster than others, some think faster. And some just see more clearly. In the end, the "magic gift" may simply be a trick of mind that enables one person to regard what lies before him without prejudice while everyone else has been blinded by learned expectations. The finest analysts often can't explain themselves. The answers just seem obvious to them. The least we could do is to investigate the possibility that some human beings have talents that we need. Yet we approach hiring intelligence professionals little differently than we do when hiring clerks for a regional claims bureau.

Agents and agent handlers are even more complex. The best spies aren't remotely like James Bond. On the contrary, they're the sort of men or women who can disappear into the woodwork. Agent handlers must have the gift of making men and women from very different cultures trust them—literally—with their lives.

Several years ago, Earl "Frosty" Lockwood, a lovely man and a longtime friend to the special-operations community, invited me to dinner in downtown D.C. Another guest at the table of six was the splendid novelist and former CIA man Charles McCarry. McCarry had been a bona fide spy and we were speaking about public misconceptions of what espionage involves. McCarry said, quietly, that his greatest advantage had been simply that people tended to overlook him. Even in a small group he became invisible. A few minutes later the waiter took our table's orders. He left without asking McCarry what he wanted, having missed him entirely.

How would you test for that "gift"?

Some things *are* testable, of course. One is language skills. We desperately need more linguists, not only in the intelligence field but in our military as well. A skilled linguist sometimes can do the work of an entire battalion—especially if he has the knack for working inside the patterns of a foreign culture. Foreign-language capabilities matter not only because we must be able to translate what the enemy says or writes, but because the ability to live in a foreign language gives an analyst or agent richer insight into native psychology than any number of textbooks and courses can do. Language remains the key to more than we can yet pin down. Arabic, when spoken by a master, has an enrapturing effect that fits it for poetic expression—but it also can entrap the speaker in grandiose phrases that glide away from reality. English is explicit. Chinese is implicit. German is topically efficient but channels thought into linear patterns.

You'll never crack the final layer unless you can live, think, and dream in the other tongue.

Our answer to these requirements to date? Buy more stuff. But cracking diplomatic codes is not nearly as important as cracking human codes. Above all, an intelligence failure doesn't mean that we overlooked some juicy bit of data gleaned from a cell-phone conversation. It means that we failed to *understand* our enemies.

The intelligence agencies should also pursue the resources to offer generous scholarships to talented young people who want to study cultures and languages, in return for a set number of years of service, much as the military does with its Reserve Officer Training Corps scholarships. Intelligence agencies likely would find, as the military does, that many of those who take the scholarships, intending to do their stint and then get out, will fall in love with the ideals of service and stay.

But *how* can we make more talented Americans fall in love with the ideals of service in the intelligence field?

Change the Culture. This is extremely difficult. Bureaucracies are inherently resistant to change, and no change is as hard to effect as a fundamental shift in organizational culture. Successful intelligence managers and executives at or nearing the peaks of careers built upon caution are unlikely to embrace risk taking of the sort required to serve our needs. There is no formula for implementing this sort of change. If anything, it's a process of accretion, of slow shifts. Only a cataclysm creates the conditions for a swift cultural metamorphosis—and even 9/11 wasn't sufficient.

Why? Because no heads rolled in the aftermath. Although intel deficiencies were only one aspect of a much greater governmental failure that allowed terrorists such a comprehensive success on 9/11, top intelligence officials should have been removed. Even if some innocent victims suffered in the administrative purge the price would have been worth it. If no one was responsible for the weaknesses that led up to 9/11 no one will expect to be responsible next time. Fear is one of the few effective tools for changing bureaucratic behavior. At present, fear is instilled in the junior ranks, inhibiting creativity and risk taking, while senior ranks and executive appointees are protected (new CIA Director Porter Goss's late 2004 massacre notwithstanding).

We need to learn to empower junior and midlevel intelligence personnel, to trust them and to prod them to break from the safe conformity and mere punctuality bureaucracies admire. We also need to raise pay scales and implement stronger merit-pay differentials: Patriots though they be, intelligence professionals have mortgages and kids to put through college like the rest of America. Far too often, I've seen talented frontline analysts driven into management positions (which are always considered promotions by the system) in which their expertise was of slight use. They needed the higher salaries to care for growing families. Yet who might have been of more value in the days before 9/11—another gray-clad manager or an experienced analyst, a longtime student of terrorism fluent in Arabic?

Of course, all systems need good managers too. But the actual intelligence work should be rewarded, not just the ability to deliver progress reports to the next higher link in the chain.

No matter how many structural changes we make and how much money we spend, if we do not bring actual intelligence work back to the forefront of the vast intelligence bureaucracy, we will never give the American people the intelligence capability they deserve.

Above all, we must fight groupthink and the inherent wish to agree with one another. Calm may be attractive to bureaucracies, but it's not a suitable atmosphere for intelligence in the age of terror. Instead of striving endlessly for consensus, we should demand blood on the floor.

Get Dirty. Unless we want to fight no end of big wars in the light of day, we must be willing to fight brutal little struggles in the dark. When we leave the moral posturing of the campus for the world beyond the greensward the common good sometimes requires uncommon savagery. Faced with evil—and there *is* evil in this world—we must at times preempt our enemies with tactics resembling their own. The safe and self-righteous will warn of "slippery slopes" and the compromise of our values. But our values cannot long survive if we allow enemies to turn the slope of history into a precipice.

Few of our intelligence officers or agents engage in violent, clandestine operations. CIA station chiefs often are known to their host governments, while a top covert agent may simply be a skilled, unobtrusive listener. But there are circumstances under which we must act outside the bounds of international law and our own codes of behavior to prevent great harm to our country and its people. We must always have sound oversight of such exceptional operations, but we cannot hold those who defend us in back alleys abroad to legal standards suited to suburbia at home.

We must recognize that we are in a great war. And in this war spies and direct-action operatives must be regarded as soldiers on a battle-field, permitted to kill hostile actors before we are killed ourselves. We will make mistakes. But better to have occasional regrets than to en-dure a series of 9/11s. If we are unwilling to fight terror and related threats with every useful tool our enemies will locate the weaknesses in our system and exploit them. For decades we allowed terrorists to exist in plain view and to act with relative impunity. More than once we had Osama bin Laden in our crosshairs while President Clinton agonized over the legality of killing him.

We will not lose our souls by fighting back, although we might lose our lives through hesitation. The greatest myth perpetrated by those who never served and never will is that we lose our virtue when we "fight dirty." Our nation and our values are far more robust than such disin-genuous claims allow. Time and again our soldiers and agents have been thrust into infernos where hellish acts required a like response. The vet-erans of those affairs overwhelmingly welcomed peace when it came. They did not become deadly outlaws, as Hollywood would have it, but returned home to become law-abiding citizens and good neighbors. The soul can bear much when faced with grim necessity. The greater danger lies in failing to respond to that necessity in time. America's historical weakness has not been that we act rashly but that we act too slowly.

We live in a world with an appetite for holocausts. Our govern-ment's preeminent duty is to ensure that no holocausts happen to us.

We must ask *every* question, no matter how uncomfortable. Despite my conviction that human rights must be a pillar of our foreign policy, I would be dishonest to avoid the issue of torture. The position that tor-ture is never defensible is far too easy, too glib. If faced with a situation in which a prisoner possessed time-sensitive information that could prevent the loss thousands of American lives, most of us would agree that torture was justified in so extreme a case. To insist that torture must always remain forbidden is the easy argument of the theoretician evading the dilemmas faced by those who must operate in the world of flesh and blood.

Experienced interrogators know that in the great majority of cases torture is counterproductive, and cooption is far more effective. Adamantly opposed to torture, Colonel Stuart A. Herrington, a retired Army veteran and one of our nation's most accomplished interrogators, stresses that generous treatment defying a captive's expectations of brutality is often the most effective way to deal with high-ranking prisoners—along with playing to their vanity and sense of importance. Humane treatment overwhelmingly works to our advantage.

But there are exceptions. We must learn to recognize them.

We cannot accept direction from a morally bankrupt world. The prime recent example of the left's hypocrisy and folly was the uproar over the possibility that Saddam Hussein might receive the death penalty. Those critics had little to say while Saddam was slaughtering his own people and they overwhelmingly opposed his overthrow. But when this mass murderer was threatened with a trial in a court of law, the left took no interest in justice for the dead or the maimed. Their sole concern was Saddam Hussein's human rights.

How on earth can we take such voices seriously?

In a just world the Saddams would die while their prospective victims live long and happy lives. America must invest its power in justice for the many, not in protection for the outlaw few. We must do what is necessary, not merely what is popular.

In this comprehensive new war thrust upon us by the apostles of terror and bigotry, our intelligence system is a crucial weapon, from the analysts at their desks in northern Virginia, to the armed men on foreign soil without local permission. At times, intelligence specialists will prove more vital than military forces. But if they are to contribute all that the age requires we must discard the myths that obstruct effectiveness and dismiss the false humanity that would protect the enemies of humankind at the expense of tens of millions.

Behind the scenes we are making progress in the use of agents, spies, and direct action. But we are only at the beginning of a new and bitter age of midnight struggles. Our intelligence system has a very long way to go.

downtown hotel, which had no running water at that moment, I went to sleep to the festive sound of gunfire.

The next morning, before the heat rose, I made my way through the gasoline-starved city on foot to the U.S. embassy, which had a staff of six and had been in existence for five months, quartered in a hotel that stood in safe isolation on the city's edge, convenient to the well-guarded presidential compound. Our temporary embassy occupied the floor immediately above the Iranian delegation. Of course, our diplomats refused to speak to the Iranians, who desperately wanted to talk. Our barricaded embassy staff was mortified to learn that I'd hitched a ride into town with one of Tehran's diplomats the night before (his car had been one of the few with gas and I had cajoled a lift by pleading my lifelong desire to see the wonders of Isfahan and other Iranian cities).

Warned not to say so much as "Hello" to those nasty Iranians, about whom we refused to learn anything that might have been of value, I was given a pat on the head and told to stay out of trouble. Since I had come as a tourist the diplomats, to their chagrin, could not easily order me to get on the next plane and disappear. Pleasant enough as diplos go, the staff complained of their workload and I learned that in five months only one of them, a woman tougher than any of the men on station, had been outside of the capital city. She had spent a weekend fishing on the Turkish border, away from any matters of concern.

I rented a car, confident that dollars would make gasoline materialize from thin air. Within twenty-four hours a "complimentary" driver appeared to help me, a young man who was, unmistakably, a fledgling member of the Armenian security services. Miffed at first, I quickly grasped that if co-opted he could get me to destinations I would not be allowed to visit on my own. He turned out to be a bewildered young man whose infant child had died for lack of medicine the winter before. As soon as he realized that I knew a bit about his country he opened up, anointing me as the representative of a better world beyond the frontier. I was that magical beast, the *American*. He was a sad boy whose country was at war.

We had a grand time. After traveling the broken roads by day he would return to his wife and his child's ghost. I washed in whatever water the hotel's floor matron had captured in my bathtub, then strolled the streets of Yerevan, a lovely place even in the worst of times, dramatically

Seven

THE DEVIL'S DIPLOMATS

Friction between our military leaders and our diplom[...]
tine. Generals focus on results. Ambassadors are pr[...]
process. Embassy staffs concern themselves with pro[...]
the shape of the negotiating table. Soldiers kill people who ne[...]
The personalities involved are antithetical.

My own early contacts with the mandarins of the State De[...]
were inauspicious. Confused by the collapse of the Soviet U[...]
horrified by the tumult in its wake, our diplomats discarded [...]
tents of their faith in favor of clinging to an empty liturgy. [...]
sadors pursued smooth relations with foreign government[...]
than advancing American interests, human rights, or democr[...]

In the summer of 1992, with war raging in Nagorno Karab[...]
United States had no military observer on the scene. I had b[...]
tained after staff college at Fort Leavenworth to work on the [...]
keystone manual, *FM 100-5, Operations* (upon which I had n[...]
whatsoever). As a recent witness to much of the tumult in East [...]
rope and the dying Soviet Union I felt that someone in uniform [...]
to have a look at the situation in the Caucasus, a region a comrad[...]
had explored the year before.

My boss, Colonel Jim McDonough, was an inspiringly pugn[...]
man whose sense of war's reality routinely collided with the fanta[...]
staff officers. Jim was perfectly willing to pack me off to Armen[...]
the end of the fiscal year was approaching and there were no [...]
funds for conflict tourism. I took leave and paid my own way. Foll[...]
a stop in Moscow, I arrived at Yerevan's airport after midnight [...]
scenes of confusion, despair, and loutish affection. Checking in[...]

strewn between mountain and gorge, with Ararat snowcapped and tantalizing across the sunburned plains.

The city was in chaos. Officially, the war was proclaimed to involve only those ethnic Armenians resident in Nagorno Karabagh, an enclave within Azerbaijan. That was nonsense only a diplomat could believe. The struggle was going badly for the Armenians just then. Each day at dusk passionate rallies in the square below the opera house saw off truckloads of men in hodgepodge uniforms. Left behind, Yerevan's women wept as their sons and husbands headed for the front. Men too old to fight cursed age-old enemies, and you did not need to speak Armenian to recognize the outrage, fear, and venom blasted from blown speakers in the twilight. As the crowds ran out of spunk and began drifting homeward, wary of the thickening night, rival gangs dueled briefly with Kalashnikovs, their flashes a shock when glimpsed at the end of an alley.

Our embassy didn't have a clue. At the end of each afternoon the staff locked themselves in. They not only had no sense of the war, but lacked any grip on the reality in the city's streets. They did, however, offer me the address of a pleasant restaurant near their hotel.

But the nadir of my experience with "our man in Armenia" came toward the end of my too brief stay (Armenia is a gorgeous, fascinating country whose breadth of character more than compensates for its shrunken boundaries). My driver and I spent the morning dodging potholes as we aimed for the eastern end of Lake Sevan. It was a wind-freshened, vivid day, with gilded light and infinite blue skies. My scheme for getting about had been to study Armenian ecclesiastical architecture, since the country is littered with ruined churches and monasteries. You can explain the desire to go anywhere by a wish to visit this shrine or that chapel. A remnant of the earliest Christian kingdom, today's Armenia takes pride in its unassailable faith. That gave me a grand excuse to go where I wanted.

My driver had done well by me, able to talk us through roadblocks I would not have passed alone. Security services rarely think matters through and the Armenians, bless them, ended by assisting me. But as we closed upon the Azeri border east of the lake, amid history-bitten hills, we came upon one last roadblock. This time even my driver's credentials failed to do the trick.

In those halcyon days when Marlboros ruled the planet and Americans were welcome in the Soviet rubble, a dollar bill or a pack of cigarettes opened most any door and lifted roadblocks. I got out of the car and in my best Russian described my adoration for all things Armenian while casually holding two packs of Marlboros in my hand.

Poor as famine itself, those guards wanted the cigarettes. They were sweating like interrogation victims in a black-and-white spy film. But they would not let us pass nor explain why.

Addled between duty and desire, one of the guards finally whispered, "If you go past this place they will kill you. There is fighting."

With all the serendipity of the poor film in which we found ourselves, the clumsy thump of mortar fire sounded along the valley, behind the next turn in the road.

Nagorno Karabagh was far away, across a swathe of hostile territory. The Armenians had not yet seized the land between their country and the habitat of their kinsmen. The firing meant that the Armenian and Azeri governments had begun shooting across the international border, making a mockery of the claims—from both sides—that the conflict was restricted to the mountains of Karabagh.

Upon my return to Yerevan I dutifully went to our embassy and told the junior diplomat on duty what I had witnessed. Practicing her diplomatic language, she called me a liar without quite using the word. The Armenian government had assured her and her superiors that there was no combat anywhere along the international border. And that was that.

Nor did that little embassy, which soon would metastasize, have a military attaché to report back to Washington. Military officers were not wanted in the realm of peace and diplomatic receptions that was certain to appear, Atlantis resurrected, in each space left vacant by the Soviet departure. What I had seen and heard did not fit the template Washington wished to impose. And reality had no weight compared to diplomatic prejudice.

In time it emerged—undeniably—that the Armenians were engaged in a counteroffensive. In a dramatic turnabout they overran Azerbaijan's hapless, overstretched forces and took their turn at conquest. Later I would see the refugee camps and disorder from the other side, in the quintessentially human domain of nagging hunger, shattered lives, and intermittent cholera. But long before that I left Yerevan embittered.

Thanks to my "free" driver we had fuel not only for my junkets, but sufficient to deliver me to the airport without the need to hitch another ride from the Iranian embassy. As we left I saw for the last time the sight I had watched each day down in the circular plaza below my hotel balcony. Too late for the overcrowded shelters and lacking relatives to take them in, a great pack of refugees from Karabagh huddled against the curving walls of the plaza, surviving on one meal a day delivered by the government. The rest of their time was spent shifting slowly out of the punishing sunlight, following the shade with their shabby possessions, a human sundial.

They never made the diplomatic cables.

———————

Still, my dark view of our diplomats lightened as time passed. The inanity and close-mindedness so widespread in the early 1990s masked a positive trend. The sudden dissolution of the USSR left more than a dozen nascent states in need of U.S. ambassadors. That meant unexpected opportunities for many talented foreign service officers who did not suit sufficiently to fill the more glamorous embassies reserved for those who, lacking substance, were grand masters of form. Many of the men and women who found themselves unexpectedly in charge of start from scratch embassies outperformed their mainstream peers, blooming in jobs that demanded a sense of reality. Even those who assumed their posts with a disdain for uniformed officers soon learned the necessity of having a capable military attaché on hand. New partnerships coalesced between youngish, unspoiled ambassadors and a generation of colorful military officers, with both parties determined to make sense of a topsy-turvy world.

In that regard, the Soviet carcass did us a last favor from beyond the grave. I have since encountered numerous foreign service officers who do not fit the worn-out pattern yet whose careers are moving ahead. The old breed lingers on (a few years ago, while I was happily larking about in Indonesia, our Jakarta embassy was locked down in fear of a madly exaggerated threat, merely persuading Indonesians that we were cowards), but the new generation is slowly renewing the creaking apparatus of our diplomacy.

Unfortunately, the machinery of international relations isn't all that needs changing. The one additional revolution we need desperately isn't just an American requirement, but a global one.

Diplomacy is *dead*. Countless zombies continue to populate embassy receptions or feed from the trough at the United Nations, but as an effective tool to solve the world's most important problems, diplomacy as we have known it is finished. And it wasn't just Anglolateral leadership over Iraq that gave it the coup de grâce. Diplomacy's corpse has been rotting for decades, its stench masked by the vodka breath of the Cold War, then by the perfume of habit in that great contest's aftermath. Diplomats fled from the plague of reality into incense clouds of illusion, pretending as hard as they could that the tired rituals they knew how to perform might exorcise the spirits of a savage age.

Diplomacy as practiced today is a nineteenth-century European form with elaborate twentieth-century accretions, all of it incompetent to twenty-first-century demands. The European model of diplomacy, to which we foolishly continue to subscribe, assumes a like-mindedness that no longer exists; a universal adherence to basic rules now honored only by the few; and a monopoly of power contained in that fraction of the globe between London and Vienna, with Moscow (or St. Petersburg) admitted to the club for special occasions.

Today power is diffuse, our enemies and even our allies break the rules whenever they find it convenient, interests are almost never coincident from one continent to another, and business goes where diplomacy fears to tread.

Behind these generalities lie fatal specifics. Europe, the continent that has exported more man-made death than any other, may have seen its power ebb, but that wretched expanse left behind two curses on our planet, both of which our diplomats embrace: flawed borders that spawn bloodbaths and a model of state sovereignty that protects even the worst tyrant. The greatest force for good in human history—the United States—has been tricked into diabolical folly by retreating Europeans. Our diplomats now do the devil's work—or at least the will of dead kings, kaisers, and czars.

Bad Borders. Imperial Europe divided the world. Even where no explorer or magistrate had yet planted a flag, Europe's ministers carved up continents to their presumed advantage. The process did not begin with the notorious "scramble for Africa" but centuries earlier, when the Portuguese and Dutch slew each other over the Spice Islands that now comprise Indonesia; when the Pope blessed the division of the non-European world between Madrid and Lisbon; when Spain subdivided its vast domains into viceroyalties, then divided them again; and as Britannia contested the appetites of France. Those who came late to the feast—Germans, Belgians, Italians—demanded full plates as well. Africa was apportioned among Europe's ruling houses with astonishing cruelty. European governments knew the boundaries of their imperial properties long before they could say with confidence what those boundaries contained.

People did not matter. Navigable rivers, mountain barriers, fertile plains, ore deposits...such was the stuff of empire. Human beings were of concern only when hands were wanted to do brute work or as purchasers of the empire's monopoly goods; otherwise, black and brown flesh was superfluous. Pencils dueled over tens of thousands of square miles, blank spaces on the maps. Crayons slashed across continents. And when the bartering ended in Berlin or London uncounted masses had been divided by diplomats who had little knowledge of—and less interest in—their existences or desires. Tribes found themselves split between German, Portuguese, and English masters, between merciless Belgians and the French. Imaginary lines descended upon jungle and savannah, followed by real penalties for their violation.

Elsewhere, the opposite phenomenon prevailed. Tribes or religious communities with histories of gory rivalry found themselves bound together within a colony destined to become a blood-soaked state. Berlin conferences...the Curzon line...the satanic horse-trading of Sykes-Picot...the Balfour Declaration...*Kolonialwaren*...the *mission civilatrice*...the missionary school...thus Europe deformed the world and deemed it good.

And when the great empires collapsed, gutted by insupportable wars and rotten with moral languor, Europe *still* had the last laugh. From Congo to Iraq, Palestine to Indonesia and the Philippines, new states inherited old borders designed in distant capitals to spite human affinities and compound hatreds. Yugoslavia, Nigeria, Pakistan—each a Frankenstein's monster of a country, cobbled together from graveyard parts. Somalia, Afghanistan, Saudi Arabia—imagined as states where only tribes existed.

In the decade and a half since the Soviet Union collapsed in a drunkard's gutter, the armed forces of the United States have been drawn into conflicts or full-scale wars in Somalia, Bosnia, Kosovo, Afghanistan, and Iraq, with lesser involvements in Rwanda, West Africa, and the Caribbean. Discreetly in Pakistan and a degree more openly in the Philippines, our special operations forces and military advisers risk their lives. And every conflict in every location where our soldiers have given blood since the Cold War's end is a legacy of Europe's determination to draw the world's borders to its own benefit—and damn the consequences.

How did we fall into such a trap, insisting that those old imperial borders were sacrosanct, then fighting to defend them? Europe's despots must be howling with glee in hell. Our obsession with intact borders, no matter their flaws or origin, is such that a Republican secretary of state tried to persuade the splintering Soviet Union to remain whole—after we had finally cracked it apart. Then his Democrat successor insisted that Yugoslavia must remain intact, continuing to demand that its ever-shrinking rump must stay together.

The locals took no interest in our dismay.

In Somalia we pretended a shifting constellation of tribes was a country. In the Balkans, even now, we pretend that Kosovo might again be a happy extension of Serbia (and that Kosovo itself is a unity, despite its insurmountable internal division). In Iraq we squandered an opportunity to do justice to the Kurds, free the Shia, and contain the Sunni Arabs by dividing the state along its natural fault lines. Instead, American soldiers and Marines died for the sake of boundaries agreed to by a Frenchman and an Englishman a century before.

We are fighting wars that we either cannot win in the long run or that we can win only at great cost. We are not just fighting against contemporary human agendas but against the tide of history. This is an age of devolution, of breakdown, of the last dismantling of empires. The great imperial orders are all gone now that the Soviet incarnation of the empire of the czars is in recession. At this stage, the miniempires are slowly cracking up: Pakistan, Nigeria, Congo...perhaps Iraq, Ukraine, Russia, or Indonesia. Yugoslavia is already gone. We are so intent on sticking our fingers in this dyke that we fail to see the waves coming over the wall.

The greatest failing of our diplomats is one of imagination—they cannot conceive of an order other than the one they have been trained to serve. If you remark to a diplomat that borders have to change he or she reacts with the horror of a sixteenth-century monk confronted with the telltale signs of witchcraft. The diplomat will tell you that no means exist to change borders. But that is an inadequate and dishonest answer. Borders *are* changing. At present they are changed—or maintained— with blood. If we do not design, in collaboration with our allies, a mechanism for amending borders more peacefully, we will not see an end to these pogroms, attempted genocides, and civil wars in our lifetimes—or long after.

The world has been made wrong.

The obstacle to making it right is the European model of government embraced by every colony set free. No minor state, however failed, willingly cedes territory to its neighbor or to an independent entity. Dictators cling until their last gasp and even elected leaders insist on their "right" to every inch of "their" soil. If one tribe or religious group aims to leave, those who would be left behind employ force to restrain them. Europe excited dreams of nationalism—nightmares, rather—where none previously existed. And now we are holding the bag as it drips gore. In some respects the legacies of colonialism are crueler and more insidious than was imperial rule itself.

We need diplomats with less regard for protocol and more respect for reality. This world is changing volcanically. Pretending that the status quo can be maintained defies both history and the immediate evidence. Borders have *always* changed. They are changing now. And they will continue to change.

The only question is *how* they will change.

The Sovereignty Con. The most outrageous scam in the contemporary system of international relations is another European

legacy, the concept of inviolable state sovereignty. The idea of sovereignty in one form or another doubtless predates recorded history (it is time to resurrect anthropologist Robert Ardrey's concept of the "territorial imperative," an insight so profound that his colleagues disowned it); however, the Europeans of the imperial age codified it, and built barriers of custom and law to guarantee that no matter how abhorrent the actions of the king, and no matter how grim the slaughter he wrought upon his people, other rulers would neither move to depose him nor interfere with his internal arrangements. Reciprocity prevailed.

The most bankrupt argument a diplomat or activist can make in defense of a dictator is that, no matter how gruesome, the actions of a state apparatus within its own borders are a sovereign matter and external powers have no right to intervene. According to such a doctrine Hitler might have been deemed a splendid fellow had he confined himself to killing German Jews.

Must America accede to a doctrine that defends the Hitlers and Saddam Husseins?

The sole justification for any government in the twenty-first century is the protection and advancement of its population. A state that kills its own people en masse has no legitimacy whatsoever—no matter what the tyrant-ridden United Nations declares.

We do not reflect. Instead, we shout our prejudices while refugees stream and tens of thousands die. Given his crimes against his own people and his neighbors, how can any moral human being argue that Saddam Hussein should have been left alone?

The moral indolence of the international community is incomprehensible to anyone with a shred of conscience. The genocide in Rwanda has been mourned theatrically in retrospect—Europeans, especially, will always weep over corpses, but will not act to protect those still alive—but the massacres never stopped around the world. If profits were not threatened and our grotesque international "order" was not disrupted, despots, demagogues, terrorists, and gangsters were free to kill and maim. As I write, a tragedy has been unfolding in Sudan's Darfur province for many months. Governments wring their hands. The UN politely discusses the situation. Delegations and special representatives are dispatched. Celebrities whiz by. A bit of aid is sent along to ease our consciences. And the slaughter continues.

Of course, in Rwanda, Darfur, and other parts of Africa the dying is done by blacks. And blather all it might about the equality of humankind, the international community continues to undervalue the lives of the darker skinned. Even the United States, which has made great moral progress, is far more apt to send its troops to another Bosnia than to sub-Saharan Africa. France *does* send its troops—but only to kill natives in defense of its dwindling empire in disguise. The West should have intervened militarily in Darfur, but with the United States committed to Iraq the continental European powers, as usual, took stock of their material interests and found that none existed in western Sudan.

The United Nations is united only in its indifference to injustice. When the United States, along with other English-speaking states, fails to lead the way the screams of the anguished and dying go unanswered.

How can we not be bewildered and disgusted by the international defense of Saddam Hussein's regime? Critics of our war of liberation posed the specious question "Why Iraq? What about the other tyrannical regimes?" Their tone suggested that Washington must have had some insidious reason for singling out the Baghdad regime. Of course, the critics did not want action taken against *any* oppressive regimes. They only wished to frustrate and embarrass the United States. Yet there were plentiful reasons why it made sense to free the Iraqi population first.

You do what is possible. In an ideal world we could remove every tyrant or junta. But we do not live in an ideal world. Some take this as a justification for doing nothing, but it only means that we must do the best we can, that we must recognize our limits (but not exaggerate them to absolve ourselves of responsibility). The struggle for freedom has to begin somewhere. The notion that if we do not do everything we are not justified in doing anything has neither logic nor moral validity.

Consider a few of the practical reasons why it made sense to remove the Iraqi regime while taking a different approach to North Korea (as one obvious example). North Korea had not invaded anyone for a half century. Saddam Hussein had launched wars that took over a million lives within the past quarter century, and he was only stymied, not penitent. The United States had no specific moral responsibility for the Pyongyang regime, but in a tragic error had briefly supported

Saddam Hussein against Iran's mullahs. Our relationship with Saddam was neither so intense nor remotely as enduring as those enjoyed by France, Russia, and China, but we're Americans, and the ways of amoral powers should not be our own. Then, in 1991, after encouraging Iraq's Shia Muslims to rise against the Baghdad regime, we abandoned them (a repetition of our behavior in Hungary in 1956). The subsequent butchery of the Shia and the regime's campaign of ecological terror against the Marsh Arabs was, in part, our responsibility—inaction in the face of terror and genocide is complicity.

Yes, Iraq's oil mattered. But it was not the sole or even the primary motivation for Operation Iraqi Freedom. On the most practical level, removing the government in Baghdad was *doable* and had the support of the great majority of Iraqis. The Iraqis had risen repeatedly against Saddam Hussein. The North Koreans have not shown the valor to repudiate their leadership. A war on the Korean Peninsula would be a bloodbath. The South Koreans and their supporters would win, but Seoul, a megacity, would be destroyed (in an act of defiance, South Korea insisted on rebuilding its ravaged capital on the same site in the wake of the Korean War, failing to foresee the increased ranges and lethality that render Seoul a hostage not only to North Korean nuclear weapons, but even to conventional artillery).

But all this swiftly becomes hairsplitting. Even had we simply flipped a coin to decide which tyrant to depose the destruction of the targeted regime would have been justified. What right can an unelected tyrant, hated by his own people, have to dictate the fate of tens of millions? How can we look away—or worse, defend the tyrant's incumbency? We cannot solve every problem, but that is no excuse for doing nothing.

A tragedy of our time is that the left has squandered the last of its moral capital by elevating rigid anti-Americanism above human rights and freedom. Campus theorists were able to hijack the left even in the United States, thanks to a splendid paradox of history. In America, the workers of the world won. The traditional leftist program for which labor leaders struggled ended in a triumph for the working man and woman, thanks to the progress of capitalism, a system whose dynamism Marx and his followers never grasped. The American worker's priority shifted from a fight for economic justice to a desire to enjoy the gains achieved, leaving the left to ideologues who now disdain the worker as fully as they despise the government he or she chooses at the polls.

Human rights and freedom should not be polarizing issues in America. They should unite us. But our domestic ideologues, in slavish imitation of their foreign counterparts, would rather see a million black or brown human beings die than accord Washington the right to intervene.

Instead, they argue that all crises should be referred to the United Nations. But the UN is hopelessly corrupt. Will a Security Council that includes France, Russia, and China ever vote to remove a bloodstained regime? When the Oil-for-Food Program scandal broke we learned that the permanent Security Council members who opposed our intervention in Iraq had been making billions of dollars by helping Saddam Hussein subvert sanctions (the sanctions that critics of the war insisted would have worked, if given time). The General Assembly will not approve the deposition of tyrants because so many of its members would have reason themselves to fear, were justice and freedom to be acknowledged as grounds for intervention.

The United States need not abandon the UN, but we need to recognize its limitations. For all its exuberant corruption the UN does a few things reasonably well (if expensively). It can conduct peacekeeping—but not peacemaking—operations in a benign environment, one in which the opposing sides simply need an excuse to refrain from fighting any longer. The UN runs useful if inefficient aid programs, supports education (if selectively), and helps protect cultural monuments. It employs out-of-work bureaucrats and politicians from the developing world who otherwise might be hatching coups at home (this observation is not meant sardonically). And the UN does some good in improving health conditions around the globe (appallingly, though, when the Bush administration announced that it would commit fifteen billion dollars to the fight against AIDS in poor countries, the reaction was to pick at the details of this generous gift—a contribution that remains unmatched by the European Union or any other entity).

But for all the mixed blessings it offers, the United Nations will not and cannot advance the cause of freedom. The body is a prisoner of its own membership. And its members will defend the sovereign privileges of tyrants over human rights every time.

The United States should not withdraw from the UN, but it should impose more rigor upon it—past efforts have been half hearted and inadequate. We should not provide the level of funding we do today and should "demote" the organization by favoring regional bodies.

Most important, we must recognize that a new century demands a new organization, one that elevates moral purpose, freedom, and common sense above inclusiveness. Let the mouthpieces of tyrants have their say at the UN. Meanwhile, we must build an Alliance of Democratic Nations, constructed around the Anglolateral core of states that form the vanguard of liberty. We need a new organization that attracts would-be members with the hope of joining an exclusive club, an association of rule-of-law democracies that cherish freedom, human rights, and the individual citizen. At present, the UN does its best to paralyze the forces of human advancement. We need an organization that not only espouses liberty and justice for all, but which acts upon its principles.

The establishment of such an organization would be met with howls of outrage from despots everywhere, and even from superficial democracies such as France. The anger would mask their fear that a body of democratic nations would be a far more effective champion of the oppressed than the "democracy" of the UN in which tyrannies enjoy an equal voice in deciding our global future.

We do not need another forum for talk. We need a body with moral force that can act. Nor can we rely forever on ad hoc alliances. We must *institutionalize* freedom at a globe-spanning level. Such a formal alliance would be diverse, including not only the indispensable English-speaking countries but states such as Poland and Hungary that have been taught the price of freedom by history. Nor should this organization have an elitist steering group such as the UN Security Council. An Alliance of Democratic Nations should be truly democratic, with each vote having equal weight—but with majority rule, not an impossible goal of achieving consensus. Individual members would be free to participate or not in future operations, military or otherwise. But we would have, at last, an international body whose purpose is to champion the oppressed rather than to codify oppression.

Such an institution would slowly gut the UN, forcing it either to amend its ways or to die a slow death. But if the UN will not act for humankind, the United States and like-minded nations can no longer afford to pretend that the UN is the only organization a tormented world requires.

Sovereignty cannot be allowed to become an excuse for unrestrained savagery. Saddam Hussein *was* a Hitler to his people and his neighbors, restrained only by the limits of his power and, at last, by a coalition that found his behavior intolerable. Removing him struck fear into the hearts of dictators everywhere. That war was revolutionary—and just. We must strive toward a world in which the tyrants—not their subjects—live in terror.

Those who objected to the removal of Saddam Hussein's regime on grounds of state sovereignty were the moral descendants of those who looked away from Hitler's crimes. The difference today is that those who condone the deeds of mass murderers pose as moral arbiters, demanding to know what right Washington or London or Canberra has to decide which governments are unacceptable. The answer has been spoken before, and has fallen on deaf ears for countless generations: When the forces of good fail to act, the forces of evil triumph. And we *are* the world's essential force for good. No amount of fashionable anti-Americanism will change that.

Sovereignty that is not earned by a government's labors for the good of its citizens has no validity. An international system designed to protect kaisers and archdukes, czars and kings is a monstrous burden on this new century. No border can be allowed to stand if its only purpose is to protect a tyrant.

We must not fear to act when action is necessary, moral, and possible. Whenever the situation allows we should act in concert with our natural allies and those apprentice states moving toward mature freedom. But when we are forced to stand alone in a just cause, we must not hesitate.

Let history judge us.

The diplomatic system we inherited without a murmur from Europe is not only inadequate but immoral. The United States of America does not need diplomats whose primary goal is to keep a terminally ill system of international relations on life support, and damn the costs. We need diplomats who view themselves as soldiers on an alternative battlefield, who are willing to break china instead of preserving it for diplomatic receptions. We need fresh thinkers, fresh voices, and, above all, *fighters* in our embassies. The status quo is repugnant. The United States must rise above it.

How can we continue to pretend that a diplomatic system "perfected" in the latter half of the nineteenth century is adequate to the needs of our own time? We might as well insist that nineteenth-century medicine is all we need for contemporary health care. We have seen fewer changes in diplomatic structures and practice than in any other formal sphere of human endeavor. We cannot allow this travesty to continue.

Contrary to the accepted wisdom of diplomacy, it is *not* always better to keep talking. There are times when even diplomats must discard their cherished protocols and take up the struggle for freedom and human rights.

Those times have arrived.

Eight

DEMOCRACY AND DEMONS

W hen Americans imagine the political desires of foreign populations we make three major errors. First, we confuse democracy with freedom. While the two are related, they are far from inseparable. Second, we imagine that all other human beings desire both freedom and democracy. This underestimates both the human capacity for fear and the innate hunger for a predictable order. Third, we imagine that the democracy and freedom desired by others are bound to reflect our own. But the American experience of freedom and democracy reflects our own needs, capabilities, and desires; other cultures may have very different longings and requirements, to say nothing of different histories.

Democracy is the most humane and successful form of government humankind has yet devised. Most human beings desire a measure of freedom. But democracy, as we know it, is a cultural art. And billions of human beings still appear willing to trade away many forms of freedom for security.

Begin with freedom. Americans assume that freedom means, above all, the liberty to change or sustain administrations with the ballot. For us, freedom is inseparable from the voting booth. We cannot imagine freedom without elections. Yet in much of the world political freedom is a concern of small elites, while the general population attaches far greater importance to the simple freedom not to be annoyed too much by government. Social and economic freedoms mean more to many than the chance to decide who heads their state. While we should never stop advancing the cause of human freedom in the broadest possible sense, we also must recognize that our priorities are not necessarily those of our neighbors.

In the great age of Arab Islam the freedom of the bazaar always found ready defenders, yet there was no expression of interest in political liberties beyond the occasional revolt of oppressed minorities (who, when successful, proved equally ready to oppress those whom they had defeated). That heritage is sustained today by the Middle Eastern businessmen who accommodate themselves to despicable regimes as long as they are allowed to conduct their affairs profitably.

Islam's prescriptive nature, its obsession with the details of daily behavior, created societies that valued order over social freedoms. Contrary to the American experience, Middle Eastern societies fear too much freedom and equate public liberty with libertinism. The American insistence on freedom of choice is confounded by a civilization that desires that the right choice be made for it.

This is an essential failing of the American imagination. We cannot see that Muslim anger toward Middle Eastern governments does not always reflect an innate human longing for freedom of choice, but merely discontent over the bad choices regimes have made. Arab civilization, especially, has conditioned populations to subservience for so long that many lack the self-confidence necessary to sustain American-style democracy. We emphasize individual choice and responsibility. In the Middle East the group prevails and individual responsibility is an alien concept. While the current tumult in the region may disrupt the historical pattern—Iraq is a crucial laboratory—the truth is that many Middle Eastern Muslims want parents, not presidents.

Nor do we understand the fears that lead foreign populations to support strongmen. Americans have lived in such unprecedented security for so long that even 9/11 failed to convince many of our citizens that the world is a dangerous place. Despite lurid reports of murder in the media, most Americans assume a level of safety in their personal lives that would be intelligible only to those Middle Eastern populations who lived under the strictest, best-ordered regimes of the distant past. We assume that the integrity of our persons is our birthright and that property rights are inviolable. Elsewhere, security of any kind has always been a gift of authority, whether that of the clan or of the ruling class.

We also enjoy lives of incomparable bounty. In China, students may ponder democracy, but the masses dream of better jobs and material possessions. Even in Russia, ever scheming to take the best from its neighbors and so susceptible to the worst they have to offer, President Putin's democracy-pinching has excited no general outcry, no strikes, no mass demonstrations such as those we saw in neighboring Ukraine in late 2004. The new czar in the Kremlin knows his people and realizes that Russians fear disorder and impoverishment while inherently trusting his mild despotism. Nor has Putin eliminated democracy: Within limits, he finds it useful, at home and abroad. Russia isn't headed back to a Stalinist autocracy, but it will not soon resemble an anglophone democracy either. Putin will protect social freedoms while improving the economy. In return, Russians will accept limits on political freedoms. Elections will continue, but the parliaments they return will decide only lesser policies. Russia will adhere to many of the outward forms of representative government while imbuing them with a Russian essence. We are seeing the slow fermentation of a Russian-brewed democracy. It may not satisfy American tastes, but it is Russian tastes that matter. We see an oppressive state apparatus and fail to realize that most Russians want a level of security that allows them to enjoy those lesser liberties permitted to them.

Even continental Europe's political culture has profoundly different priorities than do those of the United Kingdom and the English-speaking nations of the New World. Their history has stricken Europeans with fear of too much freedom, of disorder, of rampage. The welfare of the group still trumps that of the individual on the old, bloodstained continent, and protests against governments are far more likely to be about group interests than personal freedoms. The closest the United States ever came to the restricted European vision of freedom was during the peculiar regimentation of the Depression years and World War II, when our president spoke of freedom from want and from fear. That single word "from" encapsulates the differences between Americans and mainland Europeans: For Europeans, the essential freedoms are always *from* something, from unemployment, from social disparities, from need, from war, from the noise of a lawn mower on a Sunday morning. For Americans, freedom means the freedom *to do*.

European freedom is essentially passive, protective. American freedom is much closer to liberty. Europeans accept limits on personal achievement in the interests of personal security and the general welfare. Americans believe instinctively that the general welfare is best served by fostering personal achievement. Europe imposes limits on the individual for the common good. We believe that the common good is best served by individual opportunity. We look at European lives and see their limits. Europeans regard our freedom to succeed as little more than the freedom to fail. Despite the chronic gloom of our domestic intelligentsia, we are the world's optimists. Europeans are pessimists. And even if their pessimism occasionally proves well-founded, it's still the optimists who change the world.

Americans and Europeans each find the other's system disheartening. Europeans choose security. Americans choose opportunity. The fact that most Europeans and most Americans still resemble each other racially (although that's changing rapidly) obscures the deep and growing differences between our civilizations.

Americans are in love with freedom and will fight for it. Europeans cherish security, and those who threaten that security may find, to their dismay, that Europeans remain capable of extravagant barbarities when sufficiently provoked. Terrorists themselves have far more to fear from the United States, but the populations from which terrorists spring may find a wounded and vengeful future Europe prone to abrupt atrocities. Europe has no track record of behaving humanely under stress. And as we saw in the diplomatic row over Iraq, the leading countries of the old European heartlands care nothing for the freedom or well-being of non-European populations.

Freedom in Europe has never meant freedom for others. No German soldier ever liberated anyone. French soldiers keep colonialism alive where it has formally ceased to exist. Dutch soldiers looked on as ethnic Serb militiamen massacred the Muslims of Srebrenica. Even in the backwater struggles of the Balkans only the United States could guarantee the minimal freedoms of daily life.

We need to have realistic expectations of this world. Every human being doubtless would like some degree of freedom, but that longing may range from the desire of the fanatic to lash himself bloody in a public ceremony, through the freedom to buy a satellite dish or marry one's partner of choice, to the grand freedoms of America. We are fools to believe that all human beings desire—or could bear—our degree of freedom.

We have *learned* freedom.

This is not an apology for "authoritarian" regimes. Human beings deserve the freedom to shape their own lives. But we should not be too surprised when they make less of their opportunities than we hope. The road to freedom, as freedom is known to us, is long and difficult. We must beware of forcing shortcuts on others.

And freedom can be dangerous. As we saw in the days that followed Saddam Hussein's fall, or in the gangster capitalism that scarred Russia after the Soviet Union's collapse, sudden freedom is all too often interpreted as license: All that was forbidden is allowed. Most societies have ways of righting themselves after listing too far to the side of freedoms for which their people were unprepared. The greater danger arises when the sudden intoxication of liberty leads to disappointment.

Disappointed people elect demagogues. Which brings us to the dark side of democracy: Hitler came to power through the ballot box. It does not matter that the first government he formed was a minority government (the next election gave him a majority). Democracy opened a door for Hitler that the old regime would have kept firmly shut. This is less an indictment of democracy itself—the most highly evolved form of government this earth offers—than of the people who misused the tool.

Because of our own experience we view democracy as harmless. But democracy is a very sharp blade that we have been trained to handle from the cradle.

Setting aside the differences between parliamentary and presidential systems, democracy appears to work well in two kinds of states. It functions superbly in the contemporary United States, where no single ethnic or religious group enjoys a majority or a decisive plurality. Our parties must build broad coalitions and subsequent elections find interest groups switching sides. Each party may have a base of support that changes only slowly, if at all, but the decisive middle shifts its weight from one election to another: "From many, one." Our social complexity results in a magnificent, robust, mongrel political health that prevents either major party from taking all of the people for granted all of the time.

Democracy also works well in states with relatively homogeneous populations, such as Sweden or the Netherlands. Parties represent concrete interests as well as political philosophies. They do not represent religions or ethnic groups but reflect differences of opinion within one ethnic group with a single religious heritage (however withered).

But democracy rarely functions effectively in artificial states, those monstrosities designed in the colonial age in which a single tribe or religion either has a majority by itself or can muster so mighty a plurality that it dominates lesser tribes. Generally, tribal cultures have difficulty overcoming their antimeritocratic practices and group loyalties. In Africa, for example, elections often meant that the most powerful tribe, or a few powerful tribes, dominated the polls. The resulting governments viewed the outcome as legitimizing the neglect or the outright oppression of the defeated.

Much of the world reflects the African model of states in which one ethnic group dominates, making democracy a tool of oppression. Should the Tutsis of Rwanda have been more concerned with democracy than with security? What has democracy meant to the Kurds of Turkey? For that matter, what will it mean in the future to the Kurds of Iraq, should Iraq continue to exist as a unified state?

Pessimistic as this discussion sounds it is emphatically *not* intended to discourage the United States from advocating democracy or from fostering it when we have a sound opportunity. It is meant as a corrective to the mindless sloganeering from both right and left that reduces an ineffably complex human experience, the emergence of Anglo-American democracy, to a cheap, all-purpose formula.

The twenty-first century *will* see the spread of democracy. But democracy will take an increasing number of forms as different civilizations and local cultures adapt it to their traditions and needs. We have convinced ourselves that democracy will change the world, and we are correct. But the world is also going to change democracy, and we may not always be happy with the results.

As with the Russians and their choice of Mr. Putin, we may find that some populations cast their ballots in favor of a strong government, even if that means reduced personal and political freedoms. Different societies value different rights. In many, improvements in the quality of daily life will overshadow any importance attached to political debate. This may be an evolutionary process in which the full belly eventually leads to a hunger of the soul for greater freedom, but we also may find that security remains more important than choice for many human beings. To the people in fragile, tormented societies democracy may appear anything but reassuring—those in unstable circumstances crave certainty. The demagogue who delivers jobs will receive a warmer welcome than the moral leader who extends only poverty.

The freedom struggles of the late colonial age rarely resulted in the emergence of lasting democracies. From early-nineteenth-century Latin America to late-twentieth-century Africa, the revolutions and insurrections were about group empowerment far more often than they were about freedom. Among the states that gained their independence in the last half century democracy rarely got even a toehold beyond the anglophone colonies of Africa or Asia. Instead, elections were a spectacle with a predetermined outcome—when elections were held at all. The great exceptions, such as India or South Africa, that have not suffered a military coup or yet succumbed entirely to a one-party dictatorship, either enjoyed British political tutelage, however uncomfortable, or achieved independence after the deadly nonsense of Marxism had been exposed as incompetent to human requirements (but the world is always good for a surprise: Mozambique, a long tormented country with massive odds against it, is struggling toward a level of governmental and social decency rare in the developing world).

Africa, especially, seemed to squander every opportunity. Democracy appeared to be a thorough failure. Yet even that neglected continent is beginning to make impressive progress in a few key states. The lesson may be that democracy just takes time, that mistakes have to be made along the way, that the people have to come to it themselves.

Iraq will remain an important testing ground, at least as much for Arab civilization as for democracy itself. Each election, however flawed, constitutes a milestone. Iraq will be a true democracy only after the third or fourth national election—if the system is not perverted by then, reducing the ballot to a meaningless formality as in other Arab states. Yet there is reason to hope, and great cause to pray, that Iraq will prove that Arabs (and the country's more sophisticated Kurds) can build a functioning democracy.

And then we will have to see how much freedom the electorate bestows upon itself—and how much power they willingly cede to their leaders.

———————

If freedom and democracy are so difficult, why bother? Because no matter how challenging freedom may be it remains the most desirable human condition. And because despotic regimes, however attractive they may appear to multinational corporations or diplomats craving order, do not last. Their stability is an illusion. They either behave aggressively to divert domestic attention from their failings, or they collapse—often suddenly—into civil war and havoc.

Even if the freedom struggle of a subject people does not aim at liberty and democracy as we know them, we are foolish to defend dying regimes. We must return to our natural place on the winning side of history, on the side of the popular will. Those whose struggle for self-determination we have supported are far more likely to be good partners in the future. We must learn to set aside short-term diplomatic and commercial interests in favor of our long-term interests. This goes against the American obsession with quarterly earnings reports, but we must retrain ourselves to think in longer cycles.

At times, this will mean accepting unattractive but popular governments for an interim period. We must always be on guard against the rise of a Hitler, but must avoid hysterical fears of democratically elected leaders we simply don't like. We never quite seem to realize that our blatant opposition to a popular choice only strengthens the support for those foreign leaders we try to bully out of their presidential palaces. We need to be more calculating and less childishly spiteful: Stalin no, Hugo Chavez of Venezuela a provisional yes (in time Chavez will overreach and fail). Let immature electorates live and learn—don't try to stop the projector in the middle of their movie. Don't behave so stupidly—as we did with Castro, Mossadegh, and others—that we become the excuse for another country's failures.

This need to accept frustrating outcomes is especially difficult when the people's voice, interpreted through the ballot box, calls for a strict fundamentalist regime. We not only fear practical dangers but are repulsed by the threat to human rights—not least the rights of women.

This is one of the most vexing questions of our time. We Americans *must* stand for human rights around the world, and we must be willing to sacrifice now for a better future. But what do we do when democratic elections empower religious leaders who impose restrictive codes of behavior that reduce women to virtual slavery?

The short answer is that we cannot force the infantile males of the Middle East to respect women. We can encourage, cajole, and, hopefully, persuade them over time. But a confrontation over this most contentious of all human issues is apt to do little good—and may even do harm.

There is no easy answer to this vile dilemma, but the most promising, if slow, solution is playing out in Iran. The Iranians could not be dissuaded from trying religious rule. Now that they have experienced it, ever fewer Iranians find it desirable. With 70 percent of the population under the age of thirty and discontented, change is inevitable. The demise of the regime of the mullahs in Tehran is already programmed. Its collapse may not come about as swiftly as we would like, but it also could surprise us as did the Soviet implosion. We may see a violent upheaval in Iran, exploding "out of nowhere," or the theocracy may linger for another decade or two. Meanwhile, we are in a race against time: Will the ruling mullahs develop nuclear weapons before they are toppled from power?

The relevant point for this discussion is that the Iranians had to suffer such a regime to get it out of their system. Once it is gone, few will mourn its demise. Despite the current tensions over the nuclear ambitions of its rulers Iran, with its far richer heritage and more confident identity, has an even greater potential than Iraq to become and remain a humane, rule-of-law democracy. Like strong-willed children, the Iranians had to learn their lesson the hard way.

Elsewhere in the Middle East secular regimes have so discredited themselves that the rise of Islamic governments may be unavoidable—or avoidable only at a terrible cost that is finally unsustainable. The coming years are going to demand much greater sophistication on our part, a richer ability to differentiate between local conditions and to recognize the psychological requirements of disparate populations. We certainly do not wish to see the rise of zealot regimes, but we must learn to sense when the trend is unstoppable, to recognize when it's wiser to concentrate on building channels, not dams.

In any case, it is unlikely that any new religious regime arising between Morocco and Pakistan would be as repressive as that of Saudi Arabia, a grotesque anachronism that has bought America's protection for far too long. If we can tolerate the repugnant monarchy of the Saudis, we certainly should be able to stomach a democratically elected ayatollah as a president. The underlying problem, of course, is that we still have trouble telling the difference between a Muslim fundamentalist and an Islamist terrorist: The fundamentalist may never be our friend, but he need not be our enemy.

By advocating democracy and championing basic freedoms we can get much of what we need strategically. But we cannot get what we desire as swiftly as we want it. We must overcome the American assumption that a thousand years or more of traditions and prejudices can be undone with one election. We must press relentlessly for change, but we must press in the right places. And we must turn away once and for all from our Cold War–era hypocrisy, from preaching democracy, freedom, and human rights while looking away from the abuses of "our" dictators. We do not need more "allies" like the House of Saud, Reza Shah Pahlavi, Manuel Noriega, or Fulgencio Batista.

This book stresses the need to fight to win whenever we must go to war, to do whatever it takes to convince our enemies of their defeat. But when our troops deploy to defend our interests, we owe it to them to judge more acutely where those interests lie.

In the end, the best thing we can do for freedom, democracy, and human rights is to lead by example. We have learned our governing skills over centuries. Others, too, will have to learn for themselves. Democracy sometimes means that the anti-American candidate wins. And freedom can mean the freedom to reject our values, at least initially. As long as nascent democracies do not export violence we need to let them make their own mistakes.

Democracy is far more complex than we like to admit. Its success relies on so much—the rule of law, basic security, the suppression of corruption, a culture of compromise and a perceived community of interests, respect for minorities, the separation of powers in government, even individual leaders—that glib beliefs in its instant and universal applicability are as absurd as the confidence of yesteryear's campus Marxists that the revolution was coming to Topeka.

Unlike Marxism, democracy *can* work. But if we try to package it as political fast food we are apt to find it lacking in appeal to cultures with tastes of their own. Instead of asking ourselves how to make American-style democracy work in Iraq our question should be "What will a healthy *Iraqi* democracy look like?"

Next time around we need to take local conditions into account as we attempt to foster democracy and freedom. And there will be a next time.

Nine

ATLANTIS, THE
IDEOLOGICAL SUPERPOWER

> "But, proceeded the Empress, how are you sure that God cannot be known? The several opinions you mortals have of God, answered they, are sufficient witnesses thereof."
>   —Margaret Cavendish, Duchess of Newcastle

The Muslim fanatics yearning to destroy our civilization sincerely hope to build a better world. Based upon mad and heartless interpretations of the Koran, the utterances of Muhammad, and centuries of arcane Islamic law their vision of a re-ordered, globe-spanning society of the faithful is repugnant to us, but to our enemies it is the answer to God's will and human need. Desiring the best for humankind—and certain that they know what that "best" should be—these terrorist chieftains are only the latest incarnation of the monsters who appear in every culture determined to purify us of our sins and weaknesses through an unsparing application of cleansing fire.

September 11 was meant to do us good.

Nothing is more dangerous than attempts to perfect the world. And there is nothing more common than human discontent with the conditions of this world. While the unhappiness of those whose fates are miserable offers little reason for astonishment, the impatience of the more privileged with their earthly circumstances renders humankind not only the most unstable species, but the deadliest. The common man or woman prays for an improvement to his or her lot. But zealots and intellectuals demand nothing less than perfection. That quest for perfection leads to the GULag and Auschwitz.

The myth of a utopia, of a golden age lost or yet to be attained, upon the earth or in an exclusive heaven, haunts history. Nor is there any likelihood that the dream of a "better elsewhere" will be extinguished before our final hours. Did any generation pass without nostalgia for the "good, old days"? How much more powerful the human longing to rediscover the paradise without flaw in which our mightiest myths claim we were safe.

Through horrid years and halcyon days alike human beings have insisted either on looking backward to an imagined Camelot or a reimagined caliphate or on staring ahead in the hope that life's travails will end in glory beyond the grave. We seem uniquely unfitted for the here and the now. No comfort or accomplishment long contents us, and no beauty sates. We humans have an explosive capacity to convince ourselves that life must have been, must be, or will be better elsewhere. It is astonishing that we have come as far as we have, that our entire race was not done in by reverie.

Sex and violence are so riveting because they offer the only instances of unqualified immediacy in our lives (and sex does not always do so, as any veteran of its conflicts can attest). The mind or soul is inconstant, ever flittering. The most successful human beings—the happiest—appear to be those who can inhabit the moment most fully, embracing reality, if not always celebrating it. The malcontents, passive or violently active, are those who live in a "someday me," who find no satisfaction in the present or their likeliest tomorrow, who wish away the world as it exists.

Benign dreams of utopias, of perfect worlds or a paradise hereafter, take a range of forms, from the honest believer's confidence in immortality down to the National Public Radio listener's dreams of a cottage in Provence, from gated retirement communities to the insistence of life-worn hippies that Atlantis is merely veiled from the human eye, and from communes that founder because someone eventually has to do the dishes to all-inclusive Caribbean resorts. We bribe ourselves with fantasies as we drive to work each day. If those common daydreams hinder us from appreciating the moment, they rarely do us harm (although it might not do to raise one's belief in Atlantis during a job interview).

Other forms of the passion for utopias turn monstrous. Whether attempts to found the kingdom of god by force or efforts to create a godless

paradise, they invariably end in cruelty and death. When we are fortunate the suffering is not long and the deaths are few. But history is
stained crimson by utopias gone mad and littered with the bones of
wayward Edens. Among Christians, the admonition of Jesus Christ that
his kingdom was not of this earth has been ignored almost as routinely
as his warning about our fervor for earthly wealth. Among Muslims, injunctions to charity and mercy are discarded in favor of rigor and oppression. The promised land is usually drenched in blood.

The trend worsened in the modern age, as humankind rejected
God for base superstitions, from nationalism to the class struggle. Now
antimodern rebels are resurrecting the cruelest forms of religion from
the past and the postmodern world threatens to become more intolerant still. As the industrial era reached its apogee in the twentieth century, schemes to purify the world, to create perfect orders, whether in
the name of a god emperor, racial purity, the workers of the world, or a
cultural revolution killed more people through war and organized
massacre than the worst preceding centuries of plague, famine, and
war had managed to do. In an age of weapons of mass destruction religious fanatics returned from history's grave may wreak still greater
havoc—and they will insist that their god looks down approvingly, that
their deeds are blessed.

All utopian schemes, religious or secular, ultimately founder on
human complexity. The intellectual's response, whether Marxist or Islamist, is to kill and torment men and women until they behave simply.
The industrial age convinced intellectuals that humanity could be reduced to an assembly line, a new twist on the ideal society. The cost of
their failure was hundreds of millions of corpses, from Germany to
Cambodia.

Once again, Anglo-American exceptionalism served us well. We
never were seduced by madcap theories hatched by European intellectuals prescribing how societies should run. Among the healthiest of
the common traits of Americans has been our resistance to the schemes
for social engineering that plagued the rest of the world.

The anglophone tradition certainly had its utopian thinkers, although the most distinguished cases involved intellectual exercises
their own authors might have stamped "unfit for human consumption."

From the shades of Avalon and Arthurian legend (much influenced by French high-medieval notions of chivalry) down to the Puritans and Cromwell's protectorate, the fantasy certainly existed that a better world once had been at hand—or might be spanked into existence. From Wat Tyler's Rebellion through the religious revivals of the eighteenth and nineteenth centuries, Britain never lacked for those who hoped to change the world.

The remarkable thing is that the passion of the zealots never took, at least not enduringly. Even Cromwell's dreary rule resulted more from a struggle over the practical forms of government than from the faith militant (the mistake of historians long has been to consider the Cromwellian interlude and the Restoration separately, instead of recognizing how they interacted in the classic Hegelian manner to yield the synthesis that began with William and Mary). The Puritan attempt to regulate the English people too strictly hardly lasted a decade. Too heavy a hand laid on our daily lives, whether in Britain or America, incited insurmountable resistance. When faced with those of too severe a rectitude we always reply with Nell Gwyn or Madonna.

Elsewhere, the tyranny of monks or mullahs, from Spain to Saudi Arabia, lasted decades and even centuries. Hanging a handful of supposed witches in New England still fills us with disgust. Elsewhere, torture and executions pleased the masses. In the Middle East public torments delight crowds to this day. Saudi Arabia constitutes an attempt to create a divinely sanctioned utopia on earth. Predictably, it has become a pit of corruption and extravagant hypocrisy.

Creative, absorptive, and adaptive—never rigid or static—America's heritage has saved us again and again. Our Constitution assumes that men and women are *not* perfectible, and it doesn't raise the bar forbiddingly high. The American Revolution, while it changed the world and certainly seemed a revolution to successive English governments, was never about creating a utopia. As with the comparatively few other successful and enduring political revolutions, ours was about improving social and economic conditions, not about altering them fundamentally. We did not take up arms to establish a millenarian commune but to restore what the Founding Fathers viewed as the inalienable political rights of Englishmen to parliamentary representation and consensual taxation. Our struggle was not remotely about the destruction of all existing forms. Had England allowed its North American colonies to become full-fledged members of its body politic no revolution would have occurred. The English rejected us before we rejected them. We became Americans because we wanted to be English, with the full rights of Englishmen, and were refused. Our revolution moved far beyond its initial goals, but were we to be accurate we would speak of the "American Evolution."

Even the sects that fled to our shores in the earliest years of settlement, each hoping to construct the New Jerusalem amid the forests of a new Eden, proved unable to sustain their severity. When the men of God asked too much of human frailty for too long their flocks moved on—or removed them. Faith never lacked, but it was redeemed from extremism by frontier individualism and an English yeoman's skepticism (so different from the cynicism of continental intellectuals, then or now). The men and women of the Massachusetts Bay Colony turned out to be from Missouri.

And those English intellectuals who scribbled about perfect societies? One of the most valuable early lessons I received in the cruelty of intellectuals came when I read Thomas More's *Utopia* in my early teens—after purchasing a copy under the influence of one of the twentieth century's disinformation successes, the film of Robert Bolt's play *A Man for All Seasons*. I was mortified by what I read. I realized immediately that More's disciplined world—a harshly limiting place—was not one for the human beings I knew. And it certainly wasn't for me. I began to view Henry VIII more sympathetically.

Predictably, More's work appeared in an age of confusion, when the old order was breaking apart and men were forced to question verities that had endured for centuries. It is always so. Periods of social disintegration and crises of belief, of the evident failure of the old ways, always produce dreams of utopia. We see the pattern repeated as Islamic terrorists nudge their god to hurry up and return the world to a divinely prescribed order—and, not least, to make the rest of us behave.

The "moral behavior" issue is always there. A routine priority is the control of the female. Few millenarian prophets have been women. They are almost invariably embittered men who view women as the handmaidens of the devil in need of chastisement and close management, lamentable necessities to be used sparingly and with distaste.

The antifemale rage of Islamic terrorists may be extreme, but it is not unique. Susannah is *always* in trouble with the elders. Few male witches burn. Muslim fanatics mortify themselves with online pornography, then rail against the degeneracy of the West. Whether religious or secular, prophets of a paradise on earth always seek to suppress human desires (and the competitive loyalties they create).

Of course, the English-speaking tradition has not been entirely immune to this phenomenon. Even Francis Bacon's *New Atlantis* from 1627 has a cold, Puritan wind running through its pages. His imaginary paradise of "Bensalem" is described proudly by its residents as "the virgin of the world." Published after the Restoration had begun, Henry Neville's *The Isle of Pines* ends with the morals police of his cobbled-together paradise hurling a black man off a cliff for lascivious behavior. Preachers from John Knox through John Wesley on down to the Welsh fire-and-brimstone preachers of early twentieth-century chapels and the televangelists of twenty-first-century America have never stopped inveighing against the sins of the flesh. And those of us reared in the English-speaking tradition ignore them when they press a mite too hard. In America, humanity itself always wins in the end.

Elsewhere, it's different. Failing cultures take even the maddest promises of utopia seriously—whether the lies have been told in the name of Karl Marx or Allah.

———————

It has been observed that Communism was a religion without a god— although the Stalins and Maos were happy to stand in for vanquished deities and be worshipped. Communism in its various mutations never lacked for liturgy (or prudery). It suggests that, for many human beings, the idea of a god may not be as important as the promise of a utopia. In the Communist interlude—blessedly behind us—the golden age was always just around the corner waiting for one more enemy, internal or external, to be defeated. The promise of that new Atlantis, hatched by a grubby, failed son of the Rhineland, excused the sacrifice or outright murder of hundreds of millions of human beings. For its part, the German cult of National Socialism was deficient compared to the dark genius of Communism. The Nazis could only find enemies outside of the "pure" German race. The genius of Communism (like that of Islamic fundamentalism today) was its ability to find enemies anywhere and everywhere.

Was Marx indispensable to the mass horrors of the twentieth century? Probably not. The GULag had deep roots in European history. Communism wasn't a seed, but merely a fertilizer for murderous sprouts that had been nurtured since the late Middle Ages. The monopoly church of the crusading era believed no toll in human suffering was too high to "perfect" God's children. We all can cite a few of the heresies that were suppressed with horrific bloodshed—the Cathars and Hussites, for example—but there were *hundreds* of heretical movements, many no more than efforts at church reform, that the papacy suppressed with fire and sword. Early Protestants were no more tolerant, if less capable of mass suppression. The Age of Reformation, from 1517 to 1648, saw the sanctioned slaughter of more Europeans by Europeans— and Christians by Christians—than any other period prior to the twentieth century, all in the name of purifying societies, of pleasing God, of bringing about His perfect kingdom. The inquisitions and witch hunts, the Massacre of St. Bartholomew's Day and the broad moral collapse of the Thirty Years' War were all the result of dreams of establishing an earthly order that would better please God.

The notion of human perfectibility is lethal. Europe embraced it, as did many of Europe's colonial-era victims later on. For the Islamic world it was there from the start.

———————

There's always another enemy. Whether they center on the salvation of the flesh or of the soul the appetite of utopian schemes for human victims is insatiable. America's New Jerusalem has grown so generous in spirit because it was never imprisoned within a theoretical framework. We have an ergonomic utopia, designed and redesigned by countless users. Above all, our sloppy paradise accepts human variety and imperfection: Hester Prynne is vindicated, the elders of Susannah's church are exposed (didn't Jimmy Swaggart read the Bible?). Utopias tried elsewhere have all been based upon texts, either upon the inhuman designs of intellectuals or on inhumane interpretations of sacred books. They all insisted on human perfectibility. And they all failed.

The inquisition will always uncover heretics. People's courts will always discover doctrinal imperfections in the prisoner. Few Muslims will ever be pure enough to satisfy Islamic extremists. And the old men of every faith and political doctrine will always find the young worrisomely immoral.

If any proof is wanting that men and women make of religion what they will, it certainly lies in the extremist's perversion of Christ's message of human fallibility and redemption, of forgiveness, of love. Islam doesn't even bother to pardon human weakness but reaches right for the whip. In his canny memoir, *Tristes Tropiques,* the anthropologist Claude Lévi-Strauss termed Islam a "barracks religion." The epithet perfectly suits the Muslim insistence on submission (the literal meaning of "Islam"), on social discipline, on the spit and polish of forms, on the division of humanity into a male officer corps and female enlisted ranks that so cripples Islam today.

Those who inaugurate systems, religious or secular, to perfect humankind invariably find themselves frustrated by the glorious intractability of men and women. First the unbelievers or the heretics or the capitalists have to go. Then the poets go, along with the dubious books. And the "rich" peasant landholders and the adulterers have to go. Then the comrades whose revolutionary zeal appears in danger of faltering and the fellow believers whose faith may be too weak have to go too. The soundtrack for utopia consists of cell doors slamming and the shrieks of the dying, of bullets fired into the back of heads and the weeping of the survivors.

If Osama bin Laden's most idealistic followers managed to eliminate America and Israel overnight, Europe wouldn't escape. Even now Allah's butchers murder those Muslims whose faith seems heretical, deviant, or simply insufficient. To build an earthly paradise according to the blueprints of the preachers or the intellectuals you have to kill the scientists, the doctors... the insubordinate workers, the youthful sinners... and after the slaughter the Party's five-year plan is no closer to fulfillment and the world remains a repulsively sinful place, an insult to the god that killers have yoked to their discontents.

If bloodshed purified the earth we would all be walking angels.

In contrast to the American Revolution the French Revolution sought to alter everything within its grasp, from the elimination of traditional hierarchies to the price of bread, from defeating the grip of organized religion to changing the names of the months. Robespierre, Danton, St.-Just, Marat, and their ilk sought to purify their world with blood and soon drowned in it themselves. The revolution failed, although it did not lack consequences. Its myth has been far more enduring than its accomplishments.

The French Revolution was radical in both its techniques and its aims, an uproar, a great spasm. Seized by intellectuals, it swiftly lost touch with every reality but the guillotine. Generals were executed for losing battles no general could have won. Ambitions promptly exceeded capabilities. The citizen disappeared into the mob. And, inevitably, enemies were discovered not only beyond French borders among scheming aristocrats and Prussian regiments, but within the revolutionary cadres. In the sudden absence of common values and codified law the patriotic speech of one resounded as treason in the ears of another. This was a revolution that literally talked itself to death, the fate of its strongest voices prefiguring the ends of the Bukharins and Trotskys of another revolutionary era.

The people unleashed cannot endure disorder very long. They soon crave a messiah with parental authority. The French found one in Napoleon, who set Europe on the march toward the mass wars of the future. In popular emotions Napoleon stood in for a truant God. Yet there was a difference between the little Corsican, who was interested in his own glory, and prophets or *mahdis* who claim to act for the glory of their deity. Bloody handed though he was, Napoleon wanted to rule the earth, not destroy it. The true messianic temperament views the destruction of earthly forms as the short path to paradise. The secular leader, even at his worst, is drawn to the things of this world, while the religious firebrand is repulsed by them. The man who believes he acts for his god is the more dangerous of the two, but the charismatic leader, religious or secular, is humankind's bane.

We should be grateful for dull presidents.

Although the religious zealot is not merely willing but impatient to sacrifice his life for his cause, Americans should be wary of impassioned mass movements of any variety, anywhere in the world. If we examine the ease with which the French or Russians or Chinese or Cambodians leaped to a quasi-religious fanaticism even in the absence of a god, we find a collective need within populations deprived of traditional structures to believe in something greater than themselves, in a unifying cause, in some justification for their sufferings and sacrifices. Human beings are hardwired for faith. They require it almost as commonly as they require oxygen. It may take many forms, most of them benign, from identification with a football team to a quiet, luminous faith in the divine. But when the great chain of being is broken, when the heavens appear to be falling and traditions can no longer be relied upon for protection or the least certainty, men and women flock to the nearest messiah, whether he appears in religious robes or in a uniform fit for an operetta. They kneel to the man who validates their existence and offers them a purpose. Hitler gave German identity a powerful meaning, absurd as its foundations may have been. He was the perfect idol for his time and place, replacing a sense of injustice with one of pride. Osama bin Laden, like many another self-raised prophet before him, revives the threatened identity of the faithful. He does not simply tell them their faith is valid, he demonstrates its power through acts of revenge against iconic enemies. And few things satisfy humankind as profoundly as seeing the mighty suffer.

Osama bin Laden wasn't an accident. His coming was inevitable. The disarray of Middle Eastern Islam demanded that he appear. We will be fortunate if he isn't merely John the Baptist to a coming terrorist messiah—or a series of such prophets—and we must kill him to demonstrate our greater power. There will be practical results, but those are of lesser consequence. Loath though we would be to admit it, we need to demonstrate that our "god" is more powerful than his. Contrary to the wisdom of the faculty lounge, dead martyrs are far less of a menace than living killers. Others will arise in the wake of dead terrorist leaders, but that is a result not of our actions but of the disastrous state of Middle Eastern civilization. We will have to keep on killing them until they are decisively discouraged or destroyed. There is no immediate alternative.

All religions produce fanatics in unstable times. Osama bin Laden and his comrades are products of the crisis within their faith. The times made the men. And they are likely to go on making them. The arch terrorists who claim to represent pure Islam are often nihilistic in their actions, but they provide certainty—clear, incontestable answers—to those who have come to doubt themselves and the power of their creed. They offer a fascist utopia on earth and a well-regulated paradise hereafter. Above all, they remove doubt from the minds of the weak and give purpose to souls adrift and in disarray.

The American assumption is that men need something to live for. The brilliant insight of the master terrorists is that once they have been sufficiently humiliated men will as readily embrace a reason to die. The perfect apocalyptic terrorist—the suicide bomber or the hijacker who does not intend to survive—is the young man or woman for whom life is not only disappointing but intolerable, the failure who craves an end. The terrorist chiefs give their human tools a deluxe version of their desire.

Suicidal "martyrs," when they appear in significant numbers, are symptoms of a society terrified of life. Today, the spiritual wounds and material humiliations of Middle Eastern Islam cut so deep that the longing for a shortcut to paradise has infected many thousands, perhaps millions. Those who will become suicide bombers tomorrow are already the walking dead. It may be too late for any action of ours to resurrect them. In their hearts they have already left this earth behind, with all its dreads and shames. It is an experience so profoundly unAmerican that we cannot comprehend it.

After 9/11, the War on Terror, the liberation of Afghanistan, and the shattering of Saddam Hussein's Iraq we still refuse to recognize our enemies.

Above all, they are *believers*. Miserable in the here and now, like so many who went before them, they seek a better world than this earth offers them. Their utopia lies beyond the grave. They are the ultimate revolutionaries, willing to destroy all of the earth for a promised garden in paradise. They represent the age-old human quest for Utopia, for Paradise regained, for the pastures of Heaven.

Our grimmest mission in the twenty-first century will be to kill these dreamers.

Ten

THE BLOOD CULT OF TERROR

Europeans insist that the United States overreacted to the events of September 11, 2001, that they have been dealing with terrorism successfully for more than three decades, that it can be managed, that life goes on.

They're wrong.

What Europeans fail to grasp—what they willfully refuse to face—is that the nature of terrorism has changed. The alphabet-soup terrorists of the past, the IRA, ETA, PLO, RAF, and others were essentially political organizations with political goals. No matter how brutal their actions or unrealistic their hopes, their common intent was to change a system of government, either to gain a people's independence or to force their ideology on society.

The old-school terrorists Europe outlasted did not seek death (some still linger on to harass their governments today). They were sometimes willing to die for their causes, but they much preferred living to watch their enemies fall. None were suicide bombers, although a few killed themselves in prison as a political statement. Crucially, their goals were of this earth. Each of them would have liked to survive and rule in a government their faction controlled.

Now we face terrorists who regard death as a promotion. They reject secular ideologies and believe themselves to be instruments of their god's will.

They yearn to nudge their god along, to persuade him through their actions that the final struggle between faith and infidelity is at hand. While they would like to see certain changes in this world—the destruction of Israel, of the United States, of the West, of unbelievers, heretics, and Muslims whose faith is imperfect—their longed-for destination is a paradise beyond the grave.

This makes the challenge they pose fundamentally different. The new terrorists are vastly more dangerous, more implacable and crueler than their predecessors. The political terrorists of the 1970s and 1980s used bloodshed in attempts to reach finite (if often unrealistic) goals. Religious terrorists approach mass murder as an end in itself, as the deserved punishment of the wicked, as a purifying act that cleanses the world. They do not place their bombs solely for political leverage but to kill as many human beings as possible.

Yesterday's murderers of European politicians and businessmen seem almost mannerly compared to today's faith-fueled terrorists, who videotape the ceremonial decapitations of their victims. When political terrorists hijacked airplanes they hoped to draw attention to their cause. When Islamic terrorists seize passenger jets they do it to kill.

Europeans refuse to acknowledge the difference. Doing so would require deep shifts in their philosophy and practice. The threat from Muslim extremists is far more insidious than any Europe has confronted in generations, but Europeans cannot bear the reality confronting them, so they curl into denial. It will take thousands—perhaps many thousands—of European deaths to convince the continent that it is not immune to the plague of Islamic terror. The Madrid train bombings or the murder of a Dutch filmmaker in the street by the light of day inspired more narcissism than intellectual rigor.

The old terrorists were often so rabid that they had to be killed or imprisoned, but others became negotiating partners for governments. From Yasser Arafat to Gerry Adams, a handful gained international stature. It may even be argued that Adams became part of the solution, rather than simply remaining part of the problem, although Arafat remained an obstacle to the end. Characters once on the fringe of extremist movements, such as Germany's gifted foreign secretary Joschka Fischer, moderated their thinking and committed themselves to reform within the system. Ironclad doctrines and formulaic rhetoric simultaneously satisfied the old-school terrorists emotionally and limited their practical effectiveness: When all was said and done, far more was said than done.

For today's apocalyptic terrorists the existing system is evil. It cannot be reformed. It must be destroyed to make way for Allah's design. Negotiations are no more than a tool to be used in extreme situations to allow Islamic terrorists to live to kill again another day. No promises made to infidels need to be honored.

The god-haunted terrorists we face now will never become statesmen—not even at the grotesque level of an Arafat. They wish to shed our blood to fortify their faith, to impose their beliefs on a sinful world, to placate a vengeful deity.

That doesn't leave much room for polite diplomacy. Islamic terrorists have reverted to the most primitive of religious practices: human sacrifice. What else could explain the video clips of captives beheaded as they squirm and beg for life? September 11 wasn't an attack. It was an offering. Islamic terrorists are Aztecs without the art.

Europeans—and even many Americans—fail to grasp our enemy's intensity, his conviction, his blindness to all that contradicts his faith. One of our inherited myths is that all human beings, no matter how horrid their crimes, might be redeemed. That is an elevating belief, but an inaccurate one. We now face enemies who must be killed. If we intend to save ourselves and to advance the cause of human rights we must not hesitate to rid the world of those who would curtail the most elementary freedoms through the muddling of religious texts and murder.

Especially in the United States and Canada, our societies have become so humane that we cannot begin to comprehend the profoundly different mentality of our enemies. It is remarkable that none of our "experts" has recognized that Muslim terrorists have devolved to the pre-Islamic practice of human sacrifice—one of the most widespread rituals of early peoples. The extremists who invoke the name of the Prophet are not merely trying to turn back the clock. They've embraced an *ur*-theology that endless recitations from the Koran cannot disguise. Far from representing the vision of Muhammad (whose injunctions they observe selectively), the apocalyptic terrorists we face have revived the gods of the ancient Middle East, the winged devils with a thirst for blood. They may call their god "Allah" but their deeds belong to the altars of antiquity.

They are perfect representatives of the new Age of Superstition.

As a young soldier I served in Germany during the glory days of the Red Army Faction and the Red Brigades. I saw the disruptions the terrorists wrought. Just as Europeans have conveniently forgotten the Holocaust they have achieved another triumph of the will by erasing the memory of how a handful of untrained killers haunted their societies. Amateur terrorists imposed enormous costs on the continent. Governments fell. Europeans felt less secure than Americans do post-9/11. European police forces had more difficulty coping with a few dozen terrorists than the American government has had in reducing the domestic threat from global terrorist networks post-9/11.

Europeans don't want to know what's coming from the new, more virulent breed of terrorists. They insist, desperately, that terrorism remains a law enforcement problem, refusing even to consider that the entire West might face a broad, psychotic threat spawned by a failed civilization. As a result, the price Europe will pay in the coming years will be agonizing. Europe, not North America, is the vulnerable continent. Our homeland security efforts, unfairly derided at home and abroad, have made our country markedly safer. We will be struck again. But "Old Europe" is going to be struck again and again and again.

American Muslims not only become citizens—they become *good* citizens. Despite the assimilation hurdles that face every new group of immigrants, our Muslims have opportunities and hope. A disaffected few make headlines, but American Muslims overwhelmingly support their new country and do not wish it harm. They see no contradiction between faith in their god and faith in America. Our worries are their worries, and their dreams are our dreams.

Europe is another, grimmer story. Not a single European state— not even the United Kingdom—has successfully integrated its Muslim minority into mainstream society. While the UK has made the most progress, countries such as France and Germany have time bombs in their midst, large, excluded Muslim populations the native majority regards as hopelessly inferior. If you want to see bigotry alive and well, visit continental Europe. Go to inner-city Marseilles or the Muslim suburbs of Paris. Visit Berlin-Kreuzberg. Or the immigrant quarters of virtually any major city on the continent. The worst American slum offers more opportunity for self-improvement to its residents than any of Europe's soul-killing Muslim ghettos.

It wasn't a random choice by the 9/11 plotters that led them to do so much of their preparation in Europe. They knew that American Muslim communities wouldn't offer hospitality to terrorists. But Germany, France, Spain, and even Britain contain embittered Islamic minorities glad to see any part of the West get the punishment it "deserves." The American and European experiences with immigrants have been profoundly different. In continental Europe immigrants were never given a chance to become respected members of their host societies. And now they have given up trying. It is a prescription for tragedy.

As the United States becomes ever harder to strike—and as we respond so fiercely to those attacks which succeed—soft Europe, with its fateful proximity to the Islamic world, its indigestible Muslim underclass, and its moral fecklessness, is likely to become the key Western battleground in the Islamic extremists' war against civilization.

A crucial reason why continental Europeans reacted so angrily to our liberation of Iraq was that it made it harder for them to sustain their myth of a benign world in which peace could be purchased and the government welfare checks would never stop coming. America's crime was to acknowledge reality. It will be a long time before Europeans forgive us.

The one factor that will bring us closer together is terrorism. Europe will find, as it has before, that its citizens need us far more than we need them.

———————

Apocalyptic terrorists are neither new nor exclusive to Islam. Avenging messiahs have appeared in every major religion, although monotheist faiths are especially prone to attempts to jump-start Armageddon. In times of crisis, as they sense the order they know collapsing, human beings turn to religion for sustenance. Plagues make believers. When people feel they are being punished unfairly, either by nature or by the intrusion of another religion's civilization, they crave an explanation that either absolves them of personal responsibility for the disasters they witness or promises an ultimate, vengeful triumph—or both. (It will be fascinating to gauge the long-term effects—if any—of Western aid efforts in tsunami-devastated Aceh, home to Indonesia's most rigorous form of Islam.)

Islamic extremism justifies the failure of Middle Eastern civilization as the fault of the infidel, assures the faithful that they will be triumphant, and exacts revenge in the here and now. Osama bin Laden, his paladins, and rising competitors offer the complete satisfaction package: Nothing's *your* fault, Allah will win, and here's how *you* can help.

The allure of sacrificing oneself for a greater good is imperishable. Not all men and women feel it, but a startling number do, especially in times of crisis. At its noblest this impulse results in acts of great heroism. At its worst it leads young men to fly passenger jets into skyscrapers. The terrorist masters we face have a brilliant grasp of their civilization's psychology. They have developed the cult of the martyr to a level that rivals anything previously seen in Islam—or any other religion. And they have proven efficient at identifying unstable, needy young men (and some young women) who can easily be cultivated for "martyrdom."

Terror's masters seek out the confused, the malleable, the uncertain. Terrorist cadres provide their recruits with simple explanations, then reshape them and imbue them with lethal certainty. The result is that weapon of genius, the suicide bomber, the most cost-effective tactical tool of our age. Increasingly, that tactical weapon has a strategic impact.

The attractions of martyrdom—an easy solution to the individual's mundane problems and cosmic doubts—are key to the power of Islamic terrorism's appeal. The martyrdom itself becomes more important to the perpetrator than the mission. Middle Eastern Islam has been behaving suicidally as a civilization, willfully clinging to every wrong choice it possibly could have made, so a trend toward individual suicidal acts should not surprise us. Whether we speak of its Sunni or Shia populations, Islam has become a death cult for a worrisome number of believers. Shia Islam has fostered a cult of martyrs since its beginning. Now Sunni Muslims have begun to show a new propensity for religious nihilism. The terrorists are reinventing Islam, making of their book of life a book of death.

Perhaps the strictness of Islam's prescriptions for daily behavior generates a subliminal desire to escape the rules through the oblivion of death—while enjoying a divine sanction for the act. The repression of basic human impulses *never* works—the pot never stops boiling. Sooner or later the lid blows off. We ourselves know that confining young males in a military unit where they have no ready access to females helps us to create vigorous killers. The Islamic Middle East—per Lévi-Strauss again—is little more than a vast barracks where explosive young males are forever tamped down. I often joke with friends that the Middle East desperately needs a six-pack of beer. The remark is not entirely flippant.

Islamic extremism also exploits natural human pride and the importance of group identity. The young suicide bomber is accepted into something far greater than himself. Membership in the terrorist brotherhood offers him the same psychological comfort their brown shirts and armbands gave Hitler's early followers—although to a richer degree than that felt by the German *Lumpenproletariat* in its bilious stupor. As he steers his explosives-laden vehicle into a government building the suicide bomber does not feel alone. He has been persuaded that a blessed community surrounds him.

It is impossible to see how the flow of Islamic "martyrs" can be halted without changes in the Middle East so pervasive and fundamental that their likelihood is discouragingly low.

We are dealing with a failed civilization. Its members have nothing left to cling to but their faith. Every other facet of their lives has disappointed them. The fabled oil wealth of the region has been dissipated in the purchase of luxury goods that amount to little more than the beads and mirrors the West once traded with naked tribes and on architectural monstrosities that amount to lawn ornaments for a world without lawns. Not a single indispensable item is manufactured by the populations between Casablanca and Karachi. The culture is as corrupt as the commerce. And the most influential new voices among their kind insist that their god wants them to wreak vengeance upon all those who have been more successful.

Islamic terrorists are not—yet—the most dangerous enemies we ever have faced. Germany and Japan retain that title, but only because of their power and organization in the first half of the twentieth century. Should Muslim fanatics gain control of weapons of mass destruction, we will enter a new paradigm of man-made death.

Our age of technological marvels is, paradoxically, also the age of superstition's renascence. Humankind is unsure. The pace of change is without precedent. Even in the world's most successful and prosperous societies individuals struggle to cope. The means they embrace range from pressing crystals against their bodies to cure cancer to the rituals of human sacrifice conducted by Islamic terrorists. We long for an improvement in the general temper of humanity. But we shall be very fortunate, indeed, if the situation does not worsen.

Diplomats fear the instability of states. But the instability that should terrify us is that of the human soul.

We may face more conventional enemies in the coming decades. It is always foolish to prepare for a single threat or to underestimate humankind's capacity for innovative mischief. Enemies may arise from unexpected locales; crises may develop from unanticipated events. Disorienting "acts of God" could inspire terrible acts by humanity. But the one trend that appears unlikely to fade away in our lifetimes is the flight back into stern faith on the part of those who cannot adjust to the changes thrust upon their society. This age of technological wonders has conjured a rival age of primitive terrors. In an era of blinding light, many of us find that we're afraid of the dark.

A terrible error of the Western intelligentsia and its fellow travelers elsewhere was to imagine that humankind could be educated out of its dependence on religion. Whether or not God exists, He is indestructible. The 1960s magazine cover that asked "Is God Dead?" has certainly had its question answered. In blood. Humankind, or at least a substantial portion of it, *needs* a god. We need reasons, explanations, hope, comfort… and science, for all its wondrous achievements, offers only coldhearted answers. No matter how well men and women may live, only a few can bear the thought that their life is finite. And those who do not live well need a god all the more.

Whether the need for faith stems from a spiritual source or from biology, the need exists. Europe, where many societies have lost their god (but not the self-righteousness inherited from their centuries of faith), suffers a malaise that all the good harvests in Bordeaux and all the artisanal cheeses in Catalonia cannot vanquish. The stance of young Europeans toward God is mocking, its tone suggesting that any deity would need them rather than the reverse, but the European Union's liturgy cannot satisfy humankind's deepest needs. God may not reach down from above to prevent us from suffering a fatal disease, but nothing fortifies the living human being as does religious faith. When Martin Luther wrote the hymn "A Mighty Fortress is our God" he spoke to humankind's inextinguishable need for a bulwark against fear, doubt, and Old Night.

While Americans do not yet fully comprehend the men of maddened faith who wish to destroy us, we are likely to grasp their essence far sooner than Europeans. The average German or Frenchman, spiritually crippled by his Enlightenment inheritance, is as much unlike the Islamic extremist believer as a human being could be. Americans retain sufficient faith (and, we must admit, occasional extremism) to grasp what our enemies are about on a visceral level. But Europeans may have to be punished terribly before they take religious terrorism seriously, a wry situation, since Europeans engaged in more religious terrorism of their own, against heretical sects and other faiths, than Islam has over the centuries. From the annihilation of the Cathars to the Holocaust, Europe has never stinted from offering its own blood sacrifices to its god of choice.

Europe doesn't have a superior morality. It has amnesia.

For many years to come the most consistent threat to the West will arise from Islamic extremists. We will not eliminate this millenarian movement in our lifetimes, but can only tamp it down to a bearable level. The conditions the Middle East has created for itself will continue to generate terrorists. We can only hope that the impulse to embrace the new Islamic death cult doesn't spread exponentially.

Of course, hope alone is insufficient. We also must act. It is nonsense to claim that American displays of resolve only create more terrorists. The terrorists are already in the pipeline. There is no alternative to killing them unless we wish to establish vast prisons over the gates of which we write "Abandon all hope, ye who enter here."

It may be correct that we cannot kill our way out of this problem, but we can make the problem much more manageable by killing the right people. The terror war against us is a knife fight to the bone. We shall not relish the prospect, but we must display an absolute determination to confront and defeat our enemies wherever we find them. Especially in the face of mass murderers who believe they're on a "mission from God," our resolution cannot waver. As we Americans continue to expand humanity's frontiers we will have to fight proponents of blood sacrifice as morally primitive as any examples we might summon from history.

In the age of digital wonders we are at war with demons.

If international religious violence can be limited to the Islamic extremist crusade against civilization, we shall be very fortunate. As traditional systems continue to shatter and new forms of social organization—with their attendant shifts in values—produce further crises of identity and belief, we may see the rise of messianic figures from traditional religions or even the abrupt appearance of new apocalyptic cults in regions of the world we overlook or the character of which we take for granted.

Even now Christianity has returned to being a literal "church militant" in parts of sub-Saharan Africa. In addition to local terrorists who profess an addled Christianity, doctrinally rigorous movements have begun to confront Muslim expansionism on the continent. We already have seen Muslim versus Christian violence and even outright warfare within states as disparate as Sudan and Nigeria, but the age-old mutual distaste between the Arab north and black south may lead to extensive conflicts whose barbarity will astonish those who have made no time in their lives for the study of history.

The Chinese leadership's uncompromising reaction to the growth of the Falun Gong cult a few years ago was viewed in the West as proof that a Communist totalitarian spirit still guided Beijing. But the suppression of Falun Gong had little or nothing to do with the legacy of Mao. Rather, the gerontocracy in the capital knew their own history. China has seen its share of millenarian, leveling insurrections down the centuries. Over the past two hundred years the most impassioned resistance to Western encroachment, the Opium Wars, the Boxer Rebellion, and the rise of Communism have all involved violent cults (Communism may have denied God but, as noted above, it amounted to a secular religion). Well aware that the pace of change has left China's interior far more unstable than outsiders realize, the Beijing leadership feared competition—and widespread violence against its alien political philosophy—so deeply that they overreacted to a cult that might have proved not only benign, but useful.

We worry about China's growing strength, although the state remains too weak to confront us very far beyond its boundaries. Instead, we should worry about a serious downturn or collapse in China's internal development. China needs to grow at a torrid pace to satisfy its burgeoning needs and swelling expectations. A crisis that disoriented a billion people might well evoke the impassioned ghosts of China's past.

After its generations of suffering North Korea has the capacity to spawn a religious cult to replace the aberrant regime's godlike command of human life. We cannot know what to expect when the monstrous Pyongyang regime crumbles, but we may not find the people of North Korea entirely ready for rule-of-law democracy.

Latin America is experiencing the explosive growth of charismatic and fundamentalist Protestantism in regions where Rome has dominated belief for half a millennium. This is likely to be a great force for good, shattering a religious monopoly, leveling social barriers, and challenging antique prejudices. Yet we cannot afford to be blithe in our assumptions. As we focus on the sickness within Islam we had best keep an eye on other religious mutations in the developing world— even a faith we personally cherish can be perverted by demagogues and mass hysteria. Christians must be on guard against efforts to hijack their faith the way extremists seized the vanguard of Islam.

Even "Old Europe" may surprise us. A cascade of disasters might lead militant portions of the population to return to their old faiths—or even to embrace new forms of devotion. Religion, too, abhors a vacuum.

Much that sounds impossible today is only waiting for the calendar's pages to turn. We live in an age of man-wrought miracles and of man-made horrors. If we are fortunate, any return to faith in the West will be a positive development. But Europe, history's killing continent, remains the most unpredictable stretch of the globe.

As a lieutenant I lived in a village in southern Germany. On weekends when there were no maneuvers or military exercises I liked to run along the web of farm trails. Perhaps a mile from the house I rented a simple cross loomed above a spot, bypassed by the automobile age, where two medieval high roads intersected. Unadorned, the cross commemorated an event from the days when the Black Death ruled the world. As the plague swept Europe, slaughtering perhaps half of the population, Christian cults arose that resembled the flagellant processions of Shia Islam. Raggle-taggle mobs marched from village to village, lashing themselves bloody, preaching the end of the world and spreading the plague. The armed gentry of the region had caught one such procession in the open. They slaughtered everyone, man, woman, or child, to prevent them from carrying the plague inside the town walls.

We live in an age of postmodern plagues. Abundant information infects the unprepared. The globalization of lifestyles turns lethal. The pox of corruption has spun out of control in much of the world. Traditional societies grow delirious with the fever of change. Those who cannot compete on the complex terms of the age grow sick with fear and doubt. The processions of penitents insist that we all must be reformed if we are to be saved, that their god is punishing humankind. Like the flagellant preachers butchered at that German crossroads in the fourteenth century, their apostles breathe death.

The "information age" is becoming the new age of faith, for better *and* worse. Once again humankind is torn between visions of a merciful god and a punitive deity, between religious belief as luminous transcendence and faith as a man-made prison. The death cult of al-Qaeda and its affiliates represents a plunge into the darkest epochs of the past. The odd human lust to be chastised threatens to spread even more widely in the Islamic world. And there is little we can do about it except to refuse to be chastised ourselves.

No man's god is our enemy. Our enemy is the man of faith convinced that his god wants blood.

Eleven

DIGITAL DEMONS

In this new age of superstition the frailest of spirit need to believe not only in a god, but in ghosts and goblins. Every deity requires a devil to explain evil. Men and women terrified by a changing world want to believe themselves the victims of witches—or at least of the sorcerer's contemporary equivalent, the superpower, the heretic, or the Jew.

Today evil is at our fingertips. On the Internet.

The World Wide Web was supposed to mesh humanity together. Freedom of information would shed light on humankind's last dark corners. In digital bursts we would discover how much we all have in common, that "they're really just like us." Instant messaging would guarantee peace in our time.

Instead, the Internet became one of history's greatest tools for spreading hatred.

Rather than uniting the virtuous the Internet has allowed deviants of every sort to find each other and band together. Not only do extremist Web sites preach a parallel universe of conspiracies, but individuals around the world who once were ashamed of their perversions have learned they are not alone. Not only are bigots newly confident in their electronic communities, malformed souls are assured by their no longer isolated brethren that others share their monstrous tastes and revel in them. Child molesters once hid in shame, fearful of society's retribution, their existences precarious, their behavior cautious. Thanks to the Internet, pederasts today are all but unionized.

Whether fomenting terrorist attacks or victimizing the helpless, the Internet demands its pound of flesh. We did not learn that others are "just like us." Instead we have found that others are terrifyingly unlike us.

Our lives are encompassed by history's third information revolution. Each successive development struck more swiftly than its predecessor. The first such revolution was the development of scripts and writing, enabling men to give their interpretations of God and man a permanence the spoken word alone could not provide (despite the robust power of oral traditions). Writing developed painstakingly, from a crude use of uninflected symbols to the versatile alphabets that continue to evolve today. Writing allowed codification and communication. Stylus and papyrus triggered empire.

The lack of written languages may have been the decisive factor in limiting the development of imperial regimes in sub-Saharan Africa. Without written Arabic, there never would have been an Islamic empire stretching from the Atlas Mountains to the Hindu Kush. The explosive "People of the Book" were just that: human beings with texts. Without writing, whether hieroglyphics or Latin letters, attempts at empire would have been evanescent. Just as the Iraqi military crumbled before the informationally superior American forces in 1991 and again in 2003, indigenous American societies could not withstand the document-powered organizational skills of European invaders. The masters of information are the masters of the battlefield (the one impressive aspect of the Revolution in Military Affairs lies in the field of communications).

Writing allows the development of bureaucracies, without which no complex state can function. And writing gave permanence to literary art, one of the few unifying factors among humans that does not rely on fire and sword. Writing allows a decisive communion of understanding and purpose.

The second information revolution began in the middle of the fifteenth century with Johannes Gutenberg's development of movable-type plates for the printing press. The immediate effect was to undermine the prevailing religious monopoly. Prior to the production of

books, pamphlets, and broadsheets in relative mass all dissenting movements were containable, since their doctrines could be spread only by
individuals at the speed of the human foot or the velocity of a mule. The
"universal" church could cordon off ideas by cordoning off the heretics
themselves. When the troublesome congregation was exterminated, its
doctrines proved as impermanent as the flesh, decaying in the swamp of
local memory.

Books printed in volume changed the world. The monopoly on
knowledge held by clerics and their fellow travelers shattered in mere
decades. The complex of reformations that Luther's defiance unleashed
were *all* movements of the printed word, of the Bible translated—often
magnificently—into popular tongues, of prayer books whose shining
vernacular lives unto this hour, of hymnals and militant pamphlets, of
volumes of commentaries and printed sermons. Despite papal prohibitions and bonfires of banned works, the revolution of the printing press
proved unstoppable.

That second information revolution led to a great leap forward in
human freedom. It also led to a century and a quarter of the most savage warfare Europe had ever experienced, culminating in the Thirty
Years' War. If information was liberating, it was also profoundly desta-
bilizing. A flood of complex information overwhelmed data-deprived
societies. Neither the uneducated masses nor the prevailing social structures could absorb the torrent without suffering violent convulsions.
The popular mind lacked the necessary discriminating mechanisms to
judge the quality of data accurately. The early age of the printed book
produced charismatic demagogues, saints, and opportunists, madmen
and enraged defenders of the old order and, above all, individual confusion. It led directly to the rise of science and the burning of witches by
the thousands.

It was a preview of the twenty-first century.

―――――――――

The third information revolution, which has been accelerating and in-
tensifying since the mid-nineteenth century, involves the rapid trans-
mission of data over great distances through the mastery of new
scientific principles. It is difficult now to comprehend the impact of the
telegraph on everything from the rise of mass newspapers, through the

conduct of warfare and diplomacy, to travel arrangements. Coincident with the mastery of steam power, the telegraph led educated Europeans and Americans to consider themselves as "modern," to see themselves in an entirely new light. This perception of modernity was qualitatively far different from Shakespeare's "brave, new world" or John Donne's "newfangledness." Instead of the rich evolutionary sense of eighteenth-century observers (claims of revolution notwithstanding), the physically mobile classes of the mid-nineteenth century perceived a dramatic rupture with the past. Before the telegraph things might (or might not) have been viewed as "getting better," as "progressing," but after the dots and dashes collapsed time and distance contemporaries felt that the world had *changed*.

Reading texts from early Victorian England one is struck by the similarity in tone and vanity to the self-importance of our own day (although the mid-nineenth century works were considerably more artful). Anthony Trollope's novels remain as relevant now as when they first were printed. The literary-minded can see the precise dividing line between the age of sweat and the age of steam by comparing the works of Trollope and Charles Dickens. Both wrote of London and England in the 1860s. But Dickens wrote of a world of hooves and coach wheels, where debts were small, if fateful. Trollope's world is one of telegrams, steam trains, and global capitalism. Dickens's London is a city long vanquished from our experience, while Trollope's town is the one we know today. Trollope's generation was our doppelgänger, certain that all was known or soon would be deciphered and possessed of new, remarkable, and spreading wealth. Dickens was the great novelist of nostalgia, Trollope the timeless chronicler of ambition.

Since the great age of the novel the pace of change has accelerated phenomenally. The rise of the broadcast media, radio and then television, deepened the third information revolution by making large volumes of data available not only to the semiliterate, but even to the illiterate. Relatively cheap, radio swiftly became a tool for tyrants, disseminating propaganda almost as soon as it had learned to entertain (and propaganda is, of course, a vicious form of entertainment, a means of escape from unbearable realities). From Nazi Germany to Rwanda radio has been the voice of the angel of death. A more expensive medium on both the production and consumer ends, television is still in the process of penetrating the less developed regions of the world, and radio retains one propagandistic advantage—it needn't provide verifying images as television must (of course, the spread of digital technologies is already helping the Internet over the "visual proof" hurdle and will likely help television create alternative realities in the future).

Because of their limited infrastructure and technical parameters, the telegraph, radio, and television all have been subjected to measures of state control, from licensing, through government monopolies, to jamming and even the physical destruction of broadcast means. The number of bands and wavelengths was finite, allowing a degree of monitoring and sanctions far more difficult with the elusive, anarchist Internet.

Hitler was, of course, the first great master of the broadcast media, perfectly attuned to his audience. Speeches that sounded insane to outsiders struck atavistic chords in the German families huddled around their wooden radio sets (Hitler "got" the power of film, as well).

The dark genius of the Internet is that it allows the less talented and less charismatic to reconstruct themselves not only as the grandchildren of Hitler, but as the channeled voice of their god. The Internet allows human monsters to amplify, transform, and reinvent themselves as heroes to those who share their disappointments, fears, and lusts. Just as we all have heard urban legends (or a friend's complaint) about an Internet dating adventure that began with a promise of meeting a Julianne Moore or a Brad Pitt but ended in an evening spent with one of the witches from Macbeth—or with Macbeth himself.

The Internet allows us to reinvent ourselves. Nobody knows if you're Jeffrey Dahmer or St. Francis of Assisi. Or a terrorist. Until you connect with the myriad kindred spirits lurking in cyberspace. The Internet, with its rants and raves, its grotesque diversity (and anonymity), and its technological suggestion of authority, is a superb confidence builder, steroids for the twisted soul. It offers evil an unprecedented sanctuary.

We may find that the Internet didn't simply extend the ongoing communications revolution but marked the start of a qualitatively new, fourth information revolution. From the book to the DVD the information transmitted as "news" or otherwise as factual was tethered to empirical reality. Even the most lunatic propaganda had to refer to the world as recipients of the message had experienced it. Hollywood might create otherworldly images, but children knew they were no more than a fantasy.

The Internet *creates* reality. Increasingly we encounter not only twisted versions of our commonly agreed reality on the World Wide Web, but parallel, constructed realities. Through gratifying simplifications these alternative models of the world wield tremendous seductive power over those whose discontents exceed all possibility of remediation. The Internet offers a new world of excuses for life's failures, then grants the losers a chance to reimagine themselves as heroes.

There is no success or glory in the Middle East. But extremist Web sites allow the user to enter a parallel Islamic civilization where triumph is certain, enemies are dehumanized, and Arab greatness exists in the here and now. In the Middle East the Internet is the fifth horseman of the apocalypse.

———

In cultures little adept at digesting data even simple facts can be disorienting. The only remedy is an admixture of education and time, and some of the victims may fail to get well no matter the efforts others make to cure them. Information disorders are so widespread that the United States can have only a limited impact on them (although foreign aid dollars that go to secular education programs are well spent).

The Internet hate sites vending opiate fantasies of glory while inciting terrorism, ritual murder, and catastrophic destruction must be fought. We must take the War on Terror to the Internet as resolutely as we have taken it to the Middle East. It is not a matter of censorship but of self-preservation. Still in our pre-9/11 mode informationally, we do not even acknowledge the seriousness of the threat. We are not only losing the war in cyberspace, we aren't even fighting it.

We must bear the inevitable complaints from the global intelligentsia and attack the Web sites and networks of Islamic extremists with the intent to destroy, pursue, and destroy again. This is a long overdue effort. Mouthing cheap slogans about "a war of ideas," we lack the common sense and strength of will to deny our enemies the means to inexpensively, swiftly, and broadly disseminate their bigotry. Just as physical territory has to be denied to opponents in war, we have to seize and defend the key terrain of cyberspace. Sites that thrive on clips of beheadings and call for the destruction of entire states and peoples are far more effective than we have found the wherewithal to admit. Mired in past models of diplomacy and social organization, we asked the governments of Saudi Arabia, Pakistan, and others to crack down on hate speech in Friday sermons in key mosques. But the fiery hatred graven on the computer screen reaches far more potential supporters and has a greater permanence than any single sermon barked through tinny speakers. Our intelligence services must conduct "search and destroy" missions in cyberspace against our self-declared and deadly enemies.

This is not an issue of freedom of speech. This is war. And we are going to need to marshal our resources to fight it. Despite leading the Internet age in every other respect, we have neglected the need to police the digital superhighways. We exaggerate the restraints of our own laws, behave naively, and perform amateurishly. Make no mistake: Our enemies are winning the battle of ideas in cyberspace (hate is vastly more appealing than reason), while we have not even recognized this new modality of combat.

Those who worry about censorship should worry about the censorship of the voices of decency and dialogue in the Middle East. They are being driven toward oblivion by the alluring hatred preached over the Internet (and on television networks such as al-Jazeera). The same domestic critics who would be aghast were we to attack the Web sites of Islamic terrorists would howl to the high heavens if our own culture spawned equivalent sites calling for the massacre of Muslims. This is a double standard we cannot afford.

This isn't really a battle of ideas in the sense that our overcivilized thinkers mean it. It's a battle between reality and deadly fantasies, between civilization and superstition. We battle against child pornography on the Internet. Surely we should also combat the lethal pornography of terror. We have passed the cognitive equivalent of nuclear weapons into the hands of madmen. Now we must redefine weaponry and expand the dimensions of what we mean by war.

Our enemies already have done so.

Twelve

THE CANCER OF CORRUPTION

When I travel in troubled states there's a predictable moment when the eyes of a new acquaintance shift from trust to skepticism. Inevitably, the subject of corruption arises: "It is very bad here, always very bad...they always take, take...the hand is always out...." Then he or she looks at me and asks, "But how is it in America?"

When I state that in my half century of life I have never paid a bribe to a fellow countryman my interlocutor finds it impossible to believe me.

Corruption is pervasive. And it is destructive. No other single factor—not disease, civil strife, tribal loyalties, or even faulty borders—has crippled the progress of the "developing" world as severely and as inexorably as corruption has.

Yes, there is corruption in the United States. But when we discover it, we get angry. And we prosecute. Whether it's Enron or a local councilman seeking a kickback, we do not tolerate it. We refuse to let corruption become a routine aspect of our lives.

That makes us one of the world's few exceptions to the tyranny of the bribe.

Terrorism isn't the primary threat to the emergence of a rule-of-law democracy in Iraq. The terrorists can be defeated. The long-term threat is corruption, especially given the traditions of bribery in the Middle East that have been exacerbated by the decades of Saddam Hussein's rule.

If any single factor destroys the eventual development of a rule-of-law, democratic Palestinian state it will be corruption. Not the ill will of

Arab autocrats, although that's certainly a factor. And not the hostility of Muslim rejectionists toward any deal with Israel. Corruption is the cancer that could kill the highest hopes of the Palestinian people.

In Africa, corruption since independence has done more damage to states such as Nigeria, Zimbabwe, and Congo than civil war or even AIDS has. South Africa, the continent's beacon lighting the way to the future, is battling against corruption, determined that the rule of law shall prevail—but the issue is far from settled. Mozambique, a ravaged land struggling forward, faces no enemy more pernicious to its future than corruption. Every one of France's former African colonies is riddled with corruption. The French used corruption and bribes to exert control, although corruption was often a two-way street. Valéry Giscard D'Estaing, who now seeks to play the role of elder statesman, spent his years as France's president whoring among dictators and cavorting with the cannibal "emperor" Jean-Bédel Bokassa, a host who kept human steaks around for a snack.

Indonesia, the Muslim country with the greatest potential, suffers grievously from corruption. China intermittently executes a few minor officials among the tens of thousands demanding bribes, but lets corruption flourish at the top. Latin America, the continent that should have been a contender, has been stymied by corruption every time it sought to make its markets work.

South America's leading states are perfect examples of how corruption can undermine positive developments in every other sphere. While Chile made great inroads after cracking down on corruption, nations such as Argentina and Brazil have suffered tragic setbacks. After flirting with market practices their economies suffered disastrously—because corruption undercut the genius of the market. Today Latin America is going through one of its periodic flirtations with the left—which will only further impoverish the people over the long term. Capitalism, globalization, and free markets are blamed for Brazil's inequities and the collapse of Argentina's currency in recent years. But the free market was never the problem, since neither country really tried a free market. Market capitalism cannot flourish in corrupt environments. Tragically for the people of Argentina, their playboy president of the 1990s, Carlos Menem, associated himself and his regime with market economics. But Menem's government was colossally

corrupt even by Latin American standards. Competition never had a
chance. Cronyism reigned. The result was Argentine disillusion with
a free-market system that Buenos Aires never actually tried. The Ar-
gentines blamed the medicine for the cancer eating away at their national body.

We do not list corruption as a key strategic factor in our global intelligence estimates, just as we long ignored the role of religion and still
skirt the issue of Islam's oppression of women. Yet corruption has undone countless schemes for improving the lot of the common citizen or
for reforming economies. Flagrant corruption under the Shah made
the Iranian revolution appealing to many who had no other common
cause with the Ayatollah Khomeini and his acolytes.

Corruption continues to do far more damage to Mexico than U.S.
interventions ever did. Corruption robs the hope from tens of millions
of impoverished Mexicans today. *La mordida*, "the bite," poisons the national bloodstream. A threadbare Mexican saying runs "Poor Mexico;
so far from God and so close to the United States." Yet, proximity to the
United States is the only thing preventing a second Mexican revolution. Mexico's poor at least have the option (if a harrowing one) of cross-
ing into the United States for work that feeds their families back home.
Mexico's common border with the United States is its number one
strategic and economic advantage. Still, corrupt politicians and businessmen continue to play the anti-American card, even as they profit
from commerce with El Norte (not all of it legal). Paradoxically, one of
the many reasons why illegal immigrants from Mexico struggle to remain in the United States is that they respect our law enforcement system. They prefer to live where they are not subject to routine extortion,
kidnapping, random brutality, and the tyranny of the powerful.

Despots and the corrupt around the globe decry the American system. But their put-upon citizens do everything they can to live and
work in the United States.

Even India, the world's largest democracy, has suffered more from
corruption that it has from religious pogroms, demagogues, and straightforward poverty. The government launches a halfhearted campaign
against corruption now and then, but the attitude of even the educated

and successful is casual and accepting. It is as if plague raged in the streets and no one thought it worthwhile to take measures against it.

A few years ago I did an in-depth study of India for the United States Marine Corps. As I prepared for extensive travel in the subcontinent, I interviewed a range of Indian immigrants in the United States. Speaking with a finely educated young Indian woman from a privileged family—she worked, inevitably, in the information technology sector—I asked what she thought of corruption in India after living in the United States.

Her attitude was blithe: "Oh, all the corruption isn't really a problem. It's just a different system than here. Everybody knows how much has to be paid to get things done, so businessmen just factor it into their expenses. It isn't really a problem at all."

Even allowing for the defensiveness many Indians feel about their homeland (to which they rarely return to stay), the woman was absolutely blind to the insidious effects of corruption. It isn't just a matter of slipping a small bill to the traffic cop or handing over an envelope stuffed with cash to an official. That's the least of it. It's the second-, third-, and fourth-order effects that destroy societies and render governments hollow. Corruption stifles development, human, economic, and political. Even military establishments in the developing world are often so addicted to corruption that their utility approaches nil.

Nor are there any stages of economic development when corruption is "legitimate." The government shenanigans and wholesale theft of privatized corporations in post-Soviet Russia were excused by comparisons with the "robber barons" of nineteenth-century America. The analogy was insupportable. Even the robber barons met limits to their power. The rule of law, if less firm than now, already prevailed. America's nineteenth-century entrepreneurs were hard, often brutal men. But they could not control elections, or sustain their influence over administrations, or even enforce their attempts at monopoly. From a free press to free elections, Americans always possessed the tools to keep corruption from overtaking the state. Then as now the average American's reaction to an attempt at extracting a bribe was outrage.

We are imperfect. But compared to the overwhelming majority of the world's states we are paragons of integrity. Honesty, too, is a strategic factor that empowers societies and nations.

Instead of dismissing corruption as inevitable—which it is not—consider a few of the pernicious effects it has in developing countries:

- Corruption undermines public trust in the law, the state, and the financial system, demoralizing the population.
- It cripples the taxation system and promotes a culture of deception.
- It weakens financial institutions and instruments, provoking citizens to hoard precious metals (dead money that does not contribute to development) and driving high-income individuals to invest offshore, launder assets, and value property ownership over entrepreneurial risk. Corruption prevents the natural and efficient allocation of resources within an economy.
- Corruption favors large firms and fosters state-backed or state-licensed monopolies, hampering competition and industrial evolution.
- Corruption undermines attempts at innovation.
- It impedes free trade, domestically and between nations, further reducing efficiency, consumer choice, and the quality of goods and services.
- It devalues education.
- Corruption favors nepotism over merit, squandering the nation's talent and often driving the most capable workers abroad.
- It weakens currencies and the state's fiscal architecture.
- It deters, delays, or limits crucial foreign investment required for development.
- Corruption incites capital flight.
- It prevents the accurate costing essential to a complex economy.
- It skews statistics vital to government decision making.
- It inflates the man-hour costs of production.
- Not least, corruption degrades the lives of a state's citizens and undercuts respect for government across the board, creating an atmosphere of distrust and fear. The intelligentsia disengages from practical matters while the common man's ambitions are thwarted.

This list is far from exhaustive. In states from India through Egypt to Mexico corruption taints the educational system, the medical system, and the provision of basic services, from water taps to telephone connections. But the most insidious effect is the general erosion of public trust and confidence. The routine ineffectiveness and intermittent malignity of their governments reinforces the defensive ties of family and clan, as well as of nonkin associations, from the graduating classes of military academies to criminal gangs. The resulting fragmentation of the body politic makes compromise difficult and emphasizes the power of the group over the recognition of individual merit.

For the criminal there is no better guarantee of safety than a corrupt system that makes state authority complicit. For well-connected businessmen it is far easier to maintain market share in a corrupt, noncompetitive, government-licensed environment than in a free market regulated by universally applicable laws and an impartial judiciary. University professors who expect tips for high marks or even bribes for admission to essential classes are no more likely to protest against corruption than are drug lords or confidence men. Around the world many complain of corruption but few are willing to relinquish their own tiny share in the system.

Battling corruption is crucial to overcoming the world's many inequities and iniquities. If we wish to foster democracy abroad, in Iraq or anywhere else, we must fight for the rule of law. A corrupt democracy is no democracy, but simply tyranny lite.

Unfortunately for the billions of humans who suffer under corrupt regimes, reform is at best a halting affair fought at every stage by vested interests. No better example exists of the pervasiveness of corruption in human affairs than the sorry state of the United Nations.

Corruption long has been part and parcel of a UN career. For diplomats and functionaries from the developing world a UN position is regarded not only as a sinecure once obtained, but as a path to wealth. For lower-level staffers in the field UN careers have provided lifestyles they otherwise could not have achieved, as well as access to generous benefits and even, in the most deplorable cases, the opportunity to extract sexual favors from refugees, the poor, and the frightened. United Nations employees have engaged in outright criminality around the world, from graft to human trafficking. And when a violation is discovered—invariably by outsiders—the UN's response is never to prosecute, rarely to punish, and usually to transfer the offender to another post. Especially at the mid-to-higher levels, the UN is a club that protects its members no matter how despicable their acts.

The corruption in the Oil-for-Food Program, exposed through records captured in Baghdad and the testimony of its victims, is only the most recent example of the UN's theft from the poor to benefit its executives. The thievery was as enormous as it was shameless, involving billions of dollars funneled through a French bank and skimmed by UN officials and their proxies. The evidence is abundant and indisputable.

The UN's response? An internal investigation that was little more than a whitewash and the refusal to provide essential documents to outside auditors. Billions of dollars were stolen and tens of billions kicked back to Saddam Hussein. And the UN wasn't even apologetic. At the end of 2004 no one had lost his post. No charges had been leveled. The UN had not asked any governments to prosecute or even recall their nationals. Attempts by the U.S. Congress to establish responsibility for the crimes against humanity committed under the Oil-for-Food Program were stonewalled. The inbred diplomatic world even protected Secretary-General Kofi Annan's son from punishment for his involvement.

What was the real price? It cannot be measured in the hundreds of millions of dollars diverted or stolen. I saw the real cost of UN corruption with my own eyes—in Iraq. Although a few UN programs, such as demining efforts, made a useful contribution, the Oil-for-Food Program took Iraq's wealth and gave its suffering people crumbs and rags. The cost was in the children, Kurdish or Shia Arab, who died of malnutrition while funds were diverted into the accounts of UN officials and their associates. The cost was in those who died because the UN provided outdated medicines to Iraq and charged premium prices. The cost was in the dry-rotted canvas and torn plastic sheeting provided as shelter to Kurdish refugees. And the cost was, above all, in the silence of UN officials in the face of Saddam's atrocities. The cost was in the mass graves, in the refugee camps, in the UN's crime not only of silence, but of complicity.

The UN may be the most disappointing organization ever founded in goodwill. Unwilling to remove a tyrant with the blood of more than a million human beings on his hands, the UN struggled to protect him

from justice. Perhaps we should admire the UN's well-dressed criminals for their tenacity: At least they didn't take Saddam Hussein's
money and run. They stood by him to the end and would save him now
if they could. The UN was willing to let twenty-six million people suffer
so that a few of its executives and their cronies could fill their bank
accounts.

As I write, no one has been held responsible by the UN or by the Europeans—who profited hugely from the scam. The United States alone
has begun to haul the malefactors into court. Our own diplomats, terrified of distressing their fellow ambassadors and old acquaintances, have
resisted a vigorous pursuit of UN criminality.

At a minimum, those who stole from the people of Iraq should have
to help excavate the mass graves that continue to be discovered—many
of which were filled during the term of the Oil-for-Food Program. But
the thieves from the UN won't even be forced from their positions in
Manhattan, Paris, or Geneva.

Corruption is accepted as the price of doing business in the diplomatic world. We might as well shoot the innocent at random.

———————

At least the United States has sound laws for corporate activities at
home and abroad. Doubtless, American business representatives have
skirted our regulations and indulged in corrupt activities to make sales
or gain contracts. But we do not condone it. If it is detected we pursue
the criminals. Our businessmen often have complained of the unfair
advantages East Asian or European companies enjoy, thanks to their
traditions of bribery. But instead of bewailing our disadvantages the
American way would be to go after the foreign corporate criminals.
Those who foster corruption are humanity's enemies.

The European Union has fine codes forbidding bribery, as do
many individual European countries. But those laws and regulations
have the approximate force of the old Soviet constitution, which was a
splendid document to read but utterly divorced from reality. If there is
any single issue on which we should challenge Europe for the good of
humanity, it isn't support for our destruction of criminal regimes
(which Old Europe will shield until the end) but the fight against
corruption and bribery in the developing world. We need to lead the

struggle as aggressively as the British led the global war against the slave trade. As we expand our intelligence capabilities collectors and analysts should be charged to detect corruption by European corporations and governments, to build cases, and to use the evidence to prevent guilty parties from trading with or traveling to the United States.

It is unacceptable to argue that corruption is "just their way of doing business." If taking a stand against corruption is Yankee puritanism, then hurrah for puritanical Yankees. If we want to see the spread of freedom, we have to fight corruption. If we hope for the rise of new democracies, we have to fight corruption. And if we simply want a more equitable world where the average man and woman has a chance to work toward a better life, we have to fight corruption. If we want to dethrone dictators, we have to fight corruption. If we want to stop the spread of weapons of mass destruction, we have to fight corruption. Even if we just wanted to do good business over the long term, we would have to fight corruption. If we want to fight disease, we have to fight corruption. If we want to fight illiteracy, we have to fight the corruption that creates schools on paper that don't exist in fact and that controls access to a decent education. And if we want to win the battle against extremist terror over the decades, we have to fight corruption globally and implacably.

The corrupt will complain. The corrupt will fight back. But if we persist we will find the common people rallying to our side in the years ahead. When corruption loses, humanity wins. And when humanity wins, so does America.

Thirteen
THE LONGEST WAR

In January 2004, I sat over lunch in the ballroom of the Ritz-Carlton in Qatar, surrounded by Muslim bureaucrats, scholars, theologians, and journalists. While the ruling emir supplied the presiding spirit, a scattering of Western diplomats and "subject-matter experts" gave the conference a whiff of intellectual sobriety. As hundreds of us literally chewed the fat, awaiting the rants of the mullahs on the dais, the Muzak track began to play the theme from the film *Exodus*.

Starring Paul Newman as a Haganah freedom fighter, the grand old movie depicts the heroic triumph of Israel's founding. Had the hotel played the Israeli national anthem the choice could not have been more splendidly inappropriate.

I cracked up. Yearning to believe that the choice of music was a subversive act by the expat hotel staff, I had to accept that the foul-up was typical of the incompetence that plagues the Middle East, in institutions great and small, in rich countries and poor. Nonetheless, I expected someone to notice, to protest, to express outrage.

Not a head turned. So I sat there happily, listening to Ernest Gold's sweeping, gorgeous theme, a soundtrack for Israel's birth. All around me conversations burbled on between Western sycophants sniffing for project funding and Gulf Arabs incapable of hearing anything beyond hymns to their bilious majesty. It was one of those wonderful moments in life when cosmic justice prevails, and I could only think that if a civilization can't even get its soundtrack right, there may not be much hope for it.

Perhaps that's why the most extreme Islamists want to ban music.

Well-meaning souls in the West pretend that the current distemper in Middle Eastern Islam is merely a hiccup in history, but our recent military actions in Iraq only continue humankind's longest war, the struggle between the two most powerful monotheist faiths, Islam and Christianity, a death match of civilizations that began in the seventh century.

The weakness of the Islamic world over the past few hundred years created an illusion of peace, even as Europe's colonial powers fought Muslims from the mountains of Algeria and the wastes of the Sudan to the banks of the Kabul River. It is difficult to identify the span of a generation when Western and Islamic civilizations were not in conflict somewhere, either in their heartlands or on their ever turbulent frontiers. In historical terms Islam's strategic weakness is as recent as it has been misapprehended. Only two hundred years ago Islamic pirates were the scourge of Mediterranean commerce, provoking the epic deeds of U.S. Marines and sailors on the "shores of Tripoli."

But America was far removed from the realms of Islam. Unless we were annoyed we did not pay attention. As Europe sank its claws ever deeper into North Africa and the Middle East, we had no sense of the local torment. We assumed Europe's interventions to be for the good of humankind, since Europeans were white and, in those days, Christian. Sultans in Istanbul or khedives in Cairo were storybook creatures, distant, exotic, and redolent of "the degeneracy of the East." As long and brutal wars ground on between the empire of the czars and the Muslims of the Caucasus, Central Asia, or the Ottoman Empire, with vast tracts of the earth as conflict's prize, our national attention was captured only by the Crimean War, in which Britain and France propped up the Turkish "sick man of Europe" on his deathbed. Most of what we recalled of that misadventure came from one very bad poem.

Empires swelled or receded, yet Americans had no violent contact with Islam for nigh on a century, until we detached the Philippines from Spain's corroded empire and found ourselves fighting Muslim holy warriors. Drugged on faith and narcotics, the Moros were so fierce that standard-issue Army revolvers proved unable to knock them down. The famous M-1911 .45-caliber semiautomatic service pistol was developed to stop fanatics wielding swords. Ultimately, we broke Moro resistance through a combination of ferocity and development programs—a formula that has not been bettered.

If American statesmen considered Islam's domains at all, they brought to bear paternalistic goodwill. Woodrow Wilson desired a just outcome for the Middle East only to see his hopes frustrated by the diplomats of Europe, for whom the Versailles Conference was one more nasty land grab. Viewed as a potential friend by the Middle Eastern intelligentsia, the United States romanticized the region in silent films. The level of mutual misunderstanding was extreme but harmless as long as neither party had contact with the other.

Then came oil. And the Cold War. The rest is blood and folly, shame and war.

Now we face enemies so repulsed by the present state of affairs that they romanticize a gory past, painting history in black and white with a clarity of line unrivaled by yesterday's grade-school texts. The civilization of Middle Eastern Islam has seen its power collapse along with its self-respect and practical competence. Unable to compete with a West that became immeasurably dominant—after a millennium of dread before Islam's worldly power—the Middle East has spawned a breed of terrorists for whom geostrategic reality is almost irrelevant, men who inhabit a world of dreams and visions, who long to restore a glory that never existed to the degree their fantasies have stretched, and who, above all, long to punish their historical and contemporary adversaries.

Few in the West take seriously the stated goal of Osama bin Laden and his affiliates to reestablish the caliphate and restore to Islam all the lands it once possessed. But the ambition is real, if unrealistic, and its magnitude reflects both the insatiability and the implacability of today's Islamic terrorists. Al-Qaeda and its bastard offspring believe that past possession entitles them to rule much of today's India, all of Central Asia, Ukraine, southern Russia, Moldova, Romania, Bulgaria, Hungary, Greece, Albania, Serbia, Bosnia, Sicily and southern Italy, the Iberian Peninsula, and the Swahili coast of Africa southward beyond the Zambezi. Islamic extremists also claim prerogatives in lands where Muslims are resident, including still more of Europe, as well as North

America. Madmen in caves believe that they are entitled to rule the world. And they mean to do something about it.

For those who believe that negotiations and compromise are the answer the professed ambitions of our opponents should be response enough.

What happened? Islam exploded from the Arabian desert with such force—born of monotheist conviction—that it terrorized Europe for a thousand years. But Islam today counts only its own losses and not the destruction Muslim swords inflicted upon others.

Arabs make much of the Crusades, a two-century interlude of European meddling in the Levant, whose brief successes were enabled only by divisions among Muslims. Yesteryear's Hollywood fantasies of the Crusades mislead us as profoundly as their own mythmaking confuses Muslims. The truth is that the crusaders were barbarians who combined fanaticism with insatiable greed. Easily seduced by oriental luxuries, they soon became addicted to the mischief endemic to Middle Eastern politics, then as now. Greed trumped faith before the First Crusade had passed through Anatolia. Hardly had Jerusalem fallen before Muslim emirs and Christian princes banded together to oppose the interests of other Christian-Muslim alliances. Holy war came to be viewed as a nuisance by those crusaders long resident in the East. Collaboration, intrigue, and betrayal reigned, with piety the disconsolate exception.

Within the crusader states unity was as rare as innocent faith. The French sought to dominate, squabbling with the Normans. German crusaders lurched between allegiances. The Genoese and Venetians competed for commercial concessions, as ready to deal with Muslim rulers as with any Christian prince. Militant orders founded to defend the Holy Land—the Templars, Hospitalers, and the Teutonic Knights—fought against each other almost as frequently as they fought the infidel. They built up wealth and fortresses but undermined their power through crude ambitions. Christian princes looked on as Muslim armies overwhelmed their fellow Christians. Still others made pacts with the order of Assassins, the Islamic terrorists of the Middle Ages. France desired one thing, Rome another, Norman Sicily something else. The only factor that allowed the Christian presence in the Levant to survive as long as it did was the worse state of division among the Arabs.

The Mongols did vastly more damage to the Arab world than the crusaders managed to do. One of history's lost opportunities flickered by when Mongol chieftains sympathetic to frontier forms of Christianity sought to cooperate with the crusader states and Rome (Dokuz Khatun, wife of the great Hulagu, destroyer of Baghdad, was a member of the Nestorian church; Hulagu routinely massacred Muslim populations, but spared eastern Christians). But the crusaders had built up profitable trading relations with their Muslim neighbors, while the observances of the Mongol Christians repelled both papal plenipotentiaries and Orthodox clerics—who were busy scheming one against the other. Christendom's greatest opportunity to turn back the Islamic tide came to nothing. Mongol emissaries could not penetrate the web of dynastic rivalries and bickering.

Within three generations the Mongols who conquered the Middle East had turned their backs on Christ to embrace Muhammad.

In the end the Crusades proved disastrous for the West, not for the Arabs. The single sustained result of carrying the cross through Asia Minor and into the Holy Land was the destruction of the military and economic power of Byzantium, the indispensable bulwark against the onslaught of the Turks.

If there is any lesson we should draw from the vicious muddle of the Crusades, it is that the West's internal rivalries were once our undoing and might be so again—at least for Europe, exposed, infiltrated, and hated. Today, America has replaced Byzantium as the defender of the West, and just as Constantinople was reviled by medieval Europe for its divergent faith, strategy, and culture, so today is Washington.

The Byzantine empire, that last magnificent flowering of the Greeks, saved Europe time and again—until Europe betrayed and destroyed it.

Byzantium is worthy of far more respect than the greatest of Christian empires has been accorded in the West, where the scribes of the Vatican vilified the "Second Rome," after which insular Protestants took their turns at denouncing Byzantine luxury, mysticism, and policy—their complaints uncannily similar to those made about America by today's European Protestants Without God.

The empire governed from Constantinople gave the West a thousand years of security. Its armies fought countless now-forgotten campaigns in the Syrian deserts and the river valleys of eastern Anatolia, discouraging Persia and providing the only successful barrier to Arabs inspired to conquest by the prophecies of Muhammad. To us the very term "byzantine" suggests slyness, deceit, morbidity, and weakness. Yet that empire, while it could not maintain all of its possessions, fought bitterly and often brilliantly under generals such as John Curcuas and Nicephorus Phocas who had no equal in medieval Europe. Were history written fairly the epithet "byzantine" would be a byword for valor, tenacity, and enduring faith.

Constantinople's rulers have been held to a harsher standard than the inbred royal dynasties of Europe—even though Byzantium's spectacular culture glittered while Europe wallowed in savagery. From crusader propaganda to the faulty judgments of Gibbon, the West heard only of Byzantium's sins, never of its virtues. We were told of the Byzantines' moral and practical weaknesses, never of their resilience or their redeeming successes. Yet the Byzantine empire prevailed for century after century while occupying the most contested territories on earth. Anatolia, that magnet for conquerors, was the bottleneck of the world, corked by the veteran armies of Byzantium. Sturdy Byzantine infantrymen long remained the masters of the battlefield and the empire's armored cavalry proved the West's sole answer to the Arab onslaught during Islam's conquering centuries.

What became of that magnificent Christian empire? Bureaucracy undermined decisive government. The elite elevated selfishness above public service. The army was stripped of manpower to provide the funds to entertain the whims of the court and the popular hunger for amusement. And the troops who had preserved the East for Christ found themselves unaided and overwhelmed. At Manzikert in 1071 the Seljuk Turks inflicted a catastrophic defeat on a hollow army.

Even then the Byzantines proved resilient. Under strong emperors the Greeks of a weakened Constantinople fought endless wars, winning here, losing there, but remaining the rampart of Christendom. Craven emperors and dynastic struggles harmed the state from within, but Byzantium proved greater than any one man. Constantinople remained the cultural center of Eurasia.

Western Christians, not Muslims, fatally crippled Byzantine power and opened Islam's path into the West. Encouraged by an odious Venetian doge who wished to break the Byzantine grip on trade, the French and Flemish nobles who led a crusading army forged to regain Jerusalem chose to sack Byzantium instead, treating the city's Orthodox Christians as heretics, killing, raping, and mutilating the citizens of the world's most vital and beautiful metropolis. Priests, monks, and nuns were massacred. Churches were profaned, their altars soiled and smashed. Works of art that dated to the classical age were destroyed in a drunken fit of Christian zeal. The treasures that survived the sack of the city were carried off to Venice, France, or Flanders. The great cathedral of St. Sophia, the architectural and spiritual wonder of the world, saw a whore enthroned upon its altar while its arcades served as a latrine for Europe's chivalry.

The culmination of the Fourth Crusade in 1204 marked a European moral collapse that prefigured the twentieth century. After their conquest the "Franks" ruled the city with cruelty, stupidity, and avarice for over a half century, until a last surge of Greek energy expelled them from the palace above the Bosporus and cast them beyond the city's ancient walls. Shattered and shrunken, the Greek empire rose again. But its limbs were palsied. Byzantium resurrected could not long withstand the fury of the latest wave of Asian conquerors, the Ottoman Turks.

When Constantinople fell to Mehmet the Conqueror in 1453 Italian mercenaries fought on both sides, while the French refused to offer the Christian emperor of the East a single knight.

Europe's first attempt at overseas empire ended in grotesque failure. The Crusades did far more damage to Christendom than they did to the realms of Islam. But facts count for nothing in Muslim minds desperate to explain their pervasive failure.

As contemporary Muslims blame their disabilities on the Crusades (when they're not blaming Israel or America) they demonstrate to an extreme the human capacity for selective memory. By the fourteenth century the Middle Eastern Crusades were effectively over, with military orders or Italian city-states holding on to a few Mediterranean possessions, the Byzantine empire fatally weakened, and the Ottoman Turks an incandescent force. Arab power had been savaged by the Mongols, although the Mamelukes held on in Egypt after dealing the Mongols a rare decisive defeat. But the Arabs could not resist the eruption of their fellow Muslims from central Asia. Far from suffering a death blow from the Crusades, the greatest age of Islamic—though not Arab—empire was in its birth convulsions. The Turks never attained the intellectual level of the wrecked Arab cultures of Córdoba, Baghdad, or Damascus but proved themselves militarily and organizationally far better suited to the changed strategic environment.

If we Americans understand nothing of the heroic role played by Byzantium in preserving Western civilization, we know little more about the magnificence of the Ottoman empire, the most successful military state of the past thousand years and the first architectural superpower to arise since Rome. It is easy enough to overlook those lost glories given Turkey's present weakness and the elusive nature of imperial legacies in day-to-day affairs. Yet Ottoman armies were still fighting European troops to a standstill in the days of the steamboat and the telegraph, and the Ottoman collapse at the end of the Great War echoes on today, from the Balkans to Baghdad.

For our terrified ancestors, the "Grand Turk" was Satan incarnate, Antichrist in the mortal trappings of an irresistible conqueror. Centuries of Turkish wars not only shaped the collective mentality of Central and Eastern Europe, but set a pattern of French betrayal of the West and Parisian alliances with hostile Muslim states that continues to this day. Contemporary Turkey remains astride the most valuable strategic real estate in the northern hemisphere.

After an inspiring visit to Iraq in 2004, I began my trip home by walking across the Turkish border at Zakho, then climbing into a sulfurous cab with young Kurds headed for jobs in Europe and the Gulf states. That morning I had come from Suleimaniye, a city where the rule of law prevailed, undergraduates of both sexes studied side by side in university classrooms, few young women wore head scarves and none were veiled, the Internet cafés were packed, and the Kurds were embracing their new freedoms of speech and enterprise with solemn enthusiasm.

As we drove westward at an unsettling speed, with the Syrian border bristling on our left, the first Turkish city along our route was Cizre. I was in a funk, having just received a sharp lecture from a youthful Turkish customs officer who, unhappy with my stay among the Kurds, tossed around my dirty underwear while barking that Kurds were scum, Arabs were worse, America had betrayed Turkey, and—I swear by the beard of the Prophet—the Ottoman empire would return and give us all what-for.

The lieutenant had been a caricature from old spy novels, Depression-era films, and lazy memoirs, the sort of Turk who abuses his shred of authority and soils the reputation of an often admirable people. Having explored Turkey over a quarter century, and possessed of such fondness for the country that I persuaded my wife to honeymoon in its interior, I was simmering over the border affair—which had only concluded after my threats of fabulous strategic consequences drew an on-second-thought apology from the lieutenant, who was merely a bully and subject to uncertainty. I told myself, not for the first time, that the Turks were their own worst enemies.

Then we reached Cizre, where the through street is left in disrepair to impede trade with Iraq's Kurds and clouds of dust afflict the windows of the grocery shops and cafés. I had stayed overnight in Cizre en route to Iraq, in a hotel that would instantly dispel anyone's notions of the romance of the East, and I knew that the town's faint prosperity relied on smuggling and the varieties of trade that demand multiple government forms, with signatures and stamps, some of them genuine. Even sunrise over the Tigris had not redeemed the townscape.

Yet that afternoon, as my homeward route diverged from Xenophon's, Cizre shocked me. I had arrived long after dark on my journey into Iraq and left in the morning while the town still slept. Now, by the light of day, I saw a land tumbling backward. Every one of the few women in the streets was robed in black from scalp to heel, exposing only the fingers securing the folds of her garments and shadowed eyes behind the slits in her mask. Those women hurried along in pairs, as if hunted. The other salient feature of Cizre's main street was the display of racy magazines along the sidewalks and in the shop windows. The covers featured Turkish starlets and songstresses who, behind their alarming smiles, must have been wondering whether to sign up first for Weight Watchers or extreme body waxing.

It wasn't just a comic juxtaposition illustrating Islamic hypocrisy. Cizre was symbolic of a tragedy ignored by the parties in the West who insist on Turkey's value as an ally. Even as the Ankara government promises a new dawn in the European Union, the joyless night of fundamentalism is falling on Turkey's hinterlands.

Above all, the queer scene in Cizre meant that the legacy of Atatürk was dead on Turkey's eastern frontier and mortally ill elsewhere.

While his policies were far from flawless—not least as regards the Kurds, Greeks, and Armenians—Kemal Atatürk remains one of the great men of the last century. Not only did he reassemble Turkey from the Ottoman potsherds and protect it from European scavengers, he mounted a more comprehensive and thoughtful effort to modernize a Muslim country than anyone else has done. None of Nasser's nonsense nor the weird extravagance of Persian Gulf emirs approaches the integrated vision and insight of Mustapha Kemal. The former general, victor of Gallipoli, understood that it was not enough to alter outward forms—although visible changes were necessary—but that the decisive battleground of progress lay within the collective soul of the nation.

He cast aside the caliphate, banned the veil for women and the fez for men, and stressed education and personal responsibility. If his cult of personality unsettles those all too familiar with fascism and Stalinism—and even if the Turkish military remains his most durable legacy—we must acknowledge the genius with which Atatürk lifted up a defeated people and gave them back their pride, along with a purpose: to build a modern state.

Atatürk's tragedy was that of Alexander, of Peter the Great, and of Bismarck, men of genius who constructed strategic systems that required a genius to maintain them. When lesser men inherited their empires or webs of treaties they could not rise to the necessary level of performance. Atatürk retained a soldier's integrity, but those who came after him let Ottoman levels of graft insinuate themselves back into the state. Over the past fifteen years Islamists have rolled back one of Atatürk's reforms after another, winning elections because the people had grown disgusted with the corruption of the secular political parties. Even the military, the self-proclaimed defender of Atatürk's legacy, enjoys its perquisites and power to a degree that modern Turkey's founder would never have tolerated. Taken along with the mass migration of Anatolian peasants to Turkey's major cities, the results have been an urban society less cosmopolitan than it was a century ago and a return of the petty behaviors that pass for Islam among those who like their god mean.

The Ottoman empire didn't quite die at the end of the Great War. Atatürk salvaged a rump empire and gave it a sufficient transfusion of energy to enliven it for another eighty years. Now it's done.

Today much is made of Turkey's readiness, or lack thereof, to join Europe. Diplomats insist that the country is a vital link between the West and the Muslim world. Even Turkey's shortsighted betrayal of its alliance with the United States on the eve of Operation Iraqi Freedom failed to persuade Ankara's American advocates that the country is hurtling backward toward an idiot's self-destructive nationalism, religious obscurantism, and a culture of blame that tugs it toward the decayed societies of the Middle East—and certainly not Westward.

A dusty ruin today, Cizre once had been a wealthy city commanding a bend in the Tigris and built astride a vital caravan route. Its scholars were renowned; its culture alluring. Cizre's great mosque stood as a model of enlightened devotion and art (the doors are preserved in an Istanbul museum). Like Mardin, the tattered fortress city up the highway, Cizre had known glory, demanding esteem, igniting ambitions, and shaping the course of empire. Yet as our vehicle climbed the ridge above the forlorn streets I could only think of the hackneyed phrase "How the mighty have fallen!"

What I saw that day in the streets of Cizre, with its shrouded women and shabby shops, was the true death of the Ottoman empire, the low and bitter end of the world of Süleyman the Magnificent. Atatürk and his successors had played a role as pathetic as the last Byzantine emperors, heroic in their ambitions but overwhelmed by forces far greater than themselves. The Bedouins of Arabia, with their cruel religion and hatred of modernity, had conquered the Turks at last.

But what a mighty empire the Ottomans possessed for half a millennium! Even the Arab thrust into France in Islam's first burst of conquest posed far less of a danger to Christendom than did the sultans who fought their way from Bursa into the Balkans and, at last, into

Hagia Sophia, the symbol of Byzantium and the greatest monument of Christianity's first thousand years (when Muslims rage about repossessing the lost domains of their faith, one is tempted to note the Western claims on Constantinople, Antioch, Damascus, Ephesus, and, not least, Alexandria, where Christianity first discovered how to substitute bureaucracy for Christ).

The "Grand Turk" was the greatest scourge on Europe since the Black Death. It is impossible for us to recapture the terror Europeans on the continent's marches felt as Ottoman armies approached. The Balkans had already been gathered in under the sultan's banners before Constantinople's triple walls were breached. From Nicopolis to Mohács the Ottomans devoured Christian armies. Turkish fleets controlled the Mediterranean and its abundant commerce, while the sultans expanded their empire across the Arab world and outposted East Africa. The spice trade and the slave trade, the vital sea lanes and caravan routes that carried the wealth of empire all paid their tribute to the greatest city in the world and the all-powerful rulers reclining behind the Sublime Porte. Europe's survival seemed a near run matter time and again, and we forget that Crete belonged to the Ottomans until 1898, while patches of the Balkans remained Turkish until the early twentieth century. The long recession of the Ottoman empire extracted a terrible price in blood from both sides.

Two Ottoman defeats, one famous the other forgotten, saved the West. One featured hundreds of thousands of soldiers and a great battle fought before the eyes of the world. The other involved a handful of ships at the distant edge of empire. The struggle before the walls of Vienna in 1683 determined the fate of Europe. The brief encounter at Diu, off the coast of India, changed the fate of the world. The siege of Vienna is the stuff of history as pageant, but the Portuguese naval victory off the coast of Gujarat in 1509 shapes the strategy of the United States in the twenty-first century.

Fourteen
HOW THE EAST WAS WON

At three o'clock on Sunday afternoon, the twelfth of September 1683, the clang of steel on steel and the deafening gunfire subsided before the walls of besieged Vienna. A titanic battle had been underway since dawn, with the future of Europe dependent on its outcome. A cobbled together Christian relief force under Poland's King Jan Sobieski had fought its way down from the hills and into the open ground before the city, but the Ottomans resisted tenaciously. The earth had been drinking the blood of soldiers for nine hours without a decisive advantage to either side. The Christian infantry was fought out, and the Turks were bringing up their elite reserves. Weakened by hunger and disease, the garrison within the city walls lacked the strength to influence the battle. The strange lull that presages war's fateful moments settled over the plain.

An Ottoman army 140,000 strong had advanced on the greatest city in central Europe, the seat of the Austrian Habsburgs and a bulwark of Christendom that had defied repeated Turkish campaigns, assaults, and sieges. This time the sultan did not intend to fail. He had dispatched his grand vizier, Kara Mustafa, with the finest soldiery the empire could muster: the corps of janissaries formed of Christian boys taken as tribute and schooled to Muslim fanaticism, and the *Spahis*, cavalrymen who had swept away the sultan's enemies from the Danube to the Euphrates. The Muslim heart of the Ottoman army was wrapped in the muscle of tributary states: Christian auxiliaries swelled the sultan's leviathan force, the contingents of princes and noblemen whose lands had been conquered in generations past. Mercenary French artillery masters directed the Ottoman siege guns, and the king of France, Louis

XIV, had concluded an agreement with the sultan not to assist his fellow Christians against their would-be conquerors. For the Sun King, humbling his Habsburg rivals was more important than the fate of Europe. He set a pattern from which the policy of France has rarely strayed.

French diplomats had done their best to dissuade any other European states from sending troops to raise the siege of Vienna. Fearful of Bourbon malice, the states of Italy chose to remain passive, and the Habsburgs could rely upon only the remnants of their battered armies and slight reinforcements from Bavaria and a few lesser German principalities.

The numbers were not enough to defeat the massive Ottoman force. Only a single power remained with the strength to save Vienna. The Poles had defended Europe against Turks and Tatars, against Cossack raids and Muscovite barbarism, for a quarter of a millennium. Attacked on all sides in the mid-seventeenth century—by Tatars, Turks, Ukrainians and Swedes—the Poles had nonetheless preserved their state and further burnished their reputation as dauntless soldiers and devoted Christians.

France did all that policy could effect to prevent the Poles from riding southward to rescue the Habsburg Empire. The rough democracy that prevailed among the Polish nobility proved susceptible to French blandishments and threats. Poland's king could not unite his own country behind his purpose of saving Vienna. Louis XIV and his courtiers at Versailles were certain that France would soon be the dominant power remaining in Europe.

In an hour of greatness that leaves the West forever indebted, King Jan decided to march to Vienna with only his household troops and those Polish nobles willing to follow him. Defying France and his own magnates, and still threatened by the appetites of his neighbors, Jan Sobieski risked his crown and his life for his fellow Christians.

After uniting his forces with the Habsburg remnants under Charles of Lorraine, King Jan was given overall command for the looming battle. The Austrian emperor—no soldier—kept himself at a safe distance from the coming slaughter.

By three o'clock in the afternoon King Jan's plan had carried the battle within a last charge of the city walls, but the Ottomans were far from broken. On horseback atop a hill the king could see the Turkish forces rallying as the janissaries moved into the foremost lines. The Ottoman cavalry wheeled to face the Christian flank, ready to sweep down on the survivors of any failed attack. The day was warm and the sky was clear, and the smoke of the earlier fighting drifted off. For those upon the city walls or ranked on the low hills won in the day's hard fighting, the spectacle of Ottoman might unfolding must have chilled the sweat that greased their spines.

Behind King Jan stood twenty thousand horsemen, the West's last hope. Immediately at his back, the shock troops of the Polish *kawaleria* glittered in their armor, heavy cavalrymen whose equipage resembled that of the knights of past centuries. The force that would have to decide the day were those regiments of the Polish *husaria,* the greatest cavalrymen of the age and the greatest heroes Europe ever produced. Waiting in their shimmering ranks on the high ground, the Polish hussars were an otherworldly sight. Each rider's height was increased by a pair of feathered wings fixed at his back, giving him the look of a warrior angel. A Polish hussar was a mobile fortress, armored and equipped with a lance, a bow, one or two heavy dragoon pistols, and multiple sabers—all of which he wielded expertly. With each regiment arrayed in its own color—blue, green, yellow, red—and with animal pelts raked over the shoulders of their gleaming breastplates, the riders in the lobsterback helmets were feared throughout Europe's desperate frontiers. Veterans of ceaseless wars, the Polish hussars would have to break through three successive Turkish lines to gain a Christian victory.

At twenty minutes after three o'clock King Jan lifted his mace— Poland's symbol of military authority.

Trumpets blared and kettledrums thumped. The Polish cavalry began to move forward, first at a walk, then increasing their pace to a trot. Spurring to a canter, the riders maintained their ranks with iron discipline. The Turkish cavalry charged across the Ottoman front to face them, screaming their war cries and calling upon Allah.

The Polish riders broke into a gallop. Lowering their lances, they shouted, "For Jesus and Maria!" Eighty thousand hooves pounded the earth.

The forces collided with a roar and a crash of metal. Horses thudded into one another, wild-eyed, rearing, and tumbling to the earth. The lances of the first Polish rank splintered against their targets. The impact hurled the lighter Turkish cavalrymen from their saddles.

The hussars smashed through the broken troops of *Spahis,* drawing their sabers and spurring their horses back to a gallop, howling with the fury of battle and calling once more for the aid of Christ and the Virgin.

The charge was catastrophic for the Ottoman army. Dutiful to the last, the janissaries died in place, ridden down by Polish hussars exploding through their defenses, intoxicated by victory. The grand vizier fled, barely escaping as hussars reached the movable palace of his tent, sweeping through the Ottoman camp as soldiers and servants ran madly from the avenging angels of the north.

When darkness ended the last skirmishes twenty thousand Ottoman bodies littered the ground. The remainder fled in disorder. Vienna had been rescued. The myth of Ottoman invincibility, already weakened, had been destroyed. Fewer than two thousand Christians lay on the field.

The Ottoman Empire never again posed so serious a threat to the West. For centuries the names of the sultans had resounded, associated with conquests. Now the names of Christian generals would be remembered, from Prince Eugène to Suvorov and Skobelev. The Ottomans would fight on, but the empire had bled into twilight. All that remained was a long, grim, losing battle against the night as an empire famed for its diversity contracted in body and soul, reduced at last to economic capitulations to Western creditors, to cruelty in lieu of competence, and to the grisly slaughter of the empire's last minorities.

The West had won on the continent of Europe, with Christendom saved by a Polish king. Poland's thanks was dismemberment in the next century, as the rulers of Austria, Russia, and Prussia partitioned its territory and drove its heroes abroad to fight for freedom elsewhere in Europe or the Americas. Men without a country, Poles joined the struggle for freedom wherever such wars were waged—and still fought for their homeland in hopeless rebellions.

No Europeans fought longer for their freedom and the liberty of others than did the Poles. And none have received less gratitude.

Although the Ottoman Empire still seemed the mightiest power in the world as its troops besieged Vienna, its strength had been hollowed out in ways contemporaries could not understand. While Turkish armies continued to fight ferociously on land, the Muslim future had already been lost to Europe at sea.

Western scholars traditionally consider the Spanish and Venetian victory at Lepanto, fought off the coast of Greece in 1571, as the decisive battle that turned the naval tide. With hundreds of ships engaged on each side and a stunningly lopsided outcome, Lepanto was the grand sort of battle that mesmerizes the victors and gains a mythic status even before its veterans are dead. But the far smaller affair fought at Diu in 1509 had repercussions that changed the fate of empire and created a model of Western naval dominance that prevails unto this day.

In the first decade of the sixteenth century Portuguese sailors of peerless courage and astonishing ruthlessness learned to master the monsoon winds and carried Lisbon's outsized ambitions from the African coast to India. The slightest of the European powers, Portugal had gone to sea to gain what its thin population could never hope to achieve on land: an empire. Drawn by the riches of the spice trade and the lure of faulty geography, Portuguese navigators, funded by the impecunious ruling house, bullied their crews and blundered around the Cape into the Indian Ocean, a realm of wealth and strategic import so great it promises to be as essential to Western hegemony in the twenty-first century as it proved to be in the sixteenth.

The Portuguese were also intent upon spreading the Christian faith. Schooled in the savagery of eight hundred years of religious warfare on the Iberian Peninsula, they found the sword more persuasive than the Sermon on the Mount. With a handful of ships the Lusitanians seized control of the region's seaborne trade, beginning on the Swahili Coast and proceeding to western India, conquering in a manner as audacious as it was brutal. Native princes were left aghast by the Portuguese enthusiasm for atrocity—what Lisbon lacked in numbers it made up in a commitment to total war that devastated its victims psychologically, whether they were individual potentates or recalcitrant cities. With the Holy Cross and excellent naval gunnery, Portugal's miniature fleets took command of the Indian Ocean's sea-lanes in less than a decade.

The trade the Christian presence interdicted was a fundamental source of Ottoman wealth. The silks of the Far East and the spices of the still uncharted islands beyond India were the petroleum of the day, a commercial resource that translated into strategic power. Arab traders under Ottoman suzerainty had managed the trade for centuries, hugging the coasts in their dhows and bringing the treasures of the East back to coastal terminals in the Persian Gulf or along the Red Sea's shores. Every load of silk or nutmeg, pepper or mace owed a tax to the sultan's treasury.

The suddenness of the Portuguese blows found the Ottomans unprepared. Although a great Chinese fleet had come and gone in a previous century, the Turks had never been challenged in the sphere that was to prove their soft underbelly. Local emirs or Indian princes dealt with occasional piracy, but there had never been a naval threat, and the Ottoman Empire had no fleet-in-being in the region.

We forget. Imagining that our engagement in the Persian Gulf is novel—or, at most, a reprise of British interventions—we miss the true precedent for our assertion of power over our most determined enemies. Yet there is a direct lineage from those dwarfish Portuguese caravels and carracks down to the U.S. Navy's supercarriers cutting the waters of the Indian Ocean today. The strategic requirement to control the Strait of Hormuz at the mouth of the Persian Gulf was every bit as evident to Lisbon's admirals as it is to our own.

Who remembers now that the Portuguese seized Hormuz and held it for a century? Or that they terrorized the coasts of Arabia into acquiescence by disembarking at coastal settlements, massacring the males, and mutilating the women (good Christians that they were, the Portuguese did not rape their victims, and one ship's officer was executed for the crime; had he simply killed the girl, he might have survived to earn wealth and renown).

The Ottoman response was to build a fleet from scratch for the Indian Ocean with the mission of sailing to India and wiping out the Portuguese presence on land and at sea. By the reckoning of the times the European interlopers should not have stood a chance. The Turks possessed great reserves of wealth and power, and their naval might was generations away from the disaster at Lepanto. Turkish fleets and privateers in service to the sultan dominated the Mediterranean and Europe's merchants sailed at Ottoman sufferance. The sultan's fleet counted hundreds of keels and could fill the Golden Horn and line the Bosporus.

But the Ottoman strength lay in galley warfare conducted on the mild waves of the Mediterranean. The Turks might have ruled the inland seas, but they were not deepwater sailors. They had mastered neither navigation far from the littorals nor seaborne gunnery under sail. Their navy was composed of shallow-hulled vessels powered by slaves, with banks of oars suited to intricate maneuvers in coastal waters but unstable under oceanic conditions.

The Ottomans enjoyed the resources of empire, but the Portuguese had the advantages of knowledge and asymmetrical ruthlessness. Lusitanian sailors knew that a battle lost half a world away from home offered them no least hope of survival.

The Turkish admiral, Emir Hussein, set sail from the new yards at the head of the Red Sea, commanding twelve ships constructed for Indian Ocean conditions. But the emir hugged the coast as he made his way toward the enemy, lacking blue-water experience and the confidence of the Portuguese.

Still, the campaign began well enough for the Turks. Their Indian allies greeted them with scores of smaller vessels suited to coastal warfare. Then Dom Lourenço de Almeida, the son of the first Portuguese viceroy in India, blundered into a naval ambush in the port of Chaul. Fighting on with a crippling wound, young Almeida was killed and part of his squadron destroyed. Hussein and India's Muslims grew confident that the region would soon be rid of the Portuguese for good.

Lisbon's admiral-viceroy, Francisco de Almeida, saw his mission in India in a crusader's terms. Devout, stoic, and unsparing of himself or his subordinates, he did not allow himself to act rashly at the news of his son's death but methodically prepared for a climactic battle. Mustering fewer than twenty ships, he played cat and mouse with his opponent until Hussein was cornered, his capital ships at anchor and the Indian coasters interfering with the ability of their Ottoman allies to maneuver.

It was a fight to the death, all or nothing, and both sides knew it.

One of history's forgotten great captains, Almeida, who had ravished the shores of Arabia and planted the cross firmly on Indian soil, attacked at once.

Unable to get under sail or plan a response, the Turks could only defend passively, outmaneuvered and outgunned by the Portuguese. The Ottomans fought as if their ships were fortifications that happened to be on the water, unable to turn their guns or attempt an escape. Almeida's gunners blew the Turkish vessels to splinters, maneuvering to keep the native craft packed against his immobilized opponents. Nor did the Portuguese content themselves with sinking the Ottoman fleet. As the harbor's waters thickened with Muslims swimming for their lives, Almeida ordered his ship's boats into the water. His sailors slaughtered everyone they could reach.

Despite the carnage they inflicted, at the end of the day the Portuguese found themselves with hundreds of prisoners. These were tortured and mutilated in batches at ports along the coast to post the price of defying Lisbon's will.

The Portuguese maintained a presence on India's coast for almost five centuries.

Yet Lisbon's greatest glory hardly lasted a century. The Ottomans had been driven from the deep waters of the Indian Ocean, but European powers with greater depths of strength soon began to dismantle Portugal's empire. The Dutch took the far spice islands, their behavior as savage toward fellow Christians as the Portuguese had been toward the infidel. English ships drove Lisbon's governor from Hormuz. And Portugal's ill-fated union with Spain during the reign of Philip II drained the country of manpower, wealth, and resolve.

But the Portuguese had pioneered the conquest of a world of ineffable riches. The Ottoman Empire felt the loss but enjoyed such reserves of internal wealth that the opulence of the hour blinded the sultan's advisers to the consequences for future generations. The grandeur of Süleyman the Magnificent still lay ahead, an apogee of authority and culture, and successes closer at hand obscured the meaning of a naval skirmish fought beyond the reach of reliable maps.

The Ottoman Empire lived from taxes, not enterprise—except for its military endeavors. It favored trade, but lacked productivity. The treasurers of the Topkapi measured wealth in tangible terms, not in investments. Perhaps we might blame Koranic restrictions on interest and the lack of commercial banking houses for the economic ignorance of the Turks, but the ultimate source of Ottoman weakness was also the fount of its greatness: It was, above all, a military state. While Europe learned to bank, the Turks contented themselves with giving battle. Martial virtues dominated the decisive Ottoman centuries, but no amount of static military skill has ever proven a match for intellectual curiosity, innovation, and sophisticated markets. The Turks were such good soldiers for so long that they did not feel the need for other qualities until they had been fatally eclipsed.

Nor was the wealth of the spice trade all that accrued to Europe's coffers. Simultaneously, the New World bowed to the ferocity of Spain's conquistadors, soldiers trained in the last, savage wars that broke Moorish power in Grenada, Islam's last stronghold on the Iberian Peninsula and the last Arab hope in Europe. Schooled in campaigns in Andalusia's mountains, where the last Muslim footprints had to be wiped away, men such as Cortés and Pizarro brushed aside static empires unprepared for the impact of a dynamic civilization. In hardly a generation European states that had lived on the verge of poverty for centuries found themselves in possession of territories vastly greater than their Iberian homelands. Gold and silver poured into Madrid and Lisbon, sparking waves of art and inflation, military expansion, state building, Counter-Reformation devotion, and ultimately insupportable ambitions (followed by bankruptcies on a far greater scale than the medieval world had known). The Pope formally divided the world in halves, the East to Portugal, the West to Spain. Of course, the rising Protestant powers had opinions of their own...

The combination of sudden wealth from the New World with the growing revenues from the realms on the far side of the Indian Ocean funded the rise of Europe. New Spain's silver paid Velázquez and nutmeg from the Spice Isles paid Vermeer. Commerce demanded larger, sturdier, more capable ships. Fleets grew, as did the skill of their captains. In northern Europe early capitalism found its footing, along with the science necessary to maximize profit and dominate far-flung empires.

After the naval scrap off Diu Europe was unstoppable—until it stopped itself with its suicidal twentieth-century wars. Almeida sank ten Turkish ships and unleashed the West.

The strategic import of Portugal's victories at the start of the sixteenth century remains with us today. As we focus obsessively on the land mass between Suez and Samarkand, with its oil reserves and truculent populations, we miss both the crucial lesson of history and the enduring sources of Western—and American—strength: Domination of the Indian Ocean is *essential*.

Even in this era of bombers that range around the globe, control of the sea is as vital in the age of the Internet as it was in the days of Almeida and his great rival, Afonso de Albuquerque, or in the eras of Nelson or Nimitz. America's great strategic thinker, Alfred Thayer Mahan, understood that seapower was and would remain crucial to our security and authority. While naval forces today may be handsomely supplemented by airpower and the capability to intervene on land with robust strength, control of the seas remains essential to our security and trade. And in the twenty-first century, as in the sixteenth, no expanse of water is likely to be as important to Western dominance as the Indian Ocean.

The Indian Ocean was the soft underbelly of the Ottoman Empire five hundred years ago, and it remains the key to control of the Middle East today. For all of the pipelines and highways commerce has brought to the region, the wealth still moves by sea. The Portuguese victualing station at Mozambique Island, under the guns of the Fort of Saint Sebastian, served a role identical in its time to that played by Diego Garcia for American forces today. Despite the reach of our Air Force, our power still travels by sea and wants port facilities and control of the littoral. As Almeida and Albuquerque understood, control of the Strait of Hormuz and the mouth of the Red Sea means effective control of Arabia.

But the last gasp of the Arabs, the debacle of oil wealth, will pass. Substitute fuels may speed the climax, but even should we continue to rely on petroleum products throughout our lifetimes, the demographic surge in the Middle East will result in statistical impoverishment for the region, with the wealthy emirates and kingdoms increasingly under siege from without and within. And if we see the advent of alternative fuels the accelerated bankrupting of the Middle East—so richly deserved—will spawn even wilder fits of hatred and anarchy.

Like Spain in the sixteenth century, the oil-state Arabs grew so intoxicated by their newfound wealth that they neglected to diversify their economies—and saw them wither behind their ornate facades. Oil is the Arab's last advantage. It has not been and will not be enough.

We must learn to look beyond the indolence and ill temper of the Middle East to the lands of opportunity lying just where they did five hundred years ago. India is poised to play a far greater role in the twenty-first century than it did in the last one, and Indonesia, the world's most populous Muslim country, has great potential to pioneer the future of Islam in a manner both constructive and inspiring. Southeast Asia offers riches again, and Africa's Swahili Coast, long scorned, bears a promise for the future we dully ignore.

Those who insisted angrily on the importance of the southern hemisphere a generation ago were right in ways they could not understand. The human frontiers all lie to the south, save for North America. An "expanded southern hemisphere" reaching northward to the Tropic of Cancer will determine the future of the globe to a degree no conventional strategist can yet begin to accept. But whether we look for the crises of today or the possibilities of tomorrow, the Indian Ocean remains the strategic cockpit of the world.

When the Muslim civilization in its Ottoman robes lost hegemony over the Indian Ocean, Islam's decline was assured. No matter that the sixteenth century witnessed the power and the glory of the Mughal courts of India, the Safavid dynasty in Persia, or the dazzling achievements of the greatest Ottoman sultan; after Europe seized the sea-lanes from Africa to India the triumph of the West was only a matter of time.

He who controls the waters controls the world.

Fifteen
THE FROZEN CIVILIZATION OF THE DESERT

I stumbled onto the murder of Islam in Samarkand. The summer was so hot that it drained the color from the horizon, although the sky overhead was of blue enamel. Soviet power still held sway in Central Asia then, its rule grown as languid and intermittently petty as that of a bad emir. The splendor of the Registan's mosques and madrassahs, with their heretic iconography, shamed the centrally planned architecture inflicted on the city by its last conqueror. Timur's tomb waited down a lane and the towering Bibi Hanum mosque refused to fall despite the insistence of earthquakes.

The citizens adjusted their pace to the heat. Merchants lounged, confident that customers eventually must buy the little they had to offer, and anyone paid a salary by the state did his best to avoid the least hint of labor. The sanitation was such that meat burned black was a delicacy, and a bottle of salty mineral water had to be bought the instant it was sighted. Cars smoked. Unengaged young men glowered at any complexion suggesting Slavic blood. Once it was established that the visitor was an American—akin in those days to a unicorn—the tenor of welcome changed to a calculation of what might be gained from the encounter. Adorned with monuments to past reverence, Samarkand had grown as godless and torpid as it was poorly governed. The onions were good.

Once you had journeyed so far neither desert heat nor Soviet pollution was likely to stop you until you had seen all that there was to see. I made my way out beyond the tombs that still drew country pilgrims—whose religion had been reduced to hand-me-down habits—to the ruins that memorialize the last Renaissance man Islam produced.

Descended from Timur the Great—our Tamerlane and Marlowe's Tamburlaine—Ulūg Begh was a ruler, a mullah, a mathematician, a scientist, a student of medicine, a poet, a warrior, and, fatally, an astronomer. Gussied up for tourists now in the wake of the Soviet retreat, the remains unearthed upon a barren ridge are of the massive observatory Ulūg Begh designed to explore the heavens. He represented the apotheosis of Muslim intellectual achievement, a gentleman scholar of the highest accomplishments and the bitter symbol of what might have been.

The "mad mullahs" of his day murdered Ulūg Begh. His fault was to think too freely, to question too persistently, and, above all, to see too deeply. More sophisticated than any of its fifteenth-century peers, his observatory threatened the Muslim clerics of Samarkand, who yearned for the strictness of rival Bukhara, insisting that men knew all that should be known. Outdoing the papal Inquisition, they did not settle for censoring the man who pierced the heavens with his tools, but killed him, an act of regicide and cultural suicide.

Within a decade of Ulūg Begh's assassination Johannes Gutenberg had invented movable type, unleashing the torrent of knowledge that powered the West. History offers no other symmetry as perfect as that moment in the mid-fifteenth century when the most powerful civilization on earth declared itself unwilling to go forward just as its anxious competitor discovered that crucial tool of progress, the affordable book—whose spirit the Muslim world has yet to master.

If the murder of Ulūg Begh punctuates the end of Islam's intellectual glory, the symptoms long had been as evident as plague spots. At the other end of the Muslim world, in Andalusia, the last Muslim enclave struggled for its life. Fanatics of the ilk of Osama bin Laden, as well as gentler Muslims, romanticize al-Andaluz to this day, daydreaming both of its lost magnificence and of one day recapturing Grenada and Córdoba for the faith of the Prophet (the Madrid train bombings were the campaign's opening blow). But Islam's deadly romantics do not inquire seriously as to how Grenada was lost, or why the last Moors were reduced to sporting quarry for the knights of their Most Catholic Majesties, Isabella and Ferdinand.

The vanquished brilliance of Muslim culture in al-Andaluz is beyond dispute. Any architecture that survived the reconquista was profaned by every added Spanish touch. Libraries of immeasurable worth burned, their manuscripts not long before a lure to Christian scholars, who were welcomed during interludes of peace to learn from Muslims versed in Aristotle. The charge that the West regained its own heritage from Muslim Andalusia is one of the least-debatable cases before the court of history.

And there was more. Muslims will tell you of the tolerance that prevailed, protecting Jewish and Christian residents of *al-Andaluz*. Far from other centers of authority in Baghdad, Damascus, or Cairo, for centuries Moorish Andalusia escaped the clerical edicts that had begun to cripple the genius of the Middle East. The Moorish world glowed amid the general darkness.

Founded by a survivor of the dynastic struggles in the Arab heartlands, Umayyad Andalusia had no rival in the suppleness or grace of its culture. Let us grant that much to nostalgic Muslims.

The defect in the dream is that the golden age did not last, and that fellow Muslims, not the knights of Castile, Navarre, or León, precipitated its destruction. The days of grandeur reached their apogee within two hundred years of the Moors' arrival on the Iberian Peninsula; thereafter, all was a sumptuous, bitterly fought decline. The treasures that remained when Grenada fell at last in 1492 were only a shadow of the long-collapsed empire of beauty, knowledge, and exemplary governance.

Internecine strife in the tenth-century led to the importation of Berber troops from across the straits, employed first to defend Andalusia against the southward advance of the Christian knights, next against competing Muslim princes. Unity perished, an echo of the internal discord in the East that would open the Holy Land to the crusaders. If the long contest between Islam and the West offers an obvious strategic lesson, it is that the side that succumbed to internal bickering lost, while even temporary unity prevailed.

The Berber mercenaries had three reactions to their Andalusian employers: They were astonished by their luxuries and wealth; they were appalled by their lack of Islamic rigor; and they were pleasantly surprised by their weakness. In the violent madness of the tenth century the Berber Almoravid dynasty—composed of enthusiastic book burners and persecutors of Sufi mystics—established itself as the dominant power in *al-Andaluz*. The Almoravids were brutal, backward, and bigoted. They soon were replaced by another Berber dynasty, the Almohads, who surpassed them in ferocity and intolerance.

Meanwhile, the Christians to the north, militant and rough, found opportunities to extend their kingdoms across the east-west river lines and mountain ranges that grade Spain like a strategic football field. Nor were the centuries of the Reconquest shining examples of piety on either side. As the old Umayyad realm dissolved into petty feudalism and religious police states, Christian lords and Islamic nobles frequently formed alliances across confessional lines. Rodrigo Díaz, Spain's legendary hero, drew his nickname, El Cid, from the Arabic word for "chieftain," *al-sayyid*. His career was sanitized wonderfully by Charlton Heston and Hollywood, but Díaz spent much of his adulthood as a mercenary in the pay of Muslim warlords. Knowing when to jump sides was as important for soldiers in medieval Spain and Andalusia as it is for political operatives in an American presidential primary.

The destruction of Moorish Andalusia occurred in fits and starts, but never lacked brutality. Boabdil the Nasrid, the last ruler of the last ruling house in Grenada, surrendered his city to Ferdinand and Isabella in the year Americans recall for another Spanish achievement (and which Jews recall for their expulsion from the Iberian Peninsula, a tragedy that cost them a cherished homeland but which cost Spain talent it never could replace). An apocryphal tale, recounted in Western histories, Arab poetry, and world fiction, has Boabdil riding away from the Alhambra and his lost city, looking back and sobbing—to which his mother responded, "Don't weep like a woman for what you didn't defend as a man."

Their Catholic majesties had signed a treaty guaranteeing the Moors an eternal right to continued residence in the land that had been their home for eight centuries. Martin Luther, in the cold, distant Germanies, undid the promise. His reformation sparked a furious reaction from Rome, that, impotent to exterminate Protestantism, directed its wrath more successfully toward the last Moors and against those unfortunate Jews who had converted to Christianity in order to remain in their Spanish homes. One of the earliest achievements of the Counter-Reformation was the final expulsion of the Moors and the slaughter, in the names of Jesus Christ and Saint James, of any who resisted.

Their fellow Muslims beat the civilization of *al-Andaluz* nearly to death. The knights of Spain merely finished what Berber fanatics had begun.

At the other extreme of the Mediterranean the Ottoman Empire built fantastic mosques, employing craftsmen from the farthest reaches of the Islamic world. Whenever Christian lands were conquered their finest artisans were pressed into the sultan's service. Mosques, tombs, palaces, fountains...little expense was spared in decorating the empire's urban gems. The remnants may be admired today, in masterful works that delight the eye with color to hide their lifelessness.

Ottoman art reflected the deficiencies of the culture, the self-imposed limitations celebrating a world that was not supposed to change. The highest aesthetic goal was to achieve a static condition pleasing to Allah and in absolute conformity to His Word.

Just as the coincidence of the murder of Ulūg Begh and Gutenberg's discovery marked very different turning points for the Islamic world and the West, a comparison of artistic values in Europe and the Ottoman Empire in the crucial fifteenth and sixteenth centuries tells us a great deal about the weaknesses of the East—by no means evident to contemporaries—and the blossoming strength of the West.

Although the seizure of the spice trade by Europe's oceangoing powers ultimately humbled Venice and reduced the wealth of its rival city-states, Italy maintained its lead in the fine arts until the triumph of bourgeois painting in seventeenth-century Holland. The two-century span in question began with Lippi, climaxed with Leonardo and Michelangelo, and ended with the incomparable dramas on canvas of Caravaggio. It wasn't a "renaissance," a renascence. It was the *birth* of a radically new way of seeing and interpreting the world, utterly without precedent.

At the beginning of the period painting focused almost exclusively on mannered religious depictions, hardly emancipated from the rigid formulas of Byzantine icon painting or the miniaturists of the Islamic world. Suddenly human events were elevated to a new worthiness;

portrait painting flourished and biblical scenes were cast in distinctly human forms. Mistresses posed for Madonnas; the newborn Christ bawled and squirmed. By the end of the period Caravaggio's John the Baptist looked like a brooding boy toy (the artist clearly identified with Salome), while the most perfectly human religious painting in the Western tradition, the same artist's "The Calling of St. Matthew," brought religion hauntingly down to earth.

Europe's age of the conquest of new worlds was its own age of human liberation. The burst of energy that carried frail ships to New Spain or the coast of India was only another facet of the explosive genius that covered the ceiling of the Sistine Chapel. Even as Europeans slew the natives of the Indies old and new, they found a new humanity at home—not an idealized humanity of peace and good order in a great chain of being but one bursting with the will to engage the world as it is with a novel passion, with the lust to conquer, to create, to *do*.

The realistic depiction of men and women on canvas or wet plaster heralded a new honesty—heroic, ruthless, and empowering—about the human condition. When the Madonna's newly supple spine bent over a writhing infant the prison walls of the Middle Ages collapsed. The "great chain of being," the falsely idealized world of the Gothic, was forever broken.

At least in Europe. To the East, Islamic principles, interpreted with self-destructive strictness, forged heavier links for the social order's chains than the region had yet known. The art mirrored the age as the Ottomans embraced the effort already under way in Islam's heartlands to freeze time, to inhibit change, to preserve the ways already proven. At the height of their power the Turks fled into established verities, resisting the intrusion of the disconcerting changes transforming the West.

Among the Koran's prohibitions, some have been interpreted to forbid the depiction of human or even animal figures, since such representations would presume to imitate Allah's creation of life. The Arabs and the Turks generally honored the strictures, although the Persians, with their powerful pre-Islamic heritage, did not (nor did all the Turkic peoples who remained in Central Asia—the most striking facade in Samarkand's Registan square offers lions striped like tigers and Zoroastrian faces depicting the sun).

Yet even among the Turks, with their parade-ground Islam, there were exceptions. The most notable involved painted miniatures used to illustrate books. In the chronicles of a sultan's achievements, in recopied histories or in deluxe manuscripts of epic poems, gorgeous illustrations delighted the eye. But pleasure was the only purpose the miniatures served (including the soft-porn effect of unveiled princesses on the page). There was none of the Western spirit of inquiry or evolution of technique. The goal of painters at the Ottoman court was to rival the "perfection" of artists from centuries past. Even Russian icon painters had more freedom to experiment with forms. There was no Ottoman Andrei Rublev or Daniel Chyorni.

In the West the past was gone. In the East the past dictated implacable ideals. The "creative destruction" of Europe's overseas empire building, the increase in spiritual octane during the Reformation and Counter-Reformation, and the humanization of the arts met no reply along the Golden Horn. Apart from a few organizational advances, the Ottoman Empire remained within the imaginative contours of all the bygone empires of the Middle East. Faced with the revolutionary texts of the West it proved dyslexic, when not downright blind.

The figures Ottoman artists drew were as stylized as Byzantine icons of five centuries earlier, if more graceful. The same cherished figures were drawn and colored again and again and again, with only faint variations: Khosrou and Shirin, Leyla and Madjnoon, or the lesser heroes and heroines of the works of Nizami Gandjevi and his imitators. It was as if the artists of the advancing West had been forced to repeat the style of the early fourteenth century, before the Black Death led to a reappraisal of life's meaning. If there had been a distinctly Ottoman prayer it might have run simply "Don't change!"

Even the inherited works deemed fit for illustration were nothing more than elaborate cartoons. For all their interminable length, the epic poems of Nizami show no interest in actual human psychology. Emotions are mannered, the stuff of arthritic fairy tales. The stories of the beloved spied unexpectedly, pursued, lost, then regained—and perhaps lost a final time through death or betrayal—have the behavioral simplicity of low myth. They do not expand but limit human experience. It is all about outward forms and ritualized behavior. There is nothing of Chaucer's liveliness or even of Dante's earlier mischief making, and there is certainly no hint of Boccaccio's celebration of the flesh. Even at the end of the age in question, when Shakespeare was exploring every minute fold in the human fabric (except, notably, the religious impulse), the literate members of Middle Eastern societies were simply rereading the books they already knew, much as children demand to hear the same stories over and over.

Like the Shah of Iran half a millennium later the sultans hired European technicians or employed Armenian or Greek architects to manage their artillery or raise their monuments. Apart from that required for dreary bureaucratic endeavors, practical knowledge was scorned. The early Islamic curiosity about science, geography, and philosophy calcified into an obsession with religious learning (enough to qualify a man as a judge) that tolerated only those lay texts vetted over centuries. Once the jewel of Islamic literature, poetry lost its light. The yearning and rueful self-knowledge, the love of a generous god and the loving attachment to the things of the earth, the thirst for earthly wine and the symbolic vintage, all the word marvels of Hāfiz, Rūmī, Abū Nuwāz, or Fizuli inspired no worthy rivals. It was all about the past, the past, the past—as it is for today's terrorists, who cannot abide a world that changes in defiance of their longings.

The Muslim world lost interest in humanity.

Certainly the Ottoman domains, Persia, the khanates of Central Asia, and the elaborate courts of the Mughals produced works of exemplary craftsmanship: the decorations of mosques and palaces, glassware, bronzes, ceramics, baubles in precious metals and ivory, peerless swords and carpets unrivaled by the productions of later ages… but it was all about surface effects, about ornamentation and the workshop's trickery. Even at its most luxurious and vibrant Islamic art was little more than a craft. The use of color was regulated, the forms of written expression rigidly defined. Music, that other triumph of the post-Renaissance West, remained suspect and turgid. Just as Europe began its dramatic rise Islamic civilization stepped down into a tomb of its own free will.

Once the most inquisitive of faiths, Islam lost interest in new possibilities. As recently as the mid-fourteenth century Ibn Batūta had written on statecraft, strategy, anthropology, geography, and history with an audacity of purpose and clarity of sight that had no rival in the West.

He was the greatest traveler of his time—and, for all intents and purposes, the last great traveler his doomed world produced.

Many explanations have been offered for Islam's retreat into a mental fortress whose guardians were intolerant of new ideas. The Crusades and the Mongols have been blamed, along with the Black Death, militarism, economics, and general Christian nastiness. But the more convincing—if less politically correct—reason for Islamic culture stopping stone-cold dead is that civilizations are living organisms, vast creatures with constitutions of their own. Civilizations, like individuals, sicken from countless germs. To attempt to assign a single cause to Muslim cultural failure is a sport for professors desperate for an idea to call their own, but single causes do not bring great civilizations to paralysis. Rather, the complex dynamic of society begins to point one way or the other and myriad forces, decisions, and individual choices propel or impede it.

In short, if you need someone to blame for the decline and fall of Muslim civilization, blame Muslims.

One other great artistic work from the golden age of Islam must be considered. By far the most entertaining literary product Middle Eastern culture ever produced was the *Thousand Nights and a Night*, a vast storehouse of tales, many of which we have neutered to amuse children. We know the names of Sinbad, Aladdin, and Ali Baba, with their bravery and tricks, their flying carpets and fabulous voyages. But those among us who read castrated versions of those stories to children (or rent them an animated DVD) rarely have a notion of the magnitude or the viciousness of the work.

Try the nineteenth-century translation by Captain Sir Richard Francis Burton, that magnificent generator of books and scandals. "Dirty Dick" Burton was a fearless, troublesome officer who spoke twenty-seven languages infuriatingly well. His unexpurgated edition of the *Thousand Nights and a Night* runs to seventeen volumes in the edition on my shelves. The tales stray deeply into the tangled wood of the psyche, wandering through the briars and nettles of male sexual terror. A millennium old, the *Thousand Nights and a Night* is a blueprint for the contemporary misogyny among Muslims and a work that offers strategic insights of the first order into the deepest fears of our enemies.

You needn't read every volume. Pick up the first. A dozen pages should suffice to give you a feel for the work's oddity, combining the spirits of a serial murderer, the Three Stooges, a cracker-barrel philosopher, a grand dragon of the Ku Klux Klan, and a priest under indictment for preying on altar boys.

Even the framework of the tales would have brought a mighty snort from Sigmund Freud. A pair of kings, two brothers, discover that their queens have both betrayed them with black slaves, the first with a "black cook of loathsome aspect and foul with kitchen grease and grime," the second with a "big slobbering blackamoor with rolling eyes that showed the whites, a truly hideous sight." Wives and slaves are executed by the kings themselves, and by the seventh page of the vast work we have been warned that "there is no woman but who cuckholdeth her husband."

Heartbroken at the evil done by their beloved (and now quite dead) wives, the two kings take a brief road trip that climaxes when the mortal bride of a djinn commands their sexual services while her husband sleeps, adding them to her list of 570 men with whom she has merrily betrayed her husband. In the postcoital afterglow she warns the kings, "Rely not on women, trust not to their hearts, whose joys and sorrows are hung to their parts… wonderful is he and right worthy of our praise who from wiles of female wits kept him safe and kept him sound."

Unwilling to forego the pleasures of the flesh entirely the wiser king returns home and establishes the practice of taking into his bed one of his domain's loveliest virgins each night, then sending her to her death at dawn—before she can find an opportunity to betray him.

Things go splendidly for three years until, as the text coyly observes, the kingdom runs out of virgins. The vizier who pimps for the king can't locate fresh meat, nor does he mean to sacrifice his own daughters, whom he has hidden away. But to the vizier's horror his elder daughter, Sheherazade, volunteers to become the king's "bride." A student of old books and tales, she believes she can outwit the king and put an end to the slaughter roiling the realm.

Sheherazade isn't your run-of-the-mill palace bimbo. After losing her chastity she beguiles the sleepless king by telling him a story, leaving it unfinished as the dawn breaks. Unwilling to forego the tale's conclusion the king allows Sheherazade to live another day so that she might complete her story the next night. But after finishing her first tale, she promptly begins another. The procession of stories continues for a thousand nights and one more (Sheherazade never suffers from writer's block). At last the king decides that he's not going to execute her after all, but will risk taking Sheherazade for his wife, keeping her around as a sort of prototype television set.

Since this is a Muslim fable Sheherazade's desires are not considered and the ending passes for a happy one. It has a sting, though. Remarkable though she may be, Sheherazade has only survived through cleverness, by employing feminine wiles, the tricks of Eve. She'll have to be watched, and closely. One suspects that the king's harem was carefully guarded thereafter.

And in those many tales, along with Sinbad sailing the Seven Seas and Aladdin matching wits with the djinn, come ever more stories of female inconstancy, of woman's craven weakness and animal lust, of the need to keep an eye on the gals at every turn. Of course, there are idealized princesses, sorceresses, and all the stock characters, but few of the females ever quite come to life. It's a boy's book, full of high adventure, a treehouse club where the girls are never welcome. After the Koran, the *Thousand Nights and a Night* is the greatest work of literature in Muslim culture. And it is woman hating, vividly racist, and exuberantly cruel.

There has been no progress in a thousand years.

We all remember the outlines of Salman Rushdie's death sentence (since halfheartedly revoked), decreed for the liberties he took with the Prophet in *The Satanic Verses,* but fewer know of the ordeal of Naguib Mahfouz, the Egyptian writer of great conscience and commensurate talent who was stabbed nearly to death a few years ago for including in his novels mild criticisms of Muslim society. Closer to home, a Muslim fanatic murdered the Dutch filmmaker, Theo van Gogh, for taking issue with the treatment of women by Islamic fundamentalists.

Muslims do not assassinate their critics because the critics are wrong, but because the fanatics fear that the critics are right. This is a culture—an entire civilization—that lives in daily terror of demons both theological and biological. We should not be surprised when it attempts in extremis to terrorize others.

Even in contemporary Turkey, which boasts the most creative literary culture in the Muslim world (trailed by India and Indonesia), journalists and poets often have seen the inside of prison cells. Turkey's grand master of fiction, Orhan Pamuk (whose brilliant novel *My Name Is Red* contrasts the paths taken by Islamic and European art far more adeptly than I could ever do), may be living on borrowed time. Thus far Pamuk has walked his high wire with artful balance, staying just out of reach of both Islamic extremists and intolerant generals, but it will be instructive to see how Turkey deals with its single living artistic genius in the years to come.

A culture that hates and fears women simply cannot create worthy art. Nor can it create a modern society, or even a premodern hierarchy, worth living under. Women's roles were limited in medieval Europe too, and although the sequestration was not as severe as in the East, it was sufficient to stultify society. Our modern age began when a Florentine artist first dragged his girlfriend out of bed, robed her in brocade, and painted her as Mary, the Mother of God.

Culture is fate.

Sixteen

WHY IRAQ MATTERS

P resident Bush and countless Muslim voices have assured us that "Islam is a religion of peace."

Is it?

My personal conviction long has been that organized religion is what men and women make it, yet I find myself unsure of the merit of that conclusion. I long to believe that no religion is irredeemable but fear such wishful thinking may leave me as oblivious to reality as those who insist that if only we could dispense with armies and governments we would find ourselves in the midst of the Peaceable Kingdom.

Iraq will be a great test for Islam, as well as of the ability of Arabs to embrace modernity and, to a far lesser degree, of the extent of America's power to alter history.

While both Islam and Christianity have soaked themselves in blood, they bear different birthrights. Just as the stronger roles allotted to women in the Bible may help to explain the empowerment of women in Western culture, so the formative years of these two warring religious civilizations may warn us of alarming cracks in the cultural foundations of Middle Eastern Islam.

Despite their similar appetites for horror in later centuries, Christianity began as a pacifist movement while Islam was wrought in war. Do a religion's origins shape its psychology two thousand years later? Or fourteen centuries later? None of us can answer with certainty, but the question bears far more serious thought than we have directed toward it.

It's astonishing that Christianity survived. Setting aside the believer's insistence that God willed it, sending to earth His Son to get things rolling, Christianity shares with Buddhism and Jainism the ability to outlast scorn, persecution, and merciless violence through the appeal of its core message. If we pause to read the Sermon on the Mount afresh, it's striking how revolutionary it sounds. Nothing in Marx or Mao, nor in Lenin or Fanon, comes close to its rejection of mortal hierarchies, its embrace of the marginal, and, above all, its generosity of spirit. The Sermon on the Mount wasn't merely treason against a Jewish or a Roman state, but against all states. Why not render unto Caesar if Caesar is irrelevant to all that truly matters? Let the Marie Antoinettes eat cake; the poor shall eat the bread of life and the precious fruits of Heaven. Jesus Christ was so profoundly antiauthoritarian and subversive it's surprising that His picture (perhaps in a beret?) isn't on the wall of every university dorm room. The elders of Jerusalem knew trouble when it walked in on two legs.

Christ responded to violence with a rejection of violence, to suffering with a readiness to suffer. He embraced the *Lumpenproletariat* Marx dismissed as beyond rescue. He befriended those whom the privileged crossed the street to avoid. Even Satan could not provoke Him, and His worst loss of temper was with bankers (surely a pardonable lapse).

This exemplary life inspired such devotion, such a contagion of belief, that those who accepted Christ's message went mildly to their deaths at the hands of annoyed governments, refusing to fight back or dissemble their faith, expecting eternal salvation beyond the pyre or arena. For almost four centuries the church was hardly militant. Yet it endured, and grew, and devoured the greatest empire then extant.

Of course, Christianity had help from Paul, the commissar who culled, codified, and corrupted the message of Christ, down through an apostolic succession on fire with holy zeal. Paul stripped away the most radical aspects of Christ's message (especially His gentle affection toward women), allowing Christianity to survive, but also planting the seeds of later intolerance. Yet the crucial fact is that Christianity initially conquered with its message, not with fire and sword. The faith's mature barbarities obscure the miracle of its childhood. As with Buddhism, Christianity's propositions struck a thrilling chord in the suffering and dispossessed, in the frightened and abused. It was a winning proposition for losers, and it continues to draw the downtrodden today.

The childhood of Islam was that of Cain to the Christian Abel.

Muhammad survived by making war on pagan Arabs who, as soon as they were subjugated, swelled the tribal armies of Islam. In the stewpot of religions in Mecca and Medina—primarily idolatrous, but including some Jews and Christians—the force of a "for us" monotheism, a revelation dispensed directly (and, initially, exclusively) to Arabs aroused latent energies no time-traveling intelligence analyst could have predicted. Islam exploded out of the Arabian desert with such fury that it toppled empires, *always* through warfare. And the Prophet was no sooner dead than factional strife led to savage battles among the faithful, provoking the Shia secession.

In the faith's early generations the armies of Islam did not force conquered peoples to convert. The choice between embracing Islam or death came much later. Initially, the faith was exclusively Arab, imperial and wary of outside influences, even as Muslims reveled in the urban delights they seized from the worshippers of idols—or from the Christians of Alexandria or the Levant. But the economic and social strictures placed upon non-Muslims soon made conversion attractive to the opinion leaders in subject societies. The lands were conquered for Islam by the sword, but the populations were conquered by self-interest.

For many Middle Eastern and North African Christians conversion would have been eased by Islam's fierce monotheism—as were the conversions of many Balkan Christians when their homelands fell to the Turks almost a millennium later. Indeed, Sunni Islam rivals Judaism in its uncompromising monotheism, with both faiths suspicious of the hints of polytheism in the Christian trinity and, especially, in the almost Hindu Roman and Orthodox calendars of saints. The essential point is that the earliest Christian homelands were *conquered*. The Crusades that began barely four centuries later were viewed by Rome and those who took the cross as a reconquest, not as an invasion of virgin lands to which their faith had no claim.

By the gory fall of Jerusalem to the First Crusade in 1099 Christianity had become behaviorally unrecognizable. If anything, Islam had softened—Muslim chroniclers were shocked by the wholesale massacre of Muslims, Jews, and Eastern Christians in the holy city's streets. But the mild temper of Islam was as ephemeral as notions of Christians turning the other cheek. By the thirteenth century both faiths had hardened into the irreconcilable positions they maintain today.

But are the vestiges of each religion's birth still at play in the undercurrents of faith? Does Christianity's initial emphasis on nonviolence make it more amenable to compromise and coexistence? The historical evidence hardly supports it, although there is no pacifist strain at work in Islam today that rivals the antiwar voices in the West. Does the violent imagery of Islam's birth, with its stories of derring-do by the well-armed faithful, haunt the adult lives of children weaned on tales of battlefield glory won in the name of Allah? The Shia form of Islam was born not only in combat, but in a succession of disastrous battles lost through betrayals and conspiracies of the sort that poison the Middle East's psychology today.

Do religions gravitate toward a human center as they age? Or does the self-righteous strain especially evident in monotheist faiths propel all "no God but God" faiths toward belligerence? Did Christianity move toward behavioral common ground with other faiths as it matured and discovered the utility of weaponry? Islam, at least, does not seem to have lost its willingness to express devotion through violence.

That phantasmagorical rule book, the Koran, has an unedited Kerouac quality about it, as if Muhammad suffered from mood swings. Thus, justification may be found in its pages for almost any stance, from tolerance to persecution (although there is little justification for the slaughter of the innocents such as we see in Iraq as I write—only a few eccentric passages). But the same is true of the Bible. Christians did not jettison the Old Testament, with its rationales for genocide and its injunctions to godly intolerance.

Can Islam redeem itself? Can it become modern and tolerant? Can Muslim civilization rise like Lazarus? Or does its fate lie in a text that shunts women aside except as domestic slaves or playmates in Paradise, and in its early culture of the sword?

The omens are far from encouraging. In today's Middle East we see only a ghoulish spiritual revival that feeds on corpses. The great test case of our time will be Iraq.

The Bush administration made an amateur's mistake in using Saddam Hussein's ostensible possession of weapons of mass destruction as its sole rationale for eliminating his regime. Had the administration stressed Baathist atrocities, the genocide against the Kurds, and the killing fields dispersed throughout Iraq it would have been much harder for France, Germany, and anti-Americans everywhere to oppose our efforts. We could have shamed them with the corpses they sought to ignore. And we needed to be honest about our past complicity with Saddam—as well as about the craven greed of declined European states. When others pointed fingers at us for our support for Iraq in its war against Iran we could have said, "Yes, we made a mistake. Now we're going to fix it."

We also should have been forthright about oil. We didn't go to war to steal it (it would have been far cheaper to buy it), but oil security was unquestionably an issue. By insisting that oil wasn't a factor we played into the hands of cynics everywhere.

Those opportunities are lost now, but a vital one remains. With its divided population and a tradition of oppression, Iraq is the ultimate laboratory of change in the Middle East. The experiment under way will shape the region's future for decades to come.

As I write there is reason for optimism. The Iraqi elections of January 2005 were the closest thing to a miracle the Arab world has seen in a very long time. Defying death threats and bombs, millions of Iraqis stood in line to cast their ballots in the first truly free vote in the Arab world. They set an inspiring precedent. The myriad voices who insisted that "democracy can't work in the Middle East" have had to eat large portions of crow kebab. There is no guarantee that Iraqi democracy will strengthen and endure, but it made a proud and admirable debut.

For our part, we must content ourselves with the choices Iraqis make in the voting booth, even when they elect those whom we find suspect or vote to spite us. Democracy means accepting disappointments and allowing citizens to learn from their mistakes. The Iraqi role is to extend and protect the electoral process—and to write a just constitution. A state can claim to be truly democratic only after its third legitimate national election and at least one major transfer of power between parties. It is essential for Iraq to avoid another Arab variant of the "one-man, one-vote, one-time" model.

If we were troubled by the bloodshed leading up to Iraq's elections, we should be thrilled by the valor and determination of those who came out to vote, who believed that democracy was worth the risk of death.

The importance of Iraq's first free elections certainly was evident to the terrorists and old-guard Baathists. No matter the imperfections, the elections were a massive practical and symbolic defeat for their kind. The will of the people has never been respected through free and fair elections in the Middle East, not even in "golden age" Lebanon, where key government posts were apportioned in advance. All that changed in a day. Now it's up to Iraq's political parties to preserve and extend the rights the people deserve.

The elections of January 2005 undercut the terrorist and insurgent argument that we mean to stay in Iraq and exploit its resources. Iraq remains a challenge because our enemies realize the enormity of the stakes. Even a limping Arab (and Kurd) democracy that honors its own laws more often than not and generally respects human rights threatens to transform the entire region.

That is precisely why so many Middle Eastern governments have sought to inhibit the emergence of a legitimate and free Iraqi state. Short of sending in their uniformed militaries, Syria and Iran did all they could to subvert the occupation and Iraq's interim government. Turkey sulks and slows the passage of trade across its borders to a crawl. Jordan is in a defensive crouch. The Saudis have been quietly pleased to get rid of their extremist trash by neglecting to guard the routes to Iraq too closely. The lethargic government of Egypt dreads the dynamism of a true Arab democracy.

Yet even the resistance of regional states to the new Iraq has begun to soften—thanks to the terrorists. As Abu Musab al-Zarqawi and his followers engaged in no end of assassinations of Iraqi government officials, as well as of the intelligentsia, and as the car bombs targeted police stations and decapitation videos burned themselves into television and computer screens, the leadership cliques of the Arab states clinging to authoritarian models began to realize that, should the Iraqi experiment fail, terrorism will become an even more attractive tool. And their regimes are the obvious next targets.

The Saudi royal family is terrified by what it has conjured through its decades of support for religious fanatics—and it can no longer count on the United States to turn a blind eye to its sins. Desperate to secure a hereditary throne for his son, Egypt's latest pharaoh cannot afford internal discord and is now attempting to stage-manage "free" elections. Turkey has begun to have second thoughts about its intransigence, fearing that should Iraq collapse, the United States will guarantee the world's first independent Kurdish state on its borders (and a good thing, too!). Even Syria has tempered its support for the international terrorists in Iraq, although it continues to back the Baathist renegades. And the Palestinians are afraid that their post-Arafat chance for an independent state will collapse in an attempted terrorist takeover.

Only Iran's slowly eroding government of mullahs, vengeful and calculating falsely, continues to support terror in Iraq without remorse. With 70 percent of Iran's population under the age of thirty and overwhelmingly disaffected, the core members of Iran's government believe that they can only survive by exporting their Khomeinist revolution. They want a religious government in Iraq, but will settle for civil war.

Fortunately, direct clerical rule is unlikely to find much traction in Baghdad, although the influence of the mullahs may remain excessive for our tastes. Iran, on the other hand, has already passed the apogee of clerical influence.

Iraq's internal problems are terrorism, a ruthless insurgency, corruption, and ethnic and religious rivalries. Its external problem, even greater than the ill will of Arab regimes, is the global anti-Americanism, that product of failure and jealousy that makes so many leaders and opinion makers impatient to declare Iraq a failure (much harder in the wake of Iraq's first free—and massively popular—elections). Those who yearn for an American embarrassment are even more shortsighted than the Bush administration amateurs who put all of their propaganda eggs in the WMD basket.

If Iraq ultimately fails to gel as a rule-of-law democracy, America can go home. Washington will eat a few plates of humble pie, then work it off in the strategic gym. But the Middle East would be left with a terrorist homeland at its heart and the Arab world would have damning evidence that it can't compete in the race for the future, that authoritarian regimes remain its only choice. That hopelessness would leave millions more unemployed young Muslim males as prey for terrorist recruiters. Operation Iraqi Freedom did not so much create a wave of new terrorists as it drew out the legions of dead-enders bred during the West's long neglect of the extremist menace.

Now it's really up to the Iraqis. If we do not see an ever-increasing willingness to ally across ethnic and religious lines in order to defend the great opportunity that has been given them, that will be a worse sign than any series of suicide bombings. Their first nationwide elections were a proud beginning. But they were only a beginning.

Can the people of Iraq save themselves? Will they? Or must Arabs fail? Can the legacy of violence, suspicion, and betrayal bred into Islam's bones be transformed into cooperation between age-old enemies? Or will the hatreds of the Middle East trump self-interest yet again?

We do not know. Neither do the Iraqis, although they've given us reason to hope. But we had to take the chance we took. The alternative was to wait for a grand disaster.

We cannot force the Iraqis to succeed. We can put the training wheels on the bicycle of state, but the Iraqis must ride it themselves. No one can accurately calculate the odds that they will do so successfully over the long term, but the Middle East so desperately needs a success story, one Muslim state that has taken the path to modernity and democracy, that every sacrifice we have made and every loss we have suffered has been a worthwhile investment in our own future—no matter the ultimate outcome.

There are times when the fight itself matters, even if you fail in the end. Our much decried involvement in Indochina allowed the rest of Southeast Asia to develop without suffering the inhuman experiment of Communism. We did not hold the line where we hoped to hold it, but history will judge us far more charitably than our doctrinaire contemporaries. Even should our engagement in Iraq end up as no more than a long, disappointing punitive expedition, we had to act because no one else would do so.

We have carried the battle against terrorism to the breeding grounds of fanaticism in the broken civilization of the Middle East. Afghanistan is already far better off than it was, and Iraq is likely to be at least a partial, satisfactory success. But setting even those considerations aside, it remains far better to fight a war on your enemy's soil than on your own. And we have taken the war our enemies began into their heartlands.

We will not know the true outcome of our involvement in Iraq for at least a decade, possibly not for a generation. Our appetite for instant results will never be satisfied by the Middle East, where problems run so deep that the changes essential to progress will require much of this century—*if* they are embraced by the region's populations.

The chances remain strong that we will see a positive outcome in Iraq. But if that country fails, it will not be an American failure. It will be yet another tragic Arab loss.

Seventeen

THE GODDESS OF THE SOUTHERN SEAS

Whenever the State Department issues a travel warning for any location in Southeast Asia, I know exactly what I'll find when I get there: Australians drinking beer around the pool. That is what I found when I reached Solo.

After literally wading through Jakarta during the flood of 2002 I flew down to Yogyakarta, Java's cultural capital, where the women I encountered made it clear that they think Muslim fundamentalists are nuts. Our embassy, intimidated by a handful of demonstrators trudging about with placards, had declared the city of Solo, just up the road from Yogya, as much too dangerous for travelers, since Solo was the home of Abubakr Ba'asyir's extremist religious school and the headquarters for the Mujahidin Council of Indonesia. Reading the warning, one might have expected roadblocks and daylight kidnappings, followed by torture and death.

Of course, there was nothing of the sort. Solo is a pleasant, drowsy city where Australians, Americans, or anyone else may drink a poolside beer with impunity. Although Ba'asyir certainly had been involved with terrorism (as of this writing, he's under indictment for the second time), he was not about to make a mess in his own backyard. On the single occasion when a handful of students from his ratty little school got carried away and invaded a few cheap hotels in the wake of the first U.S. strikes on the Taliban, Ba'asyir called them off immediately. Like most grand advocates of terror, he does not care to put himself at risk. The local citizenry regard him as a nuisance.

Although it has nothing to do with Ba'asyir, there is, indeed, a large "fundamentalist" Muhammadiye University at the edge of the city, the sort of institution that alarms our State Department. The university has nothing to do with terror and has not produced a single violent actor. On the contrary, men and women study together on a handsome, up-to-date campus where computers are as much in evidence as the Koran. The girls dress demurely and the boys are polite. All are wonderfully curious about the United States. More than anything else the campus resembles an American Bible college, except that the Indonesian Muslim students are more interested in science. Our diplomats won't go near it.

Instead of conjuring bogeymen from nothing, our credentialed representatives in Indonesia should miss no opportunity to interact with such students or to visit the campuses of the various Muhammadiye universities as volunteer lecturers. But our diplomats and their underlings cling to capital cities, pleading crushing workloads, rancid with self-importance.

Still, there was far more to Solo than sunburned Aussies and hospitable young Muslims. The city does have a reputation for being devout (Solo's citizens had been ardent Communists in the Sukarno years; one religion served them as well as another). Its residents consider themselves impeccable Muslims, and they certainly don't have a local nightlife to rival Jakarta's libertinism. But the local folks do have a quirk or two that drives the Saudi financiers of bigotry mad.

The grandest annual event for Solo's Muslims occurs when the *susuhunan,* or sultan, opens the grounds of the *kraton,* his compact palace park, for a communal celebration. As many as thirty thousand people crowd inside the walls. Their purpose? To join the sultan—a fervent Muslim himself—in paying the city's respects to the Goddess of the Southern Seas.

Trust me: She's not in the Koran. And polytheism is the gravest offense in "pure" Islam.

Indonesia is the world's most populous Muslim country, with two hundred million of the faithful composing more than 90 percent of the inhabitants of the state's seventeen thousand islands, great and small. But the most striking thing about Islam in Indonesia is its variety, along with its commonsensical good health. Among two hundred million Muslims you can always find a few perverted believers, and anti-Americanism *is* a global fashion statement (in Indonesia, it quickly devolves into a request for aid in gaining a U.S. visa). But Islam in Indonesia ranges from the Arabian rigor of Aceh at the extreme western tip of Sumatra (devastated by the 2004 tsunami) to the surreal beliefs of the Bugis on Sulawesi—or that ceremony in Solo in honor of the Goddess of the Southern Seas.

The goddess is an old Javanese deity, a traditional protector of the island's people. Animism and folk spirits continue to play a powerful role in rural Islam, but they also retain a hold on the upper classes. If questioned, educated believers deny it at first—then they turn to a shaman or pray to a tree when their prospects look bleak. Nor is it only a matter of lingering folk beliefs. Both Hinduism and Buddhism prevailed far longer on the islands that became Indonesia than Islam has (Bali remains Hindu, while Sulawesi and other islands have significant Christian populations). On Java and the outer islands Islam itself was heavily influenced by "saints" and teachers from the last bright twilight of Sufism in the sixteenth and seventeenth centuries, before that strain of Islam became the champion of ignorance.

This matters. Because nearly all of the forms of Islam at play in Indonesia are inherently more humane than any at work in the Middle East, where the health inspired by competitive belief systems long has been squandered in spiritual dissipation. Islam *will* evolve. But it is most apt to do so on its frontiers, from Michigan to the Straits of Malacca, where it does not suffer the inbreeding that has crippled the faith of the Arabs.

With Washington's genius for missing opportunities, we warned our citizens away from Indonesia after 9/11, gutting the country's tourism industry and further limiting contact with Americans. (Before a skull spiked on a beer bottle persuaded me that I should retrace my steps, a native Christian up-country on Sulawesi asked me, at the height of a pagan ceremony, "Are there Christians in America, sir?")

When not bullying the Jakarta government over one thing or another we abandon our policy to a few mining interests and businessmen whose shenanigans would not be tolerated in our own country. And we write off the world's largest population of Muslims at a time when the faith of the Prophet has reached a decisive crossroads.

That isn't a policy. It's indolence.

The United States responded with alacrity and generosity to the tsunami that struck the Indonesian island of Sumatra on December 26, 2004. Whether our efforts will accelerate a return to healthy relations between Washington and Jakarta remains to be seen (one hopes that Indonesia, vibrant and vital, will at least hold our attention for a time), but the greatest stumbling block impeding constructive relations is the refusal on the part of the United States to understand how Javanese culture, especially, works.

The core issue dividing us has been the role of Indonesian military officers in human rights violations in East Timor and elsewhere in the 1990s—before the old regime fell and the country became a democracy. Without question, the United States should seek to advance the cause of human rights and to support justice for all. But if we mean to make a difference, rather than simply engage in counterproductive fits of public self-righteousness, we must heed the rules under which other societies function.

Public confrontation doesn't work with Indonesians. By issuing statements and holding press conferences, self-appointed human rights advocates may gain opportunities to preen, but they will not get to the guilty. Working with Indonesians you must accept that the greatest progress is made behind closed doors. Insisting that Jakarta do things the American way is a prescription for failure, not least because we put the Indonesian government—which now must answer to a proud electorate—in the position of either appearing to cave in to American pressure or standing up to Washington. Even when Indonesia's leaders want to cooperate our public condemnations force them into a combative stance. With slovenly good intentions we have managed to rally the people around abusers they otherwise would have disdained. We made the implementation of justice harder than it would have been had we pursued human rights violators more quietly and less fitfully.

It bewilders me that we insist on punishing now democratic Indonesia for deeds committed under a vanquished dictator. By that standard we should still be avoiding military contact with Germany. Indonesia not only has seen multiple democratic turnovers of power in less than a decade, but its various population groups have rejected Islamic extremism at the polls. Meanwhile, both our government and human rights organizations make a whipping boy of a state determined to become a robust, rule-of-law democracy while ignoring the vastly worse abuses in states such as Saudi Arabia, Zimbabwe, Cuba, or even Russia. Such disgraceful selectivity does not deter the world's torturers.

Human rights should not be used as a partisan political issue. The same standards must be applied universally (although the means to attain those standards will vary). This means that those on the left must be willing to condemn Fidel Castro or Robert Mugabe, while those on the right must stop making excuses for the degenerate House of Saud.

Certainly we should pursue justice against human rights abusers everywhere, nor should we ever relent in our pursuit of them. But if we seek meaningful results and not mere self-gratification or cheap applause, we must study how best to achieve justice in societies whose norms often differ profoundly from our own. Had we simply treated Indonesia's successive governments with respect and cultural sensitivity we would have advanced the essential cause of human rights much further than we have done through insults, slights, and acrimony.

Washington needs to make a new start with Indonesia, a country that already has made its own fresh start through courage and common sense. It's we who are prisoners of the past, not the Indonesians. Our posturing and proclamations have done enormous and unnecessary damage. We have undercut our own influence through our vanity and ignorance. If we wish to influence the greatly improved human rights situation in that sprawling country we need to engage Indonesia on its own cultural terms, not as if it were a recalcitrant colony. The future of Islam is in play in that most populous Muslim country. And all we do is blow raspberries from the bleachers.

———————

Indonesia matters not only because of its potential to serve as a crucible for the Islam of the future, but because of its incomparable location. A growing proportion of the oil leaving the Middle East, and the trade entering the Indian Ocean, passes through shipping choke points adjacent to Indonesia. The country's value as a strategic partner climbs still higher when Indonesia is considered as part of a greater whole, the subworld of the Indian Ocean littoral, stretching from South Africa northward along the old Swahili Coast, curving past the Arab heartlands and Iran, hastening by Pakistan, embracing the timeless prospects and frustrations of India as well as the wrenching failure of Bangladesh, lapping the eccentric successes to the east of the Bay of Bengal, then rounding Singapore to stretch across Indonesia to Australia. No portion of the globe has so great a remaining potential for development. The greater Indian Ocean will be at least as important as a strategic entity in the twenty-first century as it was in the sixteenth.

India, the centerpiece of the Indian Ocean arena, will continue to progress and disappoint. Its hi-tech city-states have begun to define an alternative model of development in which entrepreneurial locales break with the subcontinent's bureaucratic lethargy and even Hinduism's insuperable cruelty to create islands of success in a sea of failure. India's peculiar strength is that two hundred million of its billion inhabitants are perfectly willing to dismiss the fates of the other eight hundred million in order to secure their own well-being. The hardest knack for an outsider to acquire is the middle-class Indian's ability not to see the misery around him. That nonchalant cruelty allows a social ruthlessness paralleled elsewhere only by savage regimes.

India is moving forward, awkwardly and fitfully, but unmistakably. And the simple fact that the world's largest democracy continues to survive should impress us all. India is one of the few countries cobbled together by an imperial power that appears likely to maintain its territorial integrity (with the possible exception of a portion of Kashmir). There never was a unified India, not even under the Mughals, until Britain created a central administration. And India has had more obstacles to overcome than countries even more destitute and divided. The caste system is the very opposite of a meritocracy, an insidious means of resource allocation designed thousands of years ago to guarantee that the priestly and warrior castes would have first claim on power, goods, and foodstuffs in times of turmoil or famine. The message that the gods have decreed that specific classes of individuals must suffer willingly if they want a better deal in a life to come isn't exclusive to India, but nowhere else has it been so meanly perfected. While the caste system is just beginning to weaken among the educated classes (a work visa for the United States jumps a marriage partner up the caste ladder), it continues to suppress talent to a degree that cripples the country and dehumanizes the society. The most lunatic myth ever propagated in the West is that there is a humane "wisdom of the East."

The government of India has launched no end of programs to ameliorate the harsh barrier of caste; worthwhile, their effect over the years has been discouragingly slight. And the curse of caste is exacerbated by the exuberant corruption in India's government and business community (two faces of the same dominant society within a society). On top of both these plagues, the timing of India's hour of independence could not have been worse. The new state arrived just at the hour when socialism appeared to be humankind's destiny, and for almost half a century India pursued economic policies for which the word "idiotic" may be too gentle. The combination of protectionism, government-stamped monopolies, antibusiness policies, nationalization, and swollen state payrolls created an environment in which corruption not only thrived but was necessary if the economy wasn't to come to a dead halt.

The stirring rhetoric of the left has been responsible for boundless human misery. The words are lovely, the promises seductive, and the reality miserable. The first four decades after India's 1947 independence should be studied in every business school and political science department as the perfect case study in how to destroy the potential of a talented population.

And India's population *is* talented. Nowhere else in the world is there such a reservoir of reasonably well-educated (often superbly educated) citizens who remain either underemployed or unemployed. Perversely, the venal politicans in New Delhi welcome the export of their number one product—human capital—to the United States, since it both generates revenue and alleviates societal pressures back home— it's the educated, not the ignorant, who make political trouble. A gift for the United States, the flight of India's best and brightest is the surest sign of the society's disabilities.

For all this, there are hopeful indicators. A new generation of Indian leaders has begun to shrug off the straitjacket of socialist policies, while the country's youth are aggressive, hardheaded realists. The success of cities such as Bangalore and Hyderabad, trailed anxiously by Madras/Chennai, New Delhi, and a few other urban areas, signposts one path to development. Yet it is only one path, and India needs multiple routes forward. Not everyone can be employed writing software or answering telephoned complaints. This is a land of massive human potential—as well as of strategic possibilities—that deserves an even richer engagement on the part of Washington than our recent rapprochement. For all its deficiencies, India is a great potential ally and partner of the United States, and we should patiently nurture a relationship that benefits both sides by seeking common ground (even when we must briefly swallow our pride).

Meanwhile, India needs new visionaries, figures who can persuade a bigoted population to embrace systemic changes against which demagogues have warned them for generations. Calcutta, India's most seductive city, offers a classic example of what went wrong. Despite its horrid reputation, Calcutta has a resilience and style that I, for one, find inspiring. The people just won't—can't—give up. Shabby poets (isn't every Bengali a poet?) meet in coffeehouses whose walls have mottled to various shades of brown, discussing literature as if it were life's one essential; the women are as proud as they are elegant; and the corpses one occasionally jogs over during a morning run are gathered up with reasonable efficiency. The people have sudden smiles whose beauty I have seen rivaled only in Africa, although the city teems with human detritus.

The "city of dreadful night" has a population that treasures education and will sacrifice for it. It's heartbreaking to visit Calcutta's central library, housed in a decaying colonial building where students defy the heat to study sweat-blackened computer manuals that were out of date a decade ago. There is no money to buy newer texts and the young do their best with the crumbs that Communist city governments have left them.

Calcutta's tragedy was that its government meant well. Enchanted by the promises of Marx, Lenin, and homegrown crackpots, elected Communists chose policies that gave to the poor directly—and swiftly bankrupted an already impoverished city. Education was slighted in favor of make-work jobs and direct handouts (the states and cities that gave precedence to education are India's relative success stories today). Yet the Bengali tradition of learning persisted. Then, in the late 1980s, the city fathers made a mistake that cripples Calcutta's prospects unto this day.

They banned computers. From municipal offices, from businesses, from any site where their legislative powers reached. The Communists argued that computers were a capitalist plot to deprive the workers of jobs by eliminating the human factor. As a result, country cousin Bangalore became a boomtown while great Calcutta moldered. Today the hapless rulers of Calcutta realize their folly and have been trying to recover lost ground, praising computers and creating dusty business parks. But time lost in the race for prosperity can rarely be regained in such a cutthroat environment. Hyderabad, Madras/Chennai, New Delhi, Bombay/Mumbai, and other cities offer better living conditions, a more adept workforce, and, above all, the critical mass of businesses, educational institutions, and services that entice new investors to the proven ground.

Like so many other states that gained their independence before socialist economics were exposed as a merciless fraud, India still must wait for those aging politicians, professors, and opinion leaders who were infected by socialist mumbo jumbo to die off. From Africa to Latin America, the generational transition between the old believers and the new pragmatists may inaugurate the greatest positive change in the developing world since the independence years. The worst thing we could wish for developing states would be good health for those whose crackpot philosophies ruined them.

India is at the beginning of a wave of change that will last for generations and alter not only the subcontinent but all of its strategic tributaries. We need to get to the party early on.

————————

Our long-term need to cultivate a strategic partnership with India is hampered at present by the requirement to work with Pakistan against the region's terrorists. But it is unlikely that Pakistan will become a just and prosperous state within our lifetimes. Cooperation will always be welcome, but our future lies with India, to the degree that we must choose. Our goal in the Muslim realms between Fez and Islamabad will be to limit the menace the region poses, but our goal in India would be to encourage the population's extraordinary potential. While India suffers from the self-destructive pride of the poor cousin—and its military ambitions need to be tempered—Washington and New Delhi are equally to blame for past acrimony. We need to work hard, even to occasionally swallow our pride, to bury the lunatic nonsense of the Non-Aligned Movement, in which alliances between failures in the southern hemisphere pretended to rival the coalitions of the successful in the northern hemisphere. The age of empty rhetoric is dying. We need to help states such as India give birth to a new age of realism—and to recognize that lavish pronouncements are no substitute for earnest efforts.

The stakes are incalculably high. The strategic arena of the Indian Ocean includes over two billion souls, from those "Asian tigers" now missing a tooth or two to the postmodern empire South Africa is building. As I saw for myself from Burma/Myanmar to Africa, China long ago began to look south in search of strategic influence, secure oil-supply routes, and a naval outlet that challenges America's global reach. Despite our own military presence in the Indian Ocean and our recent adventures on land just to the north (Iraq is part of the same strategic calculus), we have not built up the well-rounded alliances essential to hegemony, leaving a tempting strategic vacuum for regional powers and ambitious states beyond.

This is a great danger to us, to the region, and to world peace. The hard lesson of the past five hundred years is that the Indian Ocean needs a decided hegemon, whether Portuguese, British, or, however reluctantly, American. We need not be so overt or dictatorial as were the colonial powers, but if we do not increase our de facto control of the sea-lanes and international airspace, we will only encourage the Chinese to meddle and the Indians to exceed their strategic resources— perhaps at great cost. We must have tacit mastery of the sea and sky, along with the ability to project power ashore when it proves necessary. The Indian Ocean may well become the crucial strategic cockpit of the twenty-first century.

In a sense, it already is. The oil leaving the Persian Gulf traverses Indian Ocean waters, whether on the short route to the Suez Canal or following the ancient trade routes southward along the African coast or southeast to satisfy the ever-increasing appetites of Asia. No network of pipelines could replace those sea-lanes. Interdict them, and the world grows silent and dark.

Imagine if Islamic terrorists possessed sufficient nuclear weapons to interrupt traffic through the Suez Canal—which they would not hesitate to do, since economic damage to existing regimes furthers their purposes, and such an attack would wound the West as well. Suddenly the sea-lanes off the coast of East Africa would regain an importance they had lost by the premiere of *Aida*, which celebrated the age-old dream of a navigable passage between the Mediterranean and Red seas. Whether repairs to the canal took months or years, the power that controlled the Indian Ocean sea-lanes would control the world.

It had better be us.

Oil supplies, growing commercial possibilities, potential strategic partnerships—and the enduring struggle between the West and Islam. The Indian Ocean is a laboratory of human possibilities, many of them encouraging and profound. But even in the shorter term we must recognize what the Portuguese saw half a millennium ago: Naval control of its sea-lanes and choke points commands the Middle East's sources of wealth. Then it was the spice trade; today it's the oil trade. Tomorrow it may be primarily the movement of human capital (a thankfully more benign echo of the slave trade that cursed those waters for centuries). But the Indian Ocean is at once a theater for the taking and a realm of opportunity. By nurturing alliances—and keeping our tempers—with the states beyond the Arab fringe of the ocean's littoral we can acquire a strategic insurance policy for the long term, in case Arab experiments with governmental and societal evolution disappoint us. Should things go well we may be glad to facilitate the Middle East's integration into the world. But should affairs go badly we will need to contain the region.

The Arabs remain the nagging strategic problem. Turkey may go sour or stumble forward. Pakistan could fragment or continue to muddle through. If only a crisis can be postponed, friendless Iran, Islam's stepchild, is apt to look westward again for strategic adoption. But Arab progress, if it comes, will be fitful and frustrating, slow and costly. We have no choice but to engage, yet our involvement is little more than a catalyst. The Arabs need to desire positive change sufficiently to bring it into being for themselves. We cannot afford to turn away—our enemies would only pursue us. But we need to recognize that the Middle

East is already an area of diminishing strategic returns on our investments. If we are unlucky, those returns may prove entirely negative.

Nonetheless, our obsessive, exclusive focus on the problems of the Middle East blinds us to the grand opportunities elsewhere—almost entirely in the "greater" Southern Hemisphere. Much is made of China, whether by defense contractors who intend to frighten us into extravagant purchases of arms, or by businessmen who would sell America down the river (or up the Yangtze) for a summer house in the Hamptons. But China's market will never provide as much strategic benefit to us as our market provides to Beijing. As is so often the case, a mafia of American corporations holds our policy hostage. The profit of a few costs us strategic freedom of action and dangerous trade deficits.

With our government prevented from attempting to level the playing field of trade, China is, in its very different way, as much a region of diminishing returns on our investments of strategic capital as the Middle East. Nor will Japan suddenly become a field of opportunity. We need to build constructive relationships with all of the powers of East Asia—to the extent we are able to do so without foolish compromises—but we also must realize that the much touted "Pacific century" offers us far less than we have been promised.

Look southward. Toward Africa, that perennially insulted continent. Toward Latin America, our limping twin. And toward the Indian Ocean and its powers in waiting.

Late in the last century leaders from the developing world insisted on a new world order that would hand them for free what they did not deign to earn. Fortunately for all concerned the handouts never arrived. As a result, a new sense of realism, of almost American pragmatism, is breaking out in unexpected places. There will be a "new world order" along with a shift of strategic competition, a growth in wealth, and a long overdue opening to neglected human resources. It will happen in the "expanded" Southern Hemisphere.

We are that entire hemisphere's natural partner, but we have some convincing to do.

Eighteen
NOT-SO-DARK CONTINENTS

I stood on the rampart of a derelict fortress in Mozambique staring into our future. My eyes were turned toward the Indian Ocean, past an abandoned church on the shore below, the oldest surviving European structure in the southern hemisphere. Had I turned around 180 degrees to look across the bay that separates the Ilha do Moçambique from the mainland, I might have seen a startling African future—and our own again.

Among the dreary policy circles of Washington the easiest way to derail a discussion about strategic priorities is to mention Africa. Except for the occasional congressional basket-buying excursion (if Rome's booked up and the weather's bad in Prague), Washington's sorcerers and their apprentices do *not* go to Africa. They know all they need to know: Africa is riddled with AIDS, plagued by tribal wars and strongmen, illiterate, bankrupt, and hopeless.

Except that it isn't. The general accusations may apply to specific countries, but Washington's haste to dismiss an entire continent as unworthy of our attention is in equal parts racism and intellectual sloth. It means that while picking incessantly at the scabs of the Middle East we miss unprecedented strategic developments that are changing the southern half of Africa. From Congo northward, Africa *is* in trouble—and the trouble is getting worse, from Ivory Coast to Sudan. But Africa is no more a single piece of humanity than is Europe or Asia. And a new African civilization is spreading slowly northward from Johannesburg.

While we remain happily mired in yesterday's priorities, from defending dysfunctional borders to keeping diseased regimes on life support, the Republic of South Africa is methodically building the greatest indigenous empire in Africa's history. It will be a postmodern empire similar to our own, an empire of economic power and cultural subversion, of power politics and social example, but not one of outright occupation or military oppression. Yet it *is* an empire of conscious design, sometimes unscrupulous, but largely beneficial to the region (as America's empire is beneficial to the world).

The process under way is easy to miss. When journalists or policy makers descend—briefly—on South Africa they encounter the three groups of people who remain hostile to America in developing societies: politicians imprisoned in the rhetoric of the liberation struggle; professors for whom left-wing tenets are a pleasant substitute for serious thought; and journalists whose politics rarely reflect the views of the average citizen, whether in the United States, the United Kingdom, Syria, China, or India. One of the few certainties in the tumult of civilizations is that there is no country on earth where the intelligentsia genuinely cares about the average man or woman.

Thus, our official eyes and ears, whether lawmakers or scribblers, miss the social ferment while imagining that the rear-guard action fought against the future by professors, pundits, and politicians reflects a country's yearning and its destiny.

Talk to businessmen instead. To working men and women. To anyone who must forge their way ahead through practical acumen and labor. You'll get a very different, more pro-American story. Africa is open to American influence. Only in America do the children of Africa enjoy governmental power, wealth, and respect outside of the continent of their ancestors. Cuba's model has failed. Brazil remains a land where the rich are white and the poor are black. Europe is as bigoted now as it was a hundred years ago (although it makes a half-hearted effort to hide the fact). The Arabs and their fellow Muslims were history's great slavers and they despise black skins to this day.

Where can Africa look for a model for its own development, for inspiration, for hope? Only to the United States of America. And Africans do, whether we speak of savvy businessmen in Capetown or anti-French demonstrators in Abidjan waving signs that read: "Mr. Bush, save us from Old Europe."

Unexpectedly but wisely, George W. Bush has shown more practical goodwill toward Africa than any previous president. Clinton said much but did little. He simply looked away during the Rwandan genocide. In contrast, Bush pushed for $15 billion to fight AIDS in Africa and the Caribbean. The gesture so startled the world that our traditional opponents could only complain about the largesse, demanding that those who gave nothing themselves should dictate how American funds are spent. But the effort resounded among the people of Africa.

The ravages of AIDS are real enough, even in that most hopeful of the continent's states, South Africa. From the ostentatious funerals in suburban slums to the silent misery of teenage girls wasting away in the hinterlands, the destructive fury of AIDS starts to seem omnipresent to a visitor who does more than fly in, visit a game park, then go home. Linear analysis would suggest that the infection rate—perhaps 30 percent in South Africa and as bad or worse elsewhere—will destroy Africa's future. And given the virulence with which AIDS strikes the professional class, whose earning power grants access to more sexual partners, the pessimists may prove right. Yet the Black Death, which killed between a third and two thirds of Europe's population, unleashed the energies that led to the Renaissance and the Age of Exploration. Surplus labor became deficit labor and feudalism withered. AIDS may have a similar effect on the tribal system that plagues so much of Africa today—indeed, South Africa's great strength has been the ability of its elite to build coalitions across multiple ethnic and racial lines.

Or AIDS may simply devastate an already struggling continent. We cannot know for now. But it's all too easy—and foolish—to assume the worst when much of the practical evidence runs to the contrary. Catastrophe unleashes human genius.

South Africa has deep tribal rivalries at the street level, massive unemployment and a dangerously strong political party, the African National Congress, which threatens to become immovably dominant. But it also has a great if accidental advantage that jumps it ahead of India psychologically.

The apartheid system was monstrous and inexcusable. But in another of history's paradoxes, the ability of that system to hang on into the early 1990s freed the reborn country from the worst excesses of socialism. This is certainly not meant as an apology for apartheid, which was heinous. But had the ANC managed to gain power thirty years earlier, at a time when every African state felt compelled to seek statist solutions to economic challenges, the country might have failed as badly as the former colonies to the north. With uncanny symmetry, South Africa's black majority—along with its "colored" and mixed-race residents—gained power just after the Soviet collapse and the rejection of Communism and socialism by one former Soviet satellite or subject state after another. Suddenly, the red emperor had no clothes. It was painfully evident to all except the professors and a few reality-resistant journalists that South Africa would need to embrace capitalist methods, even if they were cloaked in the slogans of the freedom struggle.

South Africa's elite—black, brown, and white—signed up for capitalism with an enthusiasm that is bringing the country an empire. Key figures within the government and the business community know full well what they are doing, although they would never admit it publicly. After grasping with surprising speed that they could all grow rich by working together, political and business leaders of every race formed coalitions that would have seemed impossible a dozen years ago.

To understand what South Africa is doing I had to go to Zimbabwe and then, a year later, to Mozambique. In Zimbabwe I got only part of the picture. The former breadbasket of southern Africa and the great African success story of the 1980s (despite massacres an indulgent West preferred to overlook), Zimbabwe has seen its economy shattered, along with the hopes of the great majority of its citizens, no matter their tribe. The country is hungry, tormented, and needlessly impoverished.

A single man did the damage: Robert Mugabe, a president for life who deals in death. Although white farmers played into Mugabe's hands by dragging their feet before turning over the least scraps of land to blacks, Mugabe's farm seizures put over a million black Zimbabweans out of work and drove the people from sufficiency down to a level of poverty at which the lines for basic foodstuffs in Harare, the capital city, were longer than any I ever saw in the Soviet Union. Except for the well connected, there was no fuel and precious little to eat. Food aid was used as a weapon by the government, and thuggish violence reigned. A few whites prospered by collaborating with Mugabe, but most fled, taking their expertise with them (neighboring countries have welcomed the extraordinarily capable—and tough—Zimbabwean farmers). So recently a jewel, the country became a disaster area where fine human beings were turned into beggars by a "hero of the liberation struggle."

The government of South Africa refuses to criticize Robert Mugabe. I assumed, at first, that this was the typical defense of a fellow freedom fighter by the aging leaders of the liberation movement, the solidarity of men who had suffered together and did not care to admit to a gloating West that one of their own had gone bad. And the South Africans argued that opposing Mugabe would only precipitate a total collapse in Zimbabwe, flooding South Africa's overcrowded squatter settlements with more refugees than the country could accommodate.

The latter explanation made little sense to me. It seemed clear that the greater danger of the crisis worsening lay in doing nothing, in letting Mugabe spend himself far beyond bankruptcy (he had been mortgaging property and granting vast concessions to the Libyans for fuel and to the mainland Chinese for goods, arms, and financial support). I couldn't understand how South Africa's leaders, who had been so perceptive in so many other regards, could fail to see the danger—or ignore the human tragedy—a mad, octogenarian dictator was visiting upon twelve million of their fellow Africans.

In Mozambique, I got it. Mozambique remains one of the world's poorest countries, ravaged by a generation of civil war (sponsored first by the Rhodesian intelligence services, then maintained by South Africa's apartheid regime). After making a herculean effort to rebuild, it was ravaged by the worst flooding in a century. But it's impossible not to like and admire Mozambicans, whether the Christians of the south, the easygoing Muslims of the north, or the practitioners of indigenous religions in the back country. (Christians and Muslims alike are quick to turn to traditional healers or seers when the going gets tough—nothing against Christ or Muhammad, but Mozambicans like to hedge their bets; in remote Muslim settlements in the north Allah slips off at twilight and witchcraft's drums still punctuate the night.)

Mozambicans are uncomplaining and hardworking, and they are not beggars. They have an almost Indian appetite for education, but schools and universities are sorely lacking. The government, after jettisoning its socialist nonsense in the 1980s, became a developmental model for the world aid community. It's even fighting corruption, although the struggle is difficult in such a poor country (Pakistani and Nigerian criminals use Maputo as a safe haven and a transit point for drugs). Elections have been quite fair by regional standards. Even bitter enemies from the civil war have found their way onto the ballot and into regional positions of authority. Considering the alternating negligence and brutality of the centuries of Portuguese colonization, Mozambique could easily have become the sort of wreck we see in once hopeful Liberia or Sierra Leone in West Africa.

But the thing that slapped me across the snout was the omnipresence of South African "partnerships," investments, businesses, and commodities. Pretoria's insiders cracked a code in Mozambique that they are now applying in Zimbabwe and elsewhere. Another perverse benefit accrued to the new South Africa because of the apartheid regime's misdeeds: The civil war funded first by Salisbury, then by Pretoria, had devastated Mozambique with horrifying thoroughness. When peace arrived at last the country needed everything and had no money for anything. Although it had undeveloped gas reserves (and possibly oil), it relied on exports such as cashews and shrimp—and even such straightforward trade had been debased by socialist inanity.

Working with Mozambican front men, South Africans began buying up the country at fire-sale prices. South African firms have built excellent toll roads in a country where the "national highways" are often rugged trails; revamped the strategic port terminals serving Maputo and its industrial suburbs; invaded the cellular communications market (essential in a country with few phone lines); built discount supermarkets and a major gas pipeline; gained authority over a crucial hydroelectric project on the Zambezi; taken over hotels, car dealerships, trade associations, and free-port facilities. And what they do not own in quiet partnerships with pliable locals they manage and control indirectly. Free Mozambique is South Africa's economic colony. On the positive side, this spurs much needed development. But it also creates a debtor nation whose policies must answer to Pretoria. (In any case, the ties are intimate: South Africa's former president, Nelson Mandela, is married to the widow of Mozambique's liberation-era hero, Samora Machel.)

Not coincidentally, the South Africans have concentrated on

transport matters. Mozambique's three main arteries into Africa's interior offer economic control over Zimbabwe, Malawi, southern Zambia, and lesser states. This is strategic genius. An economic superpower by African standards, with the region's premier military, South Africa will soon have a choke hold on the southern third of the continent.

Mozambique was the model. With astonishing cynicsm South Africa is allowing Mugabe to destroy Zimbabwe because Pretoria's cabal of insiders realize that everything Mugabe wrecks will have to be rebuilt. And Zimbabwe, already deeply in debt to South Africa, will have to turn to its southerly neighbor for reconstruction assistance. Further, Zimbabwe's fine agricultural lands, its devastated infrastructure and ruined businesses, and its share in the Zambezi hydroelectric project will all be for sale at a few cents on the dollar. Thus, South Africa continues to supply electricity, goods, and services to Zimbabwe, letting Mugabe run up the tab. Zimbabwe's suffering is to South Africa's strategic advantage.

So much for revolutionary—or African—solidarity. Even Beijing's investments in Zimbabwe will survive only at Pretoria's sufferance.

South Africa has already reached beyond the continent, as well, from headquartering corporations in London to buying the American brewer, Miller, as well as beer producers from the Czech Republic to China (where SABMiller is willing to operate at a loss for years to secure market share). South African businessmen and politicians are thinking at a strategic level that should embarrass Washington's elite.

And the South Africans, with a legacy of British law, are battling internal corruption even as they foster it abroad. While justice is not always done in South African courts and corruption remains plentiful, South Africa's business masters have realized (as Las Vegas casino owners eventually did) that more money can be made through legal means than illegally. Sailing off Capetown, I spoke with a South African businesswoman who represented an oil services firm. We were speaking about the difficulties of doing business in Africa when she shook her head and told me, "I hate going to Lagos. Nigerians are so hopelessly corrupt…"

Those were revolutionary words in Africa.

———————

While South Africa is extending its hegemony northward, the aging revolutionary generation and its acolytes are either dying off or embracing capitalism. The current president, Thabo Mbeki, lacks Nelson Mandela's stature or moral grandeur, and he succumbs now and again to the folly of antique anti-Western rhetoric or the outright madness of denying a link between sex, HIV infections, and AIDS, but he, too, will fade from the scene. The selection of its third president since the end of apartheid will be crucial for South Africa. If a capable technocrat is chosen the future is wide open for an economic boom and the expansion of Pretoria's informal empire. If an ideologue gains power, South Africa could go the way of other once promising African states such as Nigeria or Kenya.

If South Africa's vested interests behave wisely, we shall see the rise of a new political generation, friendly to business and far more open to a constructive relationship with the United States—enabling us to build an eventual alliance with Africa's dominant power (which Nigeria might have been had it not succumbed to endemic corruption, tribalism, and religious hatred). Such an alliance, if developed in concert with improved cooperation with India, a healthier relationship with Indonesia, and, just possibly, a post-theocracy community of interests with Iran, would give the United States tremendous influence over the entire Indian Ocean, as well as over regions beyond its sea-lanes. The ideal formula would be: capitalism and the rule-of-law in; China militarily out; the Arabs contained and controlled; European engagement only on equitable terms; and oil supplies assured by the United States Navy until such time as substitute fuels allow us to give the Middle East the economic coup de grâce.

———————

Beyond the strategic factors listed above there is one more great advantage to a serious and enduring American engagement with an expanded southern hemisphere: access to the human capital that will be essential to the explosive economic development possible in the twenty-first century (especially after oil dependence is eliminated). Over the last half century the United States has grown wealthier than any of us could have foreseen. That wealth is set to increase exponentially in the next fifty years—even as Europe falters and much of the world struggles. By building revolutionary, mutually beneficial relationships with the key countries and regions of the southern hemisphere (loosely defined to include more northerly states, from Mexico to Iran) we can, as once was said of the Philadelphia Quakers, "do very well by doing good."

The absurd polarities and misconceptions of the Cold War era must—and can—be overcome. The sole success of the Communist horror was its ability to poison minds against America in the developing world. Even that poison has begun—slowly—to leave the human bloodstream. But we cannot simply sit at home and expect the world to adore us. We must act—intelligently, patiently, and decisively—to build new alliances of mutual benefit between our country and those states that we have long dismissed or slighted.

No other region is as immediately important to the United States as Latin America. Our new century is much more likely to be another Atlantic century than a Pacific one. But the strategic focus will shift from Europe southward, forming a new strategic triangle between North America, South America, and Africa. Key European powers—Britain, Spain, and perhaps Portugal—will be embedded in the new strategic equation, but most of Europe will play a peripheral role at best.

Yet the level of ignorance afflicting the citizens of the United States when it comes to Latin America is appalling. Mexico is our leading source of immigrants, legal and illegal. Brazil is becoming a hemispheric great power. Countries such as Argentina, Chile, Venezuela, and Colombia offer offshore human resources that can supplement our own in a networked world. But we know less about our neighbors than we do about South Korea, a distant state of diminishing importance.

Latin America's development has been painfully slow, with heartrending setbacks. Instead of steady growth, its economies have been subjected to boom-and-bust cycles, from the silver exports of the early colonial era through the euphoric then disastrous trades in tin, beef, and narcotics. The essential problem has been the Iberian colonial legacy, which left behind values nearly as dysfunctional as those of the Middle East.

That should not surprise us, since the men who shaped Spain's and Portugal's Latin American colonies had themselves been shaped by long wars against Muslims. When two sides war for centuries while living in immediate proximity, they absorb each other's values without conscious knowledge of what's occurring. A street thug in a Los Angeles barrio today is the direct descendant of Hernando Cortés, who was formed in turn by the Muslim warriors his ancestors had battled: men who valued martial skill above all else, who despised bookishness and manual labor, and whose ideal was that of the landed gentleman who need not lift a finger except to stroke submissive women or dispense favors to his feudal underlings.

If you want to understand Latino gangs, look at the values of the Berber mercenaries who invaded Spain a thousand years ago. From the religious totems (albeit Christian, not Muslim), the superstition, the emphasis on extravagant masculinity and ready violence— even the tattoos—the street-corner drug dealer in Los Angeles is the inheritor of the values of the Muslims and Christians who took their turns ravaging *al-Andaluz.*

Most major states in Latin America won their independence in the early nineteenth century. Then they colonized themselves (as Spain itself would do after its bitter civil war). No longer ruled from Madrid, they retained its fatal values and behaviors. Democracy didn't have a chance in a world of macho posturing (had the creation of our Declaration of Independence been transferred from Philadelphia to Cartagena or Lima, the affair would have collapsed in invective, duels, and an armed coup before a draft text could have been agreed). Learning was for priests. Real men fought, amassed wealth through any means they could, and owned land. *Latifundias, estancias,* haciendas...no matter the name, such estates were feudal entities, utterly inimical to democracy.

Nor could balanced economies develop in a culture where there were only two reasons to work: first, to survive, but secondarily to grow sufficiently wealthy to never have to work again. Labor, even more than study, was demeaning—an Arab value that cripples the Middle East to this day (sweating is for Filipino wage slaves). The culture was the antithesis of the Protestant work ethic or the American assumption that labor fulfills a life. A man's aim was to wield authority, extract respect, display wealth, and enjoy leisure, to be the master of fine horses and beautiful women and to command both with hands unsullied by "peasant work."

Thankfully, the old values are breaking down, from the top to the very bottom of Latin American societies. The continent's feudalism lite is on the way out. It's rare to encounter native-born U.S. citizens who work harder than most Latino immigrants to our country. Back in their countries of origin, changes are slowly taking shape that will give the wretched of the earth better lives in coming generations.

The example of the United States, its success and its equitable society, has been essential to the transformation of Latin America. While it's easy to become hypnotized by the uproar President Hugo Chavez has wrought in Venezuela, the viciousness of narco trafficking, or the stale, conformist leftism of university students, far deeper forces are at work, from a fresh awareness of alternative ways of life (thanks to a globalizing media and the migrant-labor experience) to the multiple generations of technocrats who have been educated in the best universities in the United States. The people of Latin America *want* change. They are figuring out, through trial and error, how to achieve it.

The setbacks are frustrating, from Argentina's phony embrace of market economics under President Menem's crooked regime to the intermittent resurfacing of destructive socialist notions amid impatient electorates. Yet the change in tone from the region's politicians and opinion leaders over the past generation has been profound. Yesterday every local failure was blamed on the gringos. Today we're only occasionally at fault.

Even Mexico turned out the Party of the Institutionalized Revolution, the PRI, which had looted the country for eight decades. While the PRI may yet return to the president's office, it will never again be able to assume that it will not be held accountable. If President Vicente Fox's practical achievements have been disappointing, largely due to the truculence of the PRI-dominated congress and partly because of U.S. neglect after 9/11, the simple fact of his electoral victory changed Mexico's political landscape forever. The PRI may fight holding actions for decades, but a new age has begun.

For a century and a half, Mexico defined itself as a negative—the anti-United States—a sentiment that successive PRI governments nurtured after the revolution of 1910—17. The PRI, especially, fostered a culture of blame and hopelessness, a sense that human effort was wasted, that nothing would ever change. Now, at last, Mexicans have begun to criticize themselves, to examine their own errors with an encouraging sobriety, and to accept that cooperation with the United States is far more useful than cheap enmity.

Many obstacles and ingrained grudges remain to be overcome, but the hardest part was the beginning. If George W. Bush's second administration can revitalize its interest in Mexico and in the potential strategic partners farther to the south, history may remember the president who went to war in Iraq primarily as the man who changed America's strategic direction—all to the good.

Latin America is a natural fit for partnership with the United States. Spain has invested tens of billions of dollars in South America, in good times and bad, betting on its long-term potential. And Madrid makes much of colonial-era ties, but those connections cut two ways. If Spain shares a common language with most of Latin America (although not a congenial accent), the United States has the blood relatives of the Latin American bankers, businessmen, impresarios, and popular artists Spain hopes to cultivate. The preferred location for vacation homes for wealthy Latin Americans isn't the Costa Brava but Miami, the secret capital of Latin America.

This doesn't mean that Spain need be excluded. To the contrary, Spain is likely to become a premier American ally and economic partner once it resolves its internal dilemmas. We should not be surprised or too dismayed by outbreaks of leftist hypocrisy in Spain, since the country's "independence" from Franco's colonial rule—imposed with Berber mercenaries—is only a quarter century old. Spain is not only one of the world's youngest democracies, it's still coming to terms with the fact that it was liberated from above by King Juan Carlos, and not by a heroic struggle from below.

All that Latin America asks of us is respect. Even a pretense of respect will do in a pinch. Brazil, with a population approaching 180 million souls, can't help feeling humiliated—and angered—when we rush to consult Brussels and ignore Brasília. We do not even display good manners, let alone good sense. We know more about diseased French kings than we do about the second most populous country in our hemisphere. It would be helpful if we would occasionally do the right thing, but it often would suffice were we merely to say the right thing.

Whether frustrated by a cell-phone conversation at a neighboring table or annoyed by an aggressive driver, it's a standing joke between my wife and me to remark that "the problem with humanity is the people."

But the glory of humanity is also the people. Not the revered artists or even the battlefield heroes, but the common men and women who make societies of every sort function from day to day. And there is so much human capital going to waste south of the Tropic of Cancer, from Calcutta to Cuzco, that it's as if the streets were truly paved with gold and we just can't be bothered to look down. Strategists worry constantly about access to natural resources, but the greatest natural resource is human beings. Instead of looking at the world's poor as liabilities we need to begin accepting them as valuable commodities.

This isn't an argument for a gooey embrace of feel-good diplomacy, nor for a new paternalism, but for enlightened self-interest. The people in Brazil, South Africa, Iran, or India will determine their own futures—and thus they will shape ours, for better or worse. I argue only that we should encourage them to do well by us by doing well by them. If only we could be true to our professed values (summarized so boldly in President Bush's second inaugural address) and forgo the hospitality of the developing world's obscenely rich minority in favor of the striving majority, we would in time increase our influence far beyond that which we enjoy today.

Faced with terrorists, we must be feared. But we also should work toward the day when we might again be admired. It is not a matter of giving poor men handouts but of giving them a hand up. Power in the twenty-first century will reside increasingly with the people. We need to have the common sense to line up on the winning side. By rejecting authoritarian regimes and the artificial alliances of the past in favor of supporting the aspirations of the masses, we are much more likely to fulfill our own aspirations. We need to have the strength to stand for the good of humankind. It's the true American way.

Nineteen
MANY EUROPES

We don't have enough words. Even English, while incomparably versatile, lacks a vocabulary adequate to the world's growing complexity. Because of the gaps in our arsenal of terms we turn to linguistic shorthand, all too often obscuring that which we hope to illuminate. Consider the range of activities we encompass with the word "diplomacy" or the fateful lack of gradations when we speak of "sovereignty." Although careful when handling language, which I regard as a weapon, I find myself resorting to all too general terms, speaking of "al-Qaeda" when I mean a range of terrorist entities of various origins, differing capabilities, and complex, even contradictory, intentions. Attempting to convey a web of worlds within the world, I write of the "Southern Hemisphere," although some of the lands I mean to include lie north of the Tropic of Cancer. "Third world" is out, but does "developing world" describe Brazil, Liberia, Sudan, and Singapore equally well?

The velocity of change is such that vocabulary cannot keep pace. To enjoy a fair command of language is to confront the degree to which any language commands its employer. Vocabulary doesn't merely shape our thoughts, it condenses them into dangerous simplifications. In the world of the twenty-first century we remain trapped in twentieth century (or nineteenth century) terminology. In the field of international relations especially, deficient vocabulary leads to a lack of precision that torments the world. Nor does the difficulty lie primarily in translations from one language into another. It would not be enough to share a global language if that language were not better calibrated to postmodern demands.

The inadequacy of our strategic vocabulary becomes evident the instant we speak of "Europe." Which Europe do we mean? The freedom-breeding culture of Britain? The ethical and cultural dead zones of France, Belgium, and Germany? The rampart of hopeful new states on the continent's eastern marches? The resurgent south, where Italy has reached an overdue political maturity and Spain has come from behind to pioneer a cultural revolution? The Balkans and Greece, whose populations remain undecided as to whether they should behave as Europeans, Middle Easterners, or simply as ethnic thugs? Is Turkey truly a European state? And what of Russia, the land that bestrides two continents and embraces the worst of both?

When we speak of Europeans do we mean the Ukrainians who took to the streets in the brutal cold to insist that their country should not be sold back to Russia? Or the French, who only take to the streets in significant numbers to demand wealth without work? Do we mean the kitchen staff at Spain's forbiddingly fashionable restaurant El Bulli or Albanian gangsters? Finnish designers or Greek fishermen? Dublin's tech-sector gypsies or the impoverished Roma on the streets of Bucharest? I suspect that we rarely mean the continent's tens of millions of Muslims.

The European Union, with its fantastic goals and petty tyrannies, doesn't merely paper over cracks, as the cliché goes. It attempts to hide the ill-matched building materials of the European house, some of which are rotting behind a glittering facade. This does not mean that the European Union will dissolve—only that it will disappoint. The nasty bickering on the eve of Operation Iraqi Freedom, when President Chirac snapped at the new democracies awaiting EU integration that they ought to keep their mouths shut about supporting the Coalition, was merely a preview of many conflicts to come.

France is positioned to remain Europe's primary impediment to sensible policies, moral behavior, and meaningful international cooperation.

As the preceding chapters note again and again, France has been the cancer at the heart of Europe for centuries, ever ready to betray the rest of the continent for gains it always proves unable to consolidate or defend. If Germany is a clumsy monster, France is a poisonous snake. Were Paris's actions at least beneficial to France the intransigence and bitchy intrigues might be understandable, but the French ruling clique's pursuit of *la gloire*, of a higher status than it can support, has done more harm to the French themselves than to any of its competitors. Today the commissars produced by the *École Nationale d'Administration* feel solidarity with the ugliest Arab regimes and other dictatorships because of a shared jealousy toward more successful states and cultures.

The oddity about France is that the general population is appealing. The "French problem" isn't about the common men and women who have suffered for centuries under foolish governments. The problem lies within France's exclusive intellectual aristocracy as surely as it once stemmed from France's traditional aristocracy (a similar solution looks tempting). A tiny cadre among the country's sixty million citizens have a death grip on the government, the media, banking, and business. Iraq's Baath Party was far more inclusive than France's controlling elite. No land of opportunity, France is structured much the same way as it was in the fifteenth century, only with diminished faith and slightly improved hygiene. If a young person is not born well, does not test well early on, fails to attend exactly the right schools and universities, and is not accepted by the doorkeepers of power, he or she will never rise above the level of middle management. France is governed by the woefully inept and alarmingly inbred, and perhaps we should be grateful for the country's inability to cause even greater damage.

France's political parties represent their own interests, not those of the people. Its notorious trade unions elevate self-perpetuation over anything resembling a national interest. Its leading industries survive on subsidies, compete through bribery, and rely on industrial espionage. While the French military does a peerless job of gunning down unarmed Africans, it is incompetent at modern warfare. And France's foreign policy consists only of onanistic fantasies of undercutting American power while continuing the Gaullist tradition of embracing every Arab or African dictator (or Balkan or Russian strongman, for that matter) willing to trade bribes and share delusions.

It isn't only that the rest of Europe deserves better. The French people deserve better. But the antimeritocratic prejudices held dear by the society's controlling interests are unlikely to weaken, and the government—forever dreaming of the first Napoleon while behaving like Napoleon III—will continue to sow international discord as fervently as a rampaging cancer spreads tumors.

Secretary of Defense Donald Rumsfeld did a single useful thing during his tenure: He gave a new and wonderfully specific meaning to the term "Old Europe." If Rumsfeld failed to advance strategic thought, improve our military readiness, or employ our soldiers competently, he at least helped us out with our diplomatic vocabulary.

By "Old Europe" Rumsfeld meant the western European defenders of Saddam Hussein: cowardly Belgium, rapacious little Luxembourg, the blind German elephant, and the viral French. He had a point. Contrary to the instant myths of the left, most European countries supported the removal of the Iraqi regime. Rumsfeld isolated Europe's central problem as the age-old dance of death between France and Germany, which has begun to look more like a suicide pact.

Between them, the French-speaking and German-speaking populations of Europe have been responsible for most of the continent's internal bloodshed. From the late Tudors forward England sought to avoid warfare on the continent whenever its strategic needs permitted, while Italy sent no invading armies northward after the fall of the Western Roman Empire (until it made a shameless grab at the southern Tirol during the First World War). Adept at tormenting natives in their colonies, the Dutch lost their taste for fighting other Europeans by the eighteenth century. After 1648 Spain occasionally found itself invaded but was incapable of invading anyone else. Sweden lost its spunk shortly thereafter. Only Russia in its Soviet incarnation—inspired by the theories of an untidy German—damaged Europe with the enthusiam of the Germans or French, whether we speak of Turenne torching the churches of the Rhineland, Napoleon making war for war's own sake, or Germany's barbaric wars of conquest.

Europe has a Franco-German problem.

What shall we make of Germany, a country with all the self-righteousness of France but without the table manners? It's exasperating to hear Germans, of all people, inventing American or Israeli atrocities, forever imputing the worst possible motives to Washington and adopting a holier than thou stance when the ovens of Auschwitz have barely stopped smoking.

But therein lies the key to understanding Germany's obsession with vilifying America and Israel. The German problem came home to me almost thirty years ago, over glasses of cheap Riesling in a bare-bones bar. The Sponheimer Hof crouched down an alley that curled off a lane in Bad Krueznach—one of those lovely German towns that were delighted to herd their Jewish neighbors off to the death camps and, incidentally, where a young woman ruined her life by exchanging wedding vows with Karl Marx. I was a junior enlisted soldier interested in meeting local girls and mastering the language (mutually reinforcing endeavors) and the crude front-room bar was a meeting place for failed students, ex-students, and eternal students, along with a few strays who were unfashionably employed. The views were inevitably leftist; no money was ever wasted on deodorant, and I learned swiftly that you must let a German rant until he runs out of alcohol. It was 1977, the Rhineland winter was wet and windswept, and the characters who frequented the bar were colorful enough to hold my interest for a time.

There was one theme to which each one of them always returned: My Lai.

The Vietnam War was done, the massacre a decade past. But those Germans hugged the atrocity to their breasts. The incompetent Lieutenant Calley, who failed at an officer's fundamental responsibility, had given the sons and daughters of Hitler's veterans a great gift. An isolated tragedy with less than two hundred victims canceled every Nazi sin in the eyes of those young Germans. They embraced My Lai as the equivalent of Auschwitz, Treblinka, Bergen-Belsen, Dachau, Buchenwald, Babi Yar, the Warsaw Ghetto, and all of Hitler's invasions combined. I recall one evening early on, when I tried to argue the disproportion between our error and their formal program of extermination. I was literally shouted down. It was as if I had been reading a familiar story to children and attempted to alter the ending.

I got it. Perhaps it was the second glass of sour *Qualitätswein*, or simply an insight so obvious that even a young soldier could not mistake it, but I saw how badly those Germans, disgraced by their recent national past, *needed* to believe that America was every bit as wicked as Germany, that we were all the same—brothers and sisters in a solidarity of guilt.

At the time the Palestinian cause had already been embraced (especially in the wake of the massacre of Israeli athletes at the Munich Olympics, an event that gave Germans of all ages a shiver of dark delight), but it was still unacceptable to criticize Israel too directly or to lie about Israeli actions too obviously.

That changed with time. Today, Germans believe that the Holocaust is sufficiently far behind us to make Israel hating and Jew baiting acceptable again. Of course, the Holocaust was only yesterday—and Old Europe's sole sincere regret is that the Nazis left their work unfinished— but the new generation of Germans needs to invent Israeli atrocities just as it has to exaggerate America's missteps. Germans need to believe that Israelis are every bit as bad as their own grandparents were when they murdered Jews all morning, sat down to a steaming *Saumagen* and a mug of beer for lunch, played a quick round of cards, then murdered Jews all afternoon.

No matter what the Israelis do or fail to do, they will be blamed. When the "massacre" in Jenin a few years back turned out to be a Palestinian hoax it was a terrible disappointment to the Germans (no German paper bothered to print a front-page retraction of their anti-Israeli headlines). No nation in the world bears so great a burden of shame as do the Germans. Their only hope is to convince themselves that others are as loathsome now as they so recently were. Understanding that single truth is essential to grasping the lurches and self-defeating impulses of German foreign policy, its media bias, and the fervor, all too reminiscent of bygone rallies in Nuremberg, with which Germans young and old embrace big lies that absolve them of guilt.

My Lai has receded. Today, Germans will lecture you about our government's nineteenth-century mistreatment of Native Americans, refusing to accept that the United States might have made the slightest progress since then. Above all, their assumption of complete moral superiority is repugnant. But we have to understand that their blustering reflects weakness and shame, not strength. And their psychological need to believe that Americans and Israelis are bent on doing evil is really a desperate prayer for absolution.

Yet the moment one begins to feel some faint stirring of sympathy for today's crippled Teutonic souls, the Germans spoil it by the selectivity with which they condemn others. Anxious to damn Israel and

America, no major German student organization and no German government has been willing to condemn Saddam Hussein's genocide against the Kurds, the Turkish genocide against the Armenians, the Russian genocide through famine against the Ukrainians, or even Sudan's ongoing genocide in Darfur Province. Explicit Arab calls for the massacre of Israelis are downplayed while Germans speak indignantly of Israeli "genocide" against the Palestinians.

No other Western society is as morally bankrupt as Germany. It's a classic case of the murderer blaming his victim and suing the police who apprehended him.

Even as France attempts to portray itself as the defender of Muslims around the world and Germany pretends to flawless virtue, their behavior toward their domestic Muslim minorities makes the bygone American South look like a land of opportunity. Six million of France's sixty million residents are utterly unassimilated Muslims from North Africa or West Africa. The French treated them like dirt for decades. Now that soil has sprouted vines of hatred.

France taught its Muslim immigrants to hate the West as no madrassa could do. Repeated polls have shown that more than 80 percent of the Muslims in France believe that terrorist acts are justified. Germany's Turks, who form the majority of its Muslim population, are less supportive of terrorism but no more assimilated into society. Notwithstanding the flap over forbidding Muslim schoolgirls to wear headscarves in France, the positions of the governments in Paris and Berlin have been identical: Do nothing and hope the problem goes away (echoing President Clinton's approach to Islamic terrorism).

But those swelling Muslim minorities will not go away. With Europe's "native" populations reproducing at rates so low they will see dramatic declines across the next half century, the only residents who consistently bear enough children to increase their demographic share (even without further immigration) are Europe's Muslims. Bigoted and frightened, Old Europe has failed to think honestly about the challenge.

Meanwhile, hatred is spreading.

While France and Germany dither, Europe's smaller states may lead the way in addressing the threat from Islamic extremists. In the autumn of 2004 the ritual murder of Dutch filmmaker Theo van Gogh in a busy street shocked the Netherlands out of its complacency (which the earlier murder of a Dutch politician by an Islamist had failed to do—the first event was written off as an aberration). Decades of indulgent programs that allowed immigrants to create exclusive ghettos and avoid learning the local language had backfired. And the Dutch suddenly realized it. While reforms will be slow and there is no easy answer to the problem of Islamic minorities (many individuals have lost interest in assimilating), the Dutch have at least begun to question their past policies.

Italy, too, has begun to look for better answers, and Spain—still stunned by the 2004 Madrid train bombings—will do so. Britain's problem is massive, yet the greater opportunities offered to Muslims and the assimilation slowly working in from the edges give Britain a fonder hope of dealing with its internal Islamic crisis than other major European states enjoy. This comparison does not predict where terrorist attacks will occur—that will be a matter of terrorist strategy and opportunity—but it does suggest which countries face the most intractable problems.

On the continent the unwillingness of ethnically homogeneous populations to accept Muslims, coupled with the growing Muslim rejection of the assimilation they once would have welcomed, creates potential scenarios that verge on nightmare fiction. While human genius may prevail and Europeans may find a way to overcome their layers of discord, we would do well to keep Europe's history at the back of our minds: This is the continent that mastered genocide and perfected ethnic cleansing. Should Europe's Muslims fail to find a healthy place in their host societies in the decades to come, we may see a return of the mass deportations of minorities that Europe practiced so ruthlessly down the centuries.

The expulsion of the Jews from Spain in 1492, followed by the ethnic cleansing of the last Moors, leaps to mind as a cautionary model, but Jews and other religious minorities had already been expelled from or slaughtered by other Europeans before the Spaniards codified the behavior. Nor can we dismiss the possible return of such practices by arguing that all those atrocities happened long ago. Even setting aside

the Holocaust (which plenty of Europeans would like to do), the end of
the Second World War saw extensive ethnic cleansing in numerous
countries. The 1990s saw an unexpected refinement of the art of dis-
possessing minorities, with Serbs butchering Croats, Croats driving out
Serbs, Serbs and Croats evicting Bosnian Muslims, Serbs destroying the
homes of Kosovar Albanians, and now Kosovar Albanians squeezing
Serbs from their ancestral homelands around Priština. As all this happened Europe did little more than wring its hands. Only American intervention put a stop to the barbarities (at least for now).

The entire twentieth century was a saga of genocide and ethnic
cleansing in Europe, with Greeks driven from Turkey, Turks driven
from Greece, Chechens driven into Siberia, Poles driven from Germany and Ukraine, Germans driven from Poland and (former) Czecho-
slovakia, Hungarians scorched from Rumania, no end of small nations
diminished, displaced, or slaughtered, and European Jewry annihi-
lated.

To imagine that Europe's current charade of pacifism means that the
world's most brutal continent has changed its fundamental character
would be foolish indeed. And to dismiss out of hand the possibility that
in some future decade America may need to intervene to protect Europe's Muslims from Old Europe's wrath might prove to be no more than
the sort of wishful thinking that insisted in 1912 that Europeans would
never fight each other again, or in 1938 that Adolph Hitler wanted
only some slight redress for injustices done to Germany.

We must relearn the art of thinking the unthinkable unless we
wish to make the unthinkable probable.

––––––––––––

If Old Europe is sick, what of the rest of the continent? One of the other
Europes, that which only recently escaped from Moscow's hegemony,
is more hopeful now than it has been at any time in its history. Individual countries, such as Poland and Hungary, may have enjoyed their
golden ages, but the region as a whole, from the Baltic states to Bulgaria, has never before had such a chance at peaceful development.
From the days of the Roman Empire the region between the Balkan
mountains and the Baltic sea was either occupied by one empire or another, torn by empire's frontier struggles, or divided against itself. The

only laudable, if unintended, achievement of Soviet domination was to convince the various nations of the region that their differences with their other neighbors were trivial compared to the danger of a resurgent Russia gobbling them up one by one again. Moscow taught the states of Central and Eastern Europe to cooperate, if not quite in the manner the Politburo intended.

Certainly the East lags economically. But its greater energy and lower expectations may compensate for much of the gap between the soft-socialist societies of Western Europe and the newly free nations acquainted with socialism's harder side. If democracy has disappointed us elsewhere in the world, we should be encouraged by the enthusiasm with which Estonians, Latvians, Lithuanians, Poles, Czechs, Hungarians, Slovaks, Bulgarians, Romanians, and—despite Russian meddling—Ukrainians and even Georgians have shown for choosing their own leaders. Some states, such as Bulgaria and Georgia, have come farther faster than seemed possible even in the mid-nineties.

These states are overwhelmingly drawn to the United States, partly from gratitude and affection, but more enduringly from their sense that only Washington could and would protect them from another burst of Russian aggression (although Russia appears less and less likely ever to regain sufficient power to pretend to empire). These states do not agree with all of our policies, and we cannot expect consistent support from them, yet they remain natural allies for the United States.

They remember too well what they suffered not only at Russian hands but from Germany's iron fist. Nor have they forgotten France's coziness with Moscow during the Cold War. Recent French and German attempts at diplomatic bullying have only reminded Central and Eastern Europeans of the price they paid for previous follies committed by Berlin and Paris. While these states will naturally seek healthy relationships with France and Germany in the contexts of the EU and NATO, their interests will continue to lie in limiting Franco-German power, not in fostering it.

Given all they have suffered down the ages and particularly in the twentieth century, the current political health of Europe's newest democracies appears little short of miraculous. If there are worthy models anywhere in the world of the power and appeal of the ballot, it isn't in either of the countries the United States occupied and attempted to reconstruct after World War II, but in the states that reconstructed themselves after 1989.

In 2005, the states of Eastern and Central Europe lie farther to the West than France or Germany.

When Spain withdrew its troops from Iraq in the wake of the Madrid train bombings, many Americans dismissed the Spanish as cowards and fools for retreating in the face of terrorism. Foolish they may have been—you cannot appease religious extremists—but the charge of cowardice should be reduced to one of confusion and bewilderment. Spain is groping its way forward after half a millennium of darkness.

It's fashionable now to downplay the influence of the Inquistion and religious oppression on Spain's misshapen history, substituting economic causes or policy arguments. But if ever a country committed cultural suicide, it was Spain. The three strikes of driving out Spanish Jews, then the Moors, and following up by restricting the intellectual and practical freedoms of all Spaniards turned the greatest empire of the sixteenth century into a social and intellectual backwater with stunning speed.

If you go to the Prado in Madrid, the degeneration of the faces of Spain's kings in paintings by artists who merited better subjects perfectly reflects the decline of Spanish power and culture. The wealth that built the grim Escorial lasted long enough to buy treasures from abroad, but Spain's indigenous culture slowly congealed as the vigor of its empire weakened into unimaginative brutality. The great canvases in the Prado glorify God or the Habsburgs but leave little room for mortal beauty. The propaganda of Velázquez declines into the melodrama of Murillo, the spiritual father of black-velvet painting. Only the incandescent darkness of Goya redeems the following four hundred years (unless we count the émigré Picasso).

In Spanish-language literature there is nothing first rate after Cervantes and Lope de Vega. Pérez Galdós, Lorca, and Cela were merely the Iberian equivalents of Margaret Mitchell, Clifford Odets, and Erich Maria Remarque. Even Portugal had more to offer the world, and Spain's former colonies had to reinvent fiction and poetry after World

War II—which they did with cunning genius. At the height of the colonial era Spain extracted the lifeblood from its new colonies, but in the end the flow reversed itself. From Isabella of Castile through Philip II, Spain suffered a fateful line of rulers who loved God too much and humanity too little. Spain became the Saudi Arabia of its day, a state corrupted by its own good fortune and brought low by vicious choices.

Closing itself off from Enlightenment Europe, Spain and its far-flung empire drowsed until awakened by cries of revolution in the early nineteenth century. After losing its richest colonies, Madrid went back to sleep again, waking next to the sound of Dewey's guns in Manila Bay. Even then Spain refused to rise to the challenges of a new age. In one of history's oddest turnabouts, the country that had stunted the growth of its colonies, leaving them with sixteenth-century social structures at independence, became its own last colony, somnolent, impoverished, and incapable. By the outbreak of the Spanish Civil War—a colonial war fought at home—Japan was more industrialized than Spain.

Francisco Franco, who employed his Moroccan troops with uncompromising brutality against his countrymen, came to power not as a European leader, but as a *caudillo* in the Latin American mold, the strongman who rules by force and concentrates all power in his own hands, who "disappears" his opponents and subscribes to a fierce morality for his subjects. It was as if Cortés had come home at last.

Spain remained closer to Latin America's culture of government than to Europe's until Franco's death a mere generation ago. Madrid is now a democratic capital—and doing remarkably well, considering Spain's tragic earlier experience with elected governments. But having gained their "independence" only in 1975 (and reacting against Franco's dreary fascism), Spaniards could not help embracing much of the goofiest rhetoric of the European left. Their protests are the rebellion of political adolescents.

We should be less surprised at Spanish outbursts of anti-Americanism than at their superficiality and infrequency. We also might do well to regain some broader perspective on European America bashing: Even in Old Europe anti-Americanism today is far less rabid among the general population than it was immediately following World War II, or between 1968 and the early 1980s.

Spain is a very young democracy, with deep historical wounds.

Given our community of interests in Latin America and elsewhere, Spain and the United States are fated to be allies. But the process will take time. Spain will need to outgrow its borrowed socialist rhetoric just as the more successful African states are doing. Former prime minister Jose Maria Aznar was a visionary who recognized where Spain's long-term interests lay, but he was a man ahead of his time. His support for the removal of Saddam Hussein—which Spain's left would have applauded had it been morally serious—was too bold a step for a society still unsure of its Europeanness, its historical inheritance, and its possibilities.

As suggested elsewhere in this book, the arts are a beacon illuminating the development of immature societies. And Spain is in the midst of a cultural renaissance that ranges from film to cuisine (where it has surpassed France), from wine making to literature and fashion design. Although richer, Spain resembles Eastern Europe in the sense it gives you of pent-up energies suddenly released, of possibilities, of a future. Only Italy—another natural American ally—is experiencing the sort of social, cultural, and political leap forward manifest in Spain. Southern Europe has gone from being the continent's laggard to becoming a new and inspiring leader.

Old Europe is being surrounded by New Europe.

———————

Which leads us back to America's immediate parent and enduring ally: Britain. No expanse of water however wide has been as important to human development as the English Channel, which kept off all but a few invaders and allowed the eccentric inhabitants of one poor island to give birth to the only humane form of government the earth has ever seen.

Britannia need not be excused her sins for us to acknowledge that her virtues eclipse them. The development of England and the lands her people settled and formed has been so unique that one wonders if language so shapes consciousness and character that it helps to explain the slow but steady miracle of English-speaking democracy. Perhaps character and consciousness shape language. Perhaps our freedom is a random accident of historical interactions and a peculiar isolation. Perhaps it's genetic. Or willed from above. At our present level of ignorance we cannot settle on a single answer with any confidence. But democracy— our robust brand of freedom—exists. Perhaps that is enough.

While it's frustrating to see the intelligentsia of southern England attempt to discard their incomparable inheritance in favor of imitating the Stalinism lite of their French counterparts, the anti-Americanism of England's chattering classes is natural enough: No parent likes to be displaced by an overachieving child. We should not make too much of it. The voices at the BBC or the *Guardian* who applaud the maddened claims of Islamic terrorists and excuse gory dictators to spite America are simply the grandchildren of the Fabian socialists, with their self-dramatizing silliness, and those 1930s pacifists who complained that Britain spent too much on useless armaments, such as the Spitfire.

English-speaking intellectuals on both sides of the Atlantic can't help envying the respect accorded their continental counterparts (who insisted, until the sorry end, that the Soviet Union was the power of the future and who rather liked Hitler for getting rid of their Jewish competitors). Intellectuals in the United Kingdom and the United States are virulently hostile to democracy because the voters couldn't care less what professors think. In Old Europe the common man remains a functional serf conditioned to heed his betters. Americans and Brits respond to intellectual nannying with mockery.

It's a wonderful proof of the health of English-speaking societies.

If only those Britons resentful of America opened their eyes they might be more contented. They should be proud parents, rather than resentful ones. If London no longer controls half the world directly, isn't it better to influence the world with your ideas—democracy, the rights of the individual, equal justice before the law—than to rule it with colonial administrators and quinine-dosed regiments? English values won history's sweepstakes. The London elite declines to see it.

Perhaps the English-speaking triumph is simply too vast for the mother country to comprehend so soon. Yet the truest cliché in international relations is that the English Channel is wider than the Atlantic Ocean. The most important alliance in the history of humankind is that between the English-speaking nations.

That will not change.

Twenty

EXPANDING AMERICA'S GLOBAL SUPREMACY

I was a soldier. Every institution imbues its members with particular prejudices. Because of my emotional commitment to the Army I long believed in the unassailable supremacy of land power. I studied Carl von Clausewitz, the great philosopher of war, and have weighed his propositions over the years. I wrote about him and argued his preeminence. More out of duty than deep interest, I also read the American naval theorist Alfred Thayer Mahan, then ignored his proposition that sea power was the essential military component for states such as the United States and Britain. Clausewitz, with his focus on large armies and war's complexity, was more congenial to an Army officer than Mahan, who seemed little more than a historian drawing simplistic conclusions.

Clausewitz was a genius. But Mahan was right.

Clausewitz was a son of Prussia, a land power, and he could no more see beyond Europe's shores than Robert E. Lee could doubt the strategic primacy of northern Virginia. Mahan, a U.S. Navy officer who died in 1914, thought in global terms. Had he lived a decade longer Mahan doubtless would have integrated the potential of airpower into his proposition that control of the seas was the indispensable component of strategy for the United States. Thus, we might have been spared the destructive influence of Giulio Douhet, the greatest charlatan in military history, who insisted that airpower alone would win the wars of the future.

Mahan never suggested that sea power by itself would win our wars, only that we could not win great wars without adequate sea power. Like Freud, Mahan got many of the practical details wrong but got the big picture right: For the United States, the need to establish a presence on a foreign shore is intermittent, but the requirement for global access is constant. Our ability to respond promptly disheartens potential enemies. That freedom of strategic maneuver is guaranteed by our mastery of the sea—and today, of the skies as well.

This does not mean that our ground forces, the Army and the one-foot-in-the-water Marine Corps, are in any way superfluous or that they might be reduced in size. On the contrary, our land-power components are markedly too small for our global responsibilities and their ranks should be increased by a solid 20 percent. When ground forces are needed they are needed in large numbers, as Rumsfeld and his incompetent civilian subordinates proved yet again in Iraq. There remains no substitute for boots on the ground in a formidable array when hostile regimes must be chastised or enemies pursued into a continent's interior.

Nor can we any longer contend with emergencies by generating large, sufficiently competent armies from the raw material of draftees. Given the geometric increase in the complexity of military organizations and equipment over the past thirty years, there is no alternative to robust, professional ground forces. Even in the primitive days of the Second World War, our Navy had to buy time in the Pacific—which it did with fierce brilliance—until we could deploy adequate numbers of ground troops to engage Japan's army effectively. We could not repeat such a conjuring act today. America's twenty-first-century global challenges demand substantial forces-in-being.

World War II had to be won by ground forces, but the role of sea power was decisive. The difference may seem too fine a point, but grasping it is essential.

This means that our Navy has a vital future, but it also means that the Navy must abandon its dreams of fighting Soviet fleets that no longer exist. As our recent conflicts demonstrated, today's Navy is ill designed and improperly structured for postmodern global warfare—yet it continues to buy ships and submarines whose cost is inversely proportional to their utility. We need a Navy that delivers massive amounts of firepower; instead, we have a Navy whose specialty is merely delivering itself, as if showing up for work is more important than actually working. Despite cosmetic changes across the past decade the Navy still thinks in the combat geometries of the bygone age of Nelson and Nimitz. In the twenty-first century the Navy needs to create the doctrine and pursue the means for naval power to influence conflicts as far inland as Central Asia—while maintaining undisputed command of the sea.

We have a magnificent Navy, but not the proper Navy for the times.

A few years ago, at the Naval War College in Newport, Rhode Island, I asked a few senior officers, "What will be the twenty-first-century equivalent of American gunboats on Chinese rivers?" My point was that eighty years ago our Navy still remembered its tradition of river warfare from the Civil War, when naval and ground forces learned to cooperate and win campaigns in the heart of a continent. I did not mean that we needed to build shallow-draft gunboats to sail up the Yangtze, but that the Navy needs to return to its discarded capability to influence land warfare deep in a continent's interior, not just on littorals. The naval paradox is that while control of the seas (and skies) is fundamental to U.S. strategy, the actual fighting demanded of us will overwhelmingly occur inland: The model is Vicksburg (or Fallujah), not the Battle of Midway, while the model for command of the seas may resemble more closely British efforts to destroy the international slave trade than the battle of Trafalgar.

The incomprehension on the part of the naval officers with whom I chatted was total (although I suspect a few of them were slow to answer because they were pondering how to turn my question into a defense of the misbegotten Virginia-class submarine). The Navy may not need small boats, but it could use some big ideas.

Our Navy needs to think in revolutionary, not evolutionary, terms. We are on the cusp of a revolution in naval affairs as profound as that which occurred five centuries ago, when European powers first mastered the global projection of power with oceangoing men-of-war.

The positive aspect of all this is that our Navy, with its unblemished tradition of service, will find its way forward in time. The service that should worry every American concerned with our security is the Air Force.

Our most technically advanced service is also the least attuned to the changing world around us. Instead of designing (affordable!) aircraft to meet our security requirements it demands the aircraft that nostalgic senior officers, craven officials, and a corrupt defense industry prefer to foist upon it. I grow so outraged when I consider the Air Force because I recognize its vital role in defending our country and furthering our interests. Control of the skies is equal in importance to the control of the seas; indeed, these two dimensions of warfare have been inseparable since the 1940s. The sea is a power dimension of volume, but the air is the realm of speed, and while you can control the sea from the sky to a great degree, you cannot yet control the sky from the sea, except locally. Our strategic position demands control of the seas, but that in turn requires control of the skies.

And what do we find in the Air Force today? Worthy officers from the mid-grades down, but an ethically bankrupt, blatantly corrupt, and strategically oblivious Department of the Air Force and Air Force Staff. The service is a degenerate organization whose doctrine is inept, whose purchases are counterproductive, and whose leadership is interested only in bureaucratic self-perpetuation, not in our national defense.

We need to break the Air Force into two components, subordinating its strategic assets to the Navy, which then would control the integrated sea-lanes and airspace essential to our global reach. The aircraft that support land campaigns and ground combat would be reassigned to a revived Army Air Corps, providing a seamless capability to engage ground targets in three dimensions. We have eliminated service branches before, from the horse cavalry to the coastal artillery, when they no longer served our defense needs. Eliminating an entire failed service should not be taboo, although it would be extraordinarily difficult given the number of entrenched interests that would have to be overcome. Congressmen would rise to defend wanton purchases made in their electoral districts. Senior officers would wrap themselves in the flag and threaten biblical cataclysms upon our country if the Air Force were to give up a single VIP aircraft. Ever unscrupulous, the defense industry would fight with all of its resources against the prospect of greater scrutiny and the demand for improved performance.

Just as the military structures of the nineteenth century did not suffice for the last century, those of the twentieth century demand to be revised to suit the requirements of our own age. The Army and Marines are revamping their doctrine and organizations under the tutelage of warfare. Now the Navy has to learn to see beyond its obsession with self-protection to envision a dramatically increased offensive capability applicable in every environment, sea, air, and land.

If it can summon the will to reform itself, the Air Force needs to purge its senior ranks ferociously and return to a focus on warfare, rather than simply operating as a slush fund for the defense industry. It must return to the ideals of service from its current culture of self-service. Or it should be broken up and reapportioned as described above.

Before speaking at a recent Air Force "off-site" I arrived in time for a briefing that astonished me with its disregard for strategic reality. When my turn came to speak I asked the senior officers present, "Just how irrelevant do you intend to be?"

That is the first question an honorable secretary of defense would ask our Air Force leadership.

Meanwhile, America's leading military thinker, Alfred Thayer Mahan, is thumping the living daylights out of Europe's broken-down champion, Carl von Clausewitz, in the ring of history. The latter remains essential reading for serious officers, but his propositions, from the supposed superiority of the defense in warfare to his trinity of the state, the people, and the military, are collapsing one after another—nor were they ever fully applicable to the American way of war. Writing near the end of the nineteenth century, Mahan provided the blueprint for expanding our global supremacy in the twenty-first century. His proposition was clear-eyed and straightforward, useful and unadorned by elaborate theories. In other words, Mahan was an archetypal American.

———————

Of course, there is far more to strategy than military capability—although strategy without strength amounts to begging mercy from one's executioners. The military enables strategy but does not constitute a strategy in and of itself. Every arm of government plays a role today, from the Department of Agriculture to the Federal Bureau of Investigation, from the Federal Reserve to the Department of Education. All of these must be subordinated to a grand purpose to the degree that they affect the foreign and security policies of the United States. It will require uncharacteristic vision on the part of our leaders, and that vision must never be permitted to calcify into a formula. Our strength lies in our unchanging values coupled to the flexibility to alter our practical policies as required.

The master strategy we should employ in the coming decades is simple to outline, although, of course, many devils lurk in the details. It rests upon two pillars: national interests (to include those of our allies) and human rights.

The need to pursue our national interest is self-evident, while support for human rights is too often qualified by a largely imagined need to preserve alliances of convenience. Nothing so damages the credibility of the United States as our willingness to overlook human rights abuses for a minimal, brief advantage, whether in Saudi Arabia, Uzbekistan, or China.

While the ineptitude of the State Department long has played a role in such folly, the most powerful defenders of criminal governments are found among our corporate leaders. Business has no conscience. Corporate executives are delighted to exploit patriotism when it may be to their advantage, but they shed their red-white-and-blue scruples the instant a foreign murderer or an anti-American regime dangles profits in front of them. If multinational corporations are allowed to continue to steer our foreign policy, they will continue to elevate profits over people and sales above security.

In this age of devolution, of the breakdown of old orders and the rise of the popular will, our future lies with the global masses who ride aging motorbikes, not with the few who travel in corporate jets. If only our corporate leaders could think beyond the quarterly earnings report they would realize that a rigorous insistence on human rights is to their long-term benefit as well. It is far easier to do business with a population whose struggle for human rights and freedom you have supported than with one whose oppressors you greedily embraced.

Human rights are not a "soft" issue. The deplorable lot of billions of human beings is the hardest issue of all. *Fighting* for human rights—as we have done recently in Iraq, Afghanistan, and the Balkans—is a worthy American purpose, as well as a wise one. The age of the dictators is waning. Some despots may survive longer than others, but we should stand on the right side during their reigns if we expect to be on the victorious side thereafter. During the Cold War we may have had some justification for supporting "our" dictators. But the Soviet Union is gone and China has decided that "to grow rich is glorious." We continue to overlook the misbehavior and malevolence of regimes such as that of Saudi Arabia from a combination of inertia and greed. We *must* return to the strategically wise, morally essential tradition of American support for the oppressed. To do otherwise is unworthy of our country and destructive of our global ambitions.

Support for human rights will not make foreign populations love us overnight—there are too many psychological burdens for failed societies to overcome. But, in time, it would elicit a new respect toward us.

Nor does support for human rights have anything to do with the nonsense of our domestic left, which enjoys the rhetoric of the human rights struggle but doesn't mean a word of it. If conservatives want a worthy issue with which to drive leftists into a corner, the human rights struggle is ideal. When it comes to the suffering of the wretched of the earth, the left quite likes things as they are, since misery in the face of Western wealth is one of the few issues remaining to them. The left will not back any serious endeavor to rid the world of tyrants or to bring an end to genocide—and certainly not if the effort requires military force, which it almost invariably does.

Had President Bush been wise enough to employ human rights arguments in his quest for international support for the liberation of Iraq, he might have embarrassed even the French into less public forms of treachery. The administration should have bet fewer chips on now-you-see-'em-now-you-don't weapons of mass destruction and more on Saddam Hussein's crimes against humanity. Instead, we tossed aside the most formidable moral argument for our actions. Our response to every French or German complaint should have been an enlarged photo of Kurds or Iraqi Shias in mass graves, not cartoons of mobile weapons labs.

Of course, even arguments in favor of halting genocide won't reach everybody in the faculty lounge. Our domestic leftists are in such moral disarray that they would gladly allow tens of millions of brown or black human beings to suffer horribly in order to frustrate a presidential administration for which they feel distaste. The American left has sunk to a level at which it exploits foreign misery when it suits prevailing prejudices but ignores no end of mass graves, torture, manmade famines, ethnic cleansing, mass rape, kidnapping, and unjust imprisonments if acknowledging their existence might result in a dictator's forcible removal by the English-speaking world. The left has every right to choose godlessness, but it becomes a public menace when it embraces mindlessness.

The truth about our contemporary left is that it despises those human beings who lack a college degree, hates the workers of the world for enjoying the quality of life capitalism has given them, and believes it should be allowed to dictate policies that voters overwhelmingly reject. The only time human rights issues genuinely interest the left is when an American soldier makes a mistake.

Human rights should not be a left-wing, right-wing, or even a centrist issue. Support for human rights should be a universal issue.

Nor does a strategic struggle for human rights imply weakness or laxity. If we wish to defend and advance the human rights of the great majority of any population, we must be willing to employ force against the malevolent fraction of 1 percent of that population intent on inflicting its will upon the rest. Military action in the interests of human rights is not a contradiction in terms but all too often the only way to wrest power from cabals of thugs and murderers. American soldiers fighting on Luzon sixty years ago or in Iraq today have done far more for human rights than the legions of self-righteous "peacekeepers" who descend on ruined countries to bury the dead. We must never let the argument "peace at any price" protect the enemies of humanity. When the left argues for peace with a dictator they embrace the peace of the dungeon.

The cause of human rights should be pursued through every means we have. At times that means killing the enemies of humanity. When the good angels refuse to carry swords Lucifer commands the plains of Heaven.

What practical measures should we take to steer our national strategy toward the future?

International Organizations. The United States should neither leave the United Nations nor try to destroy it. We should subvert it. While demanding public accountability and maintaining the moral high ground with the UN, we should miss no opportunity to diffuse its remaining authority to other international organizations. Even the European Union could be manipulated as a counterbalance to the UN. When dealing with international organizations, overall our policy should be to seek unity when it is to our advantage, but to divide and rule when necessary. We do not want a multipolar world of power blocks, but multipolarity among international bodies should be our goal. We need to quietly undermine the UN while building up alternate organizations, until the UN is only one of several centers of authority among which we might always find a source of legitimacy for the actions events demand.

Meanwhile, we should press for a series of reforms at the UN, the first of which would be to add India and Brazil (*not* Germany) to the Security Council. We should champion India and Brazil even though they would often vote against us, especially at first. We can accept that price in the interests of building long-term bilateral alliances with these two vital states. Meanwhile, artful efforts to undercut the power of the Security Council in particular and the UN in general would dilute the negative effects upon our foreign policy.

We need to appear to be on the side of a different future, not of a club of "great" powers whose membership was frozen in the wake of World War II. To that end, we should dangle a European Union seat on the Security Council before Brussels *if* the EU chair replaces the French seat. We should miss no opportunity to embarrass and weaken the French by letting them reveal themselves as unwilling to sacrifice a shred of national power for the greater good of Europe. After India and Brazil have become members of the Security Council we should campaign for the inclusion of South Africa, if that country continues to progress. In dealing with the UN, we should: deflate the organization as a whole; inflate the key powers with whom we wish to build future alliances; and work relentlessly to divide the blocks that consistently vote against us. Make the bad kids fight over the candy.

We also need to accept that a new age needs a totally new organization that would eventually render the UN obsolete—a death by natural causes. It is time to pursue a globe-spanning, formal alliance of democratic states, fleshed out upon a skeleton of the primary English-speaking nations but open to other genuine rule-of-law democracies.

The UN is so dictator-ridden and sick with corruption that it will rarely, if ever, call a tyrant to account. The world needs a body with greater moral legitimacy and greater physical force. A new alliance of democratic states should adopt the spread of freedom as its goal. No member state should have a fatal veto, and the organization must avoid the paralysis of bodies such as NATO that require unanimity for action by asking only for a two-thirds majority of member votes before intervening in trouble spots (dissenters could, of course, sit out the specific operation).

Our efforts to build an inclusive world organization in the UN have failed humanity. This time we need to create a rigorously exclusive organization that states must aspire to join, an elite club of legitimately elected governments.

The tyrants represented in the UN General Assembly would howl, but they need to relearn their weakness. The UN has become a tool for protecting apprentice Hitlers. The twenty-first century demands a more supple, moral, and capable body. But for now the way to deal with the UN is to lock it in a vigorous embrace rather than throwing a tantrum and running away. Kill the UN slowly through poisoned kisses.

And never miss a chance to expose a corrupt UN official.

North America. Of all the world's rule-of-law states, no two require a spell on the psychoanalytical couch more than Germany, with its ghosts, or Canada, with its determination to become the Mexico of the twenty-first century. While Mexico itself has begun to get over its crippling habit of defining itself as the anti-United States, Canada appears determined to take up the role. This is unfortunate, since Canada could be of great help in building a better world, if only it would stop pretending that sending peacekeepers to twiddle their thumbs amid ruins is the moral and practical equivalent of fighting for justice.

It is all too easy to grow angry at Canadian strategic freeloading and petty jealousy, but there is no benefit to Washington in confronting the Great White North. World events will shock Canada out of its dreams of perfect safety and superior virtue. Meanwhile, Washington should strive to work constructively with Ottawa whenever possible while ignoring the petulant criticisms from the north. Our strategic investments, however, would be better placed in Mexico, with its greater reserves of human capital, larger potential market, and utility as a bridge to Latin America.

Lock Mexico in a double-armed embrace. Despite its enduring problems—above all, corruption—and the inevitability of future disappointments, Mexico is overdue for a serious, forget-the-past strategic partnership with the United States. Unlike Canada, Mexico does have a number of legitimate grievances against us, including the disgraceful treatment of those Mexicans who must risk their lives to cross our border to do work we demand be done. But there is no divide between us that cannot be bridged with fortitude and patience. Help Mexico become a success and we help ourselves in a variety of ways, from gaining a useful partner, reducing international crime, and building out a deep market to better managing immigration. Democrats and Republicans need to agree on the need for a long-term, multiadministration program of tenacious engagement with Mexico. No relationship is of greater strategic immediacy.

Europe. Not all Cold War strategic models are irrelevant. Think of France as a two-bit Soviet Union. Then think containment and eventual rollback. We should miss no clandestine opportunity to undercut the French, and we should exploit all diplomatic situations in which the French can be embarrassed and weakened. We should *not* seek a premature rapprochement with Paris. France needs to be broken as an international influence. To that end, we should concentrate on further developing our relationships with the new democracies of Central and Eastern Europe, on deepening our relationship with Italy, and on overcoming our disagreements with the present Spanish government (Spain is so important that we should be willing to come out on the short end now and then if doing so leads Madrid to strengthen bilateral relations). Portugal, too, should receive an abundance of American support, even when it is not reciprocated.

Of course, we will always need to maintain our close relationship with the United Kingdom. There will be feuds and misunderstandings, but we must avoid overreacting and thus giving ammunition to

Britain's hard left, the offspring of the spiritual marriage of Virginia Woolf and Stalin. Prime Minister Tony Blair has been one of the most morally courageous leaders of our time and, as long as he remains in power, we should go out of our way to help him prove to his own electorate that London has been Washington's indispensable partner, not an obedient subordinate. Keep the family healthy, even when a sibling misbehaves.

After the shame of Srebrenica, when its troops looked on fecklessly during the worst massacre on European soil since 1946, the Netherlands seems to be shaking off its moral lethargy in favor of a new sense of reality. Denmark has proven surprisingly sound in its strategic choices (having the Germans as one's neighbor doubtless helps), and the rest of Scandinavia, when not supportive of U.S. initiatives, seeks to do no harm. We should pursue a more calculated, better attuned policy to strengthen the relationships we already enjoy in Northern Europe, and to build alliances where none presently exist.

We would be foolish ever to trust Germany again and must shift key military bases to Eastern Europe, but we need to pretend a friendship toward Germany that we no longer feel. As we contain France by building stronger relationships with the countries that surround it, the rollback phase of our anti-Gallic strategy should be to divide Germany and France. We need not achieve complete success so long as we make Berlin an unreliable partner for Paris and sow doubt between the two capitals.

Eastern Europe is the new West. We should continue to nurture our relationships east of the old Iron Curtain, where freedom is not yet taken for granted and security concerns remain immediate. From heroic Poland to surprising Bulgaria, the old barrier states that withstood the onslaught of Islam for centuries (and, in some cases, suffered under Islamic rule for hundreds of years) are again the frontier of our civilization. Warsaw is far closer to Washington than either city is to Paris or Berlin.

What more can be said about the startling valor of the people of Ukraine, who belatedly cast off a government of Communist thugs in mufti to insist amid the cold of an eastern winter that they would no longer tolerate the theft of elections or the theft of their country? Defying not only their self-appointed masters but threats from a Kremlin reverting to old habits, the Ukrainians demanded freedom—and got it. Another frontier has opened for the development and consolidation of freedom, human rights, and justice.

Russia remains the most frustrating country in the world. I long have lived in awe of the literature, art, and music of Russia's golden and silver ages but find myself asking if Stalin's attempts to exterminate the genius of the Russian people might not have been successful after all. Even the Ukrainians, who seemed almost beyond hope, stood up for freedom. But as President Vladimir Putin stripped away one freedom after another in Russia the Russians accepted it as dully as serfs bowing to the will of a brutal landlord. Are any people in the world as disappointing as the Russians?

Despite the fascinating hold the country has had on me throughout my adult life, I stopped going there after 1996. It was simply too heartbreaking to watch the Russians get freedom utterly wrong, to embrace, as their ancestors had done, the worst of the West, while retaining the worst of the East. The Russians wear you down. Then, a few years ago, I accepted an invitation from NATO to speak at a conference on terrorism in Moscow (I was brought in to stir things up a bit, which I did, to the dismay of the French ambassador). I had a free morning, so I walked through the streets in the glittering cold, heading down along Tverskaya, around Red Square, across the river, and through the alleys to the Tretyakov Gallery, my pilgrimage stop in Moscow.

Once a visitor breaks free of the thrall of the icons, the remainder of the collection tells the story of Russia's last three centuries, beginning with its emulation of the West and climaxing with a storm of home-grown genius that far surpassed the powder room—print inconsequence of fin-de-siècle art in Europe. As always happens in the Tretyakov Gallery, I began to hope again, to believe that such glory must be indestructible. Then I rejoined the conference at the Ministry of Defense, where Russian generals pickled in alcohol treated their subordinates like slaves and the postconference reception featured hundreds of glasses of vodka stacked atop one another, covering entire tables (the scene begged for Jim Carrey at his wildest). The Russian junior officers present lurked near the buffet, eating hungrily when their superiors were not watching too closely. The generals drank with that mean joviality natural to Russians in positions of authority.

The NATO contingent returned to its hotel by bus, passing by the concentrated prosperity of downtown Moscow, the new shopping center outside of the Kremlin, and the designer shops on the boulevards. Except for the luxury automobiles and electric lights it might have been 1902, not 2002. Russia had returned to its prerevolution model of a heavy-handed state, a magnate aristocracy, a struggling middle class, and the vast *chyorni narod,* the humble people who plod on, forever disappointed in their minimal expectations, fearful, suspicious, diseased, ill nourished, and drunk. I decided that I had been right a dozen years before when, amid the mad euphoria about Russia's future as a model democracy, I had insisted that "a weak Russia is a good Russia."

Just ask the Poles. Or the Ukrainians. The Russians may treasure Pushkin as their literary god, but Dostoevsky understood their devils.

The Middle East. We should stress human rights, no matter the short-term cost. We should pursue terrorists without restraint, no matter the disingenuous criticism we must bear. And we should continue to do whatever lies within our power to help Iraq become a democratic, rule-of-law state—no matter how imperfect and subject to criticism that state may be. We cannot force the Iraqis to succeed, but we must not be anxious to accept their failure. Above all, we must be resolute and patient.

It is hard to be hopeful about the Middle East, given the pitiful state of Arab civilization. But we have no choice for now and must remain engaged, fighting terror in its homelands rather than in our own. Until we accept the need for a pursuit of alternative fuels with the intensity of the Cold War–era "space race" the region's oil reserves will continue to demand security guarantees. Our oil dependence remains a glaring strategic weakness, of benefit to our oil corporations and oil service companies, but to no other Americans. We need a research crusade, backed powerfully by both of our political parties, to develop alternative-fuel technologies.

The obvious reason why the administration of George W. Bush has played sleight-of-hand with the alternative-fuels issue is that it is, however virtuous in other regards, an oilman's presidency. But one begins to suspect an even deeper motive behind the reluctance to reduce our thirst for Middle Eastern oil: the fear that if oil revenues paid to the Middle East stop or are sharply reduced, the combination of sudden bankruptcy with the massive youth bulge in the region will lead to anarchy.

Let it be so. Our priorities are reversed. We must take care of our own security and economic well-being before worrying about the fate of degenerate sheikhs and bloated emirs. If we believe it worthwhile to break addicts from their drug habits, might there not be value in breaking the Middle East of the oil habit that has persuaded its governments that balanced economic development, social progress, and political reform are unnecessary? Decayed regimes should not be kept on life support at our expense. We might find that the death of the oil regimes would lead to a better, reborn Middle East.

How could it be worse?

We will have to intervene repeatedly in the Middle East in the coming decades, given the dead-end cultures and the violence they breed. But if our interventions are still required to protect oil supplies twenty-five years from now, the fault will be our own. Our policy toward the Middle East should be: engagement wherever there is hope; containment where there is no hope; preventive military action against terrorists; an urgent effort to reduce our dependency on oil; and the long-term goal of reducing our involvement in the world's least promising region, freeing resources that can be used more advantageously elsewhere.

East Asia. We have little hope of expanding our influence in East Asia and must be content to preserve what influence we have for as long as possible. While we must always be prepared for a conflict with China, we should stop looking for one and reassess our strategic requirements in the region. Meanwhile, we must break the hold of corporate America on our China policy long enough to insist that Beijing allow its currency to float against the dollar. We also need to take immediate steps whenever we suspect that the Chinese are dumping products on the American market. Fair and free trade with China is desirable, but we cannot allow China to exploit an imbalance of trade created through de facto protectionist policies. While the United States likely will always run a trade deficit with the rest of the world, the imbalance with China is artificial, unacceptable, and strategically unsound. This is the key issue for us in East Asia—not North Korea, which is, frankly, a local problem.

We should remove our ground troops from South Korea, a process already begun. Our most useful contribution to a war on the Korean Peninsula would be airpower, not land forces, of which the South Koreans have more than enough. While their presence was necessary in past decades, American troops stationed in South Korea amount to stagnant strategic capital today.

Encouraging a larger Japanese military role in the world is a misstep. We should let Japan find its own way forward without appearing to succumb to American pressure. Japanese society is still in a transition that began a century and a half ago. The last time a false acceleration occurred the results were disastrous. It is far more important for Japan to reform its education, banking, and business sectors than it is for Tokyo to send a few ships or a handful of troops to a mission in which its people have no interest. Japan may one day become an indispensable military ally, but there's no hurry: The old animosities toward Tokyo remain more current in Asia than Americans are willing to accept.

The Great South. Opportunity lies in that "expanded Southern Hemisphere" stretching north to the Tropic of Cancer. If ever there were a time to engage in a "dogs of the Dow" strategy, making policy investments in regions whose stocks are out of favor, it's now. The belt of opportunity stretching from Indonesia westward (and eastward) to Chile will not soon amass the collective wealth of the North, but the low levels of development in many of the states mean that the potential for strategic returns is immeasurably greater in the South. In real estate terms, Europe is condemned to in-fill construction and China isn't selling. The South offers vast opportunities for growth.

We must develop and pursue a long-term, bipartisan strategy that builds sincere, mutually beneficial partnerships with the lands of the South. This will not take vast resources, but it will take time and steadiness. As we've seen in disappointing countries from Zimbabwe to Venezuela, the South will have ugly setbacks. But when our efforts temporarily fail in one country we simply need to stay the course and avoid overreacting. Looked at too broadly, the South will appear to be failing for decades to come. We need to help foster individual success stories that eventually inspire their surrounding regions—while enhancing America's global security and power.

On a practical level, we should pursue a web of alliances anchored on Australia and running from Indonesia to India and (eventually) Iran, South Africa, and across the South Atlantic to all of Latin America. Indonesia matters because of its strategic location and because it could provide a model for a humane Muslim state, but we must learn to treat Jakarta as an equal partner instead of behaving as a brawny study-hall monitor. India is the strategic Manhattan, the prime real estate in a crucial region, as well as being the world's largest democracy, with a huge and talented population. We shall have to wait and see how the current nastiness with the Iranian government plays out, but Iran, too, is strategically positioned and has no friends in its neighborhood. If Tehran is not quite Washington's natural ally, Washington is nonetheless Tehran's natural ally. South Africa will control the progressive, exemplary southern third of a long-troubled continent. And Latin America is finally approaching political and economic maturity. Taken together, these states form a strategic cordon that controls not only the "soft underbelly" of the irksome Middle East, but the vital complex of civilizations ringing the India Ocean and its subsidiary seas.

If the menu for this strategic feast features a decade or so of humble pie, we should welcome the bargain.

Like the Indian Ocean, the South Atlantic is of as much strategic import today as it was in the sixteenth century. Our blithe neglect of Latin America amounts to the longest running strategic folly in our history. We need to return to the common sense of President James Monroe, who had a better grasp of the importance of the other states in our hemisphere than do the countless identical think tanks that continue to redraft each other's studies. But we also need to move beyond the growls of the Monroe Doctrine to construct a network of vital, respectful, mutually advantageous relationships with the other leading states of the Western Hemisphere. Nor should we ignore those states of lesser size, as we tend to do until they slip into crisis.

We Americans have always thrived on frontiers, and the last human frontier lies to the south. We will need to remain engaged in the Northern Hemisphere, but we must stop being obsessed by it. European history may be interesting, but it only illuminates Europe (the true dark continent). Our country is composed of citizens from every smallest part of the globe. While maintaining our essential values, we need to engage their old homelands more creatively. The English-speaking world is the basis on which a brighter global future can be built, but we must reject old models of statecraft that have entrapped our strategic thought and deformed our policies. We must return to America's ideals.

The surest way to expand our global supremacy in the twenty-first century is to turn our attention from the lands of yesterday and extend a hand to the struggling lands of tomorrow. Charity is less a requirement than common decency, and respect will achieve far more than foreign aid. Our security does not lie in preserving a loathsome Eurocentric past, but in building a better future elsewhere.

We can do it.

Index